Definiteness in a Language without Articles – A Study on Polish

Adrian Czardybon

d|u|p

Hana Filip, Peter Indefrey, Laura Kallmeyer, Sebastian Löbner,
Gerhard Schurz & Robert D. Van Valin, Jr. (eds.)

Dissertations in Language and Cognition

3

Adrian Czardybon

2017

Definiteness in a Language without Articles – A Study on Polish

d|u|p

**Bibliografische Information
der Deutschen Nationalbibliothek**
Die Deutsche Nationalbibliothek verzeichnet diese
Publikation in der Deutschen Nationalbibliografie;
detaillierte bibliografische Daten sind im Internet
über http://dnb.dnb.de abrufbar.

D 61

© düsseldorf university press, Düsseldorf 2017
http://www.dupress.de
Einbandgestaltung: Doris Gerland, Christian Horn, Albert Ortmann
Satz: Adrian Czardybon, Thomas Gamerschlag
Herstellung: docupoint GmbH, Barleben

Gesetzt aus der Linux Libertine
ISBN 978-3-95758-047-4

Für meine Familie

Contents

1	**Introduction**		**1**
2	**Theoretical basis**		**9**
	2.1	The distribution of the definite article in English and German	9
	2.2	Approaches to definiteness	13
		2.2.1 Familiarity	13
		2.2.2 Uniqueness	16
	2.3	Löbner's approach to definiteness	18
		2.3.1 Inherent uniqueness and inherent relationality	18
		2.3.2 Concept types	19
		2.3.3 Shifts and determination	20
		2.3.4 Semantic vs. pragmatic uniqueness	22
		2.3.5 Scale of uniqueness	25
	2.4	Mass/count distinction	30
	2.5	Definiteness strategies discussed in the Slavistic literature	35
3	**Demonstratives**		**43**
	3.1	Criteria for the grammaticalization of definite articles	44
	3.2	Polish determiners and the paradigm of *ten*	46
	3.3	Previous studies on demonstratives in Polish	49
	3.4	My analysis of *ten*	55
		3.4.1 The occurrence of *ten* with pragmatic uniqueness	55
		3.4.1.1 Deictic SNs	55
		3.4.1.2 Anaphoric SNs	57
		3.4.1.3 SNs with complements establishing uniqueness	63

	3.4.2	Definite associative anaphors	65
		3.4.2.1 Part-whole DAAs	67
		3.4.2.2 Relational DAAs	68
		3.4.2.3 Situational DAAs	71
	3.4.3	The occurrence of *ten* with semantic uniqueness	72
		3.4.3.1 Complex ICs	72
		3.4.3.2 Lexical INs/FNs	73
		3.4.3.3 Proper names and personal pronouns	75
	3.4.4	Factors which enable the presence of *ten* with [+U] nominal	75
	3.4.5	Summary	77
3.5	Slavic comparison		79
	3.5.1	Upper Silesian *tyn*	80
	3.5.2	Paradigms of the determiners in the investigated languages	83
	3.5.3	The occurrence of the determiners with pragmatic uniqueness	85
	3.5.4	The occurrence of the determiners with semantic uniqueness	92
3.6	Conclusion		93

4 Aspect — 97

4.1	The semantics of aspect	97
4.2	Morphological realization of grammatical aspect in Polish	103
4.3	The interaction of aspect and definiteness	107
4.4	Incrementality	111
	4.4.1 Incremental theme verbs	111
	4.4.2 Aspectual composition	113
	4.4.3 Filip's approach	114
	4.4.4 Evidence against the equation of definiteness and Perfectivity	116
4.5	Definiteness conditions - Polish data and analysis	118
	4.5.1 Strictly incremental theme verbs	118
	4.5.2 Incremental and non-incremental theme verbs	123
4.6	Aspect, definiteness, and concept types	126
4.7	Conclusion	127

5	**Differential object marking and case alternation**	**129**
5.1	Differential object marking	129
5.2	Split case alternation	133
	5.2.1 The Polish case system and animacy	133
	5.2.2 Negation	138
	5.2.3 Summary	141
5.3	Fluid case alternation	142
	5.3.1 Verbs of giving and taking	143
	5.3.2 The incremental theme verbs *eat* and *drink*	150
5.4	Conclusion	155

6	**Information structure**	**159**
6.1	Theoretical background	159
	6.1.1 What is information structure?	159
	6.1.2 Thetic sentences	160
	6.1.3 Mathesius' (1929) definition of theme and rheme . .	161
	6.1.4 Lambrecht's (1994) definition of topic and focus . .	162
6.2	Information structure in Polish	166
	6.2.1 The unmarked topic-focus structure and its influence on definiteness	166
	6.2.2 Czardybon et al.'s (2014) study on word order and definiteness	169
	6.2.3 The concept type distinction and information structure	175
	6.2.4 The ranking of concept types, information structure, and determiners	180
6.3	Slavic comparison	181
6.4	Conclusion	187

7	**Conclusion**	**191**
7.1	Summary	191
7.2	Questions for future research	196
7.3	The decision tree	198

Appendix: The distribution of the Slavic determiners
under investigation 207

References 223

List of Figures

1. Mass/count distinction 31
2. Subdivision of grammatical aspect 100
3. The interaction between information structure, word order, concept types, and definiteness in Polish 188
4. Decision tree for the (in)definiteness of NPs in Polish, part one 202
5. Decision tree for the (in)definiteness of NPs in Polish, part two 204
6. Decision tree for the (in)definiteness of NPs in Polish, part three 205

List of Tables

1	The four noun types with regard to inherent relationality and uniqueness	19
2	Congruent and incongruent determination	21
3	Distribution of the definite articles in English, colloquial German, Fering, and Maori	30
4	The four types of nouns and the mass/count distinction	35
5	Paradigm of the standard Polish determiner *ten*	47
6	The frequency of the determiners with anaphoric NPs in written Polish	59
7	The frequency of determiners with anaphoric NPs in spoken Polish	62
8	The frequency of *ten* with NPs combined with complements establishing uniqueness in Polish	65
9	Determiners in the investigated Slavic languages	84
10	Distribution of the investigated West Slavic determiners with DAAs and complex ICs	95
11	Verb classes and their distinguishing properties	98
12	Summary of the tests to determine the (im)perfectivity of verbs	104
13	Classification of nouns based on Löbner (2015)	126
14	Case endings of feminine nouns like *kobieta* 'woman' in Polish	133
15	Case endings of neuter nouns like *okno* 'window' and *dziecko* 'child' in Polish	134
16	Case endings of masculine nouns like *dom/ptak/student* in Polish	135
17	Split case alternations in Polish and their interaction with the definiteness of direct objects	142
18	The distribution of the partitive genitive with eat and drink in the investigated Slavic languages	155

19	Summary of the fluid case alternations in Polish and their interaction with definiteness	156
20	Summary of the distribution of the genitive of negation and partitive genitive	157
21	Correlation between syntactic position and definiteness of NPs	170
22	Interaction between word order, sentence stress, and definiteness of the Polish bare NP	173
23	Interaction of concept types, information structure, and definiteness	177
24	Correlation between syntactic position, definiteness of NPs, and underlying concept type	178
25	Summary of the interaction between information structure and definiteness in Polish, Czech, Slovene, and Russian with [−U] nouns	185

List of Abbreviations

1	First person	N	Neuter
2	Second person	NEG	Negation
3	Third person	NOM	Nominative
A	Anaphoric	OBJ	Object
ACC	Accusative	P	Personal
ACM	Accumulative	PAR	Partitive
ADJ	Adjective	PART	Particle
AUX	Auxiliary	PASS	Passive
CLS	Classifying particle	PF	Perfective
COP	Copular	PL	Plural
COPM	Comparative	POSS	Possession
COMPL	Complementizer	PREP	Preposition
DAT	Dative	PROG	Progressive
DEF	Definiteness	PRON	Pronoun
DEL	Delimitative	PROX	Proximal
DEM	Demonstrative	PRS	Present
DET	Determiner	PST	Past
DIM	Diminutive	Q	Question particle
DIST	Distal	REFL	Reflexive pronoun
DISTR	Distributive	REL	Relative pronoun
DUP	Reduplication	SG	Singular
EXCL	Exclusive	SUB	Subject
F	Feminine	T/A	Tense/aspect
FOC	Focus	TOP	Topic
GEN	Genitive	VOC	Vocative
IMP	Imperative		
IMPF	Imperfective		
INDEF	Indefiniteness		
INESS	Inessive		
INS	Instrumental		
LOC	Locative		
M	Masculine		

1 Introduction

The aim of this thesis is to investigate how definiteness is expressed in Polish, a language which is claimed to have no definite and indefinite articles (cf. Pisarkowa 1969: 47, Szwedek 1974: 203, Kryk 1987: 45, Błaszczak 2001: 2, Mendoza 2004: 166, 292, Tęcza 2007: 337). The central question is how the difference in definiteness is indicated between *a woman* in (1) and *the woman* in (2) in Polish:

(1) A woman entered the room.
(2) The woman entered the room.

In English, the definite article *the* and the indefinite article *a* express the category of definiteness explicitly. It has to be emphasized that definiteness is a "linguistic universal" (Cummins 1999: 171) and thus is relevant "in all languages, but in many languages it is not grammaticalized" (Lyons 1999: 278). For Polish, Szwedek (1974: 203) states that "[a]lthough there is no article in Polish we seldom have doubts whether a noun in a text is definite or indefinite". According to Szwedek, Polish is articleless, but from a typological perspective, Polish is hardly an exception. Most Slavic languages are articleless and Dryer (2015a, WALS) showed that, from a sample consisting of 620 languages, 243 (thus about 39 %) have no definite article.[1] With regard to indefiniteness, the majority (55 %) of the languages in his sample (296 out of 534) have no indefinite article (Dryer 2015b, WALS).[2] If the category of definiteness is universal and also relevant in articleless languages, there must be some means to indicate that a nominal phrase is definite or indefinite in Polish, which will be dis-

---

[1] The remaining 377 languages either have a definite word distinct from the demonstrative (216), a demonstrative word used as a definite article (69), or a definite affix (92) (Dryer 2015a, WALS).
[2] The remaining 238 languages either have an indefinite word distinct from the word for 'one' (102), an indefinite word the same as the word for 'one' (112), or an indefinite affix (24) (Dryer 2015b, WALS).

cussed in the following chapters. Polish is not investigated in isolation, however: the study is complemented by comparisons with other Slavic languages and also with a Polish dialect called 'Upper Silesian', which differs from Polish[3].

My thesis is structured as follows: Chapter 2 starts with a discussion of the distribution of the English and German definite articles. This serves as the basis for the evaluation of the two main approaches to definiteness, namely 'familiarity' and 'uniqueness'. My analysis is based on Löbner's (1985, 2011) theory of 'Concept Types and Determination' (CTD). Löbner's (1985, 2011) distinction of the four concept types (sortal, relational, functional, individual) results from the two properties of inherent uniqueness and inherent relationality. In his theory, it is essential that definite NPs signal non-ambiguous (or unique) reference, i.e., that there is only one referent which fits the definite NP (Löbner 2011: 281, 284). Following Löbner (2011), I will speak of definite NPs also in the cases in which no definite article is present to explicitly mark an NP as definite. What is crucial is that "[d]efinite NPs presuppose unique reference [whereas] indefinite NPs presuppose the possibility that reference is not unique" (Löbner 2011: 316). I will demonstrate that there are other ways than the definite article to indicate unique reference. This study is delimited to four means for expressing unique reference, which will be called 'definiteness strategies'. Each strategy will be investigated independently from the others, although they interact in a complex way, which will be shown at the end of the thesis. Furthermore, the interaction of the concept types with the strategies will be taken into consideration, which has not been done before to the best of my knowledge.

Chapter 3 focuses on the demonstrative *ten* in Polish, which is one of the few explicit definiteness strategies. The main goal of this chapter is to provide a detailed analysis of the distribution of *ten* in Polish and its interaction with the four concept types. The investigation of the occurrence of *ten* also serves as the basis for answering the question as to whether *ten* is still a demonstrative or has achieved the status of a definite article.

---

[3] I use the term 'Polish' in the sense of 'standard Polish', which includes standard spoken and written Polish, but excludes Polish dialects.

The interaction of aspect and definiteness is the topic of the fourth chapter. I will discuss the difference between perfectivity and imperfectivity and how they are expressed in Polish. It can be observed that if special conditions are met, the perfective aspect imposes a definite interpretation upon the direct object. In this chapter, I analyse a number of factors which contribute to this effect, such as the properties of the direct object, the verb and the perfectivizing prefixes.

In chapter 5, I will discuss the claim that the differential case marking of direct objects interacts with definiteness. Direct objects of a small number of verbs allow for a case alternation between accusative and genitive case. I will show that in some contexts the genitive has a partitive function and leads to an indefinite reading of the direct object. However, the case alternation with the partitive genitive is more restricted and less accepted by Polish speakers than stated in the literature and a straightforward link between genitive indefiniteness, on the one hand, and accusative definiteness, on the other, cannot be drawn.

Chapter 6 is concerned with information structure and how it interacts with definiteness. Information structure is associated with the order of constituents in a sentence and the placement of the sentence stress in Polish. The primary function is to have an optimal transfer of information in a discourse. My analysis is based on Lambrecht's (1994) approach to information structure. The central question of this chapter is how information structure, the syntactic position of an NP, its definiteness, and its concept type interact. I will present the unmarked topic-focus structure in Polish and complement the qualitative work with a quantitative study on word order and definiteness in Polish.

One important source for the Polish data in this thesis is the National Corpus of Polish (Narodowy Korpus Języka Polskiego "NKJP")[4]. All examples taken from this corpus are marked by 'C' and were additionally checked with my informants. For some special contexts (such as different types of associative anaphors) and in order to have minimal pairs, I made up examples by myself and checked them with informants as well. It was necessary to include direct elicitation tests such as grammaticality

---

[4] The Polish corpus is balanced and consists of about 250 million words, whereby 10 % are spoken data (Przepiórkowski 2012: 28f.).

judgements and cloze tests[5] in my questionnaires since relying solely on corpus data is insufficient according to Matthewson (2004). He argues that a corpus only provides positive evidence, but negative evidence can only be gained by direct elicitation. The cloze test was applied to investigate the distribution of the demonstrative *ten* in chapter 3 while the grammaticality test was used to investigate the acceptability of genitive direct objects in chapter 5. In chapter 6, additional data is taken from Mirkowicz's (2008) Polish translation of George Orwell's novel *Nineteen Eighty-Four* for the study of information structure. This was necessary because the NKJP does not consist of coherent text passages of more than 40 to 70 words (Przepiórkowski 2012: 54). A coherent text, however, plays a crucial role when it comes to deciding whether an NP is definite or not in Polish. Also in chapter 3 on demonstratives, the novel was the basis for the investigation of the frequency of determiners in written Polish. For spoken Polish, I made use of the recorded telephone calls published in Pisarkowa (1975) as well as recorded conversations published in Lubaś (1978).[6]

The majority of my informants with whom I worked were 20 to 35 years old and thus represent the younger generation. They were all native speakers of standard Polish and mostly monolingual. My questionnaires were filled out by speakers living in and outside of Poland. In order to see whether these two groups differ in their judgements, they were treated separately. This was necessary since, for example, Jarząbkowska (2012, quoted after Peterson 2016: 120ff.) shows that speakers of Polish living in Germany are influenced by German with respect to the overt realization of pronominal subjects. In contrast to German, Polish is a pro-drop language, i.e., pronouns as subject NPs are normally omitted (Swan 2002: 155ff.; Bartnicka 2004: 291). However, Polish speakers in Germany use pronominal subjects twice as often as Polish speakers living in Poland according to her. In my study, the

---

[5] A cloze test consists of sentences in which the element in question is left out indicated by a gap. The informants have to decide whether and, if so, which element is missing.
[6] By spoken Polish, I mean spontaneous speech such as conversations and not considering spoken Polish such as political speeches which can have characteristics of written language.

speakers did not show differences with respect to the use of the demonstrative or the acceptability of genitive objects. The data for the other Slavic languages in chapter 3 were also collected by a questionnaire (cloze test) and/or taken from the literature. Unless indicated otherwise, the examples are collected by me.

I would like to conclude this introduction and thank a number of people for their help and support. First of all, I want to express my deepest gratitude to my supervisor Sebastian Löbner for encouraging me to write about this topic. His continuous advice, inspiring discussions and brilliant questions and suggestions throughout the years greatly improved this thesis and made me strive towards my goal. Without his guidance, this thesis would not exist.

I would also like to thank my second supervisor Hana Filip for the fruitful discussions and helpful ideas from which especially the chapter on aspect benefitted a lot. I am also grateful to her for making me aware of relevant literature and for her comments concerning the Czech data.

Albert Ortmann has been my post-doc mentor even before my thesis. I am so thankful for all the detailed comments he has made during these last few years. He has always been willing to discuss various aspect of my thesis or read a chapter. I am really grateful for his support.

I wish to present my special thanks to Jens Fleischhauer for reading and commenting on every chapter of my thesis. He has always had time for discussions which helped me not to get lost. The work with him was so inspiring and I learnt so many things that helped me to write my thesis.

I would also like to thank Robert D. Van Valin, Wiebke Petersen, Oliver Hellwig, Christian Horn, Doris Gerland, Ljudmila Geist, Jennifer Kohls, Syuzan Sachliyan, Koen Van Hooste, and Yulia Zinova for discussing various aspects of my thesis with me and for giving me insightful comments. Furthermore, I thank Thomas Gamerschlag for helping me with the layout of my thesis. All remaining errors are my own!

Without the help of my faithful informants, I would not have been able to write my thesis. They dedicated a lot of time answering my questions and filling out my questionnaires. I am thankful to the following people for providing me with data or for helping me to find enough informants: For Bulgarian Ekaterina Gabrovska, Syuzan Sachliyan; for Bosnian Sabina Derendelic; for Croatian: Ivo-Pavao Jazbec; in particular, I want to thank Eva Lehečková from the Charles University in Prague for helping me to find a sufficient number of Czech informants: Pavlína Bednářová, Ondřej Červ, Ondřej Dufek, Inka Dvořáková, Eva Flanderkova, Hana Gabrielová, Kristýna Horáková, Jiří Januška, Jakub Jehlička, Adam Kriz, Adéla Limburská, Jana Lukavská, Helena Maleňáková, Jan Mašek, Jiří Pergler, Anna Plasová, Hana Prokšová, Kateřina Šormová, Kristýna Tesařová, Kristýna Tomšů, Katerina Veselovska, Karolína Vyskočilová; for Kashubian Róman Drzeżdżón, Adam Hebel, Artur Jablonski, Marika Jelińska, Magdalena Kropidłowska, Karolina Serkowska; for Mandarin Chinese Lei Li; for Russian Veronika Fadeeva, Julia Klimatschow, Tatiana Netesova, Anastasia Ogorodnikova, Polina Piskunova, Alexander Rakhimov, Nikolai Skorolupov, Sergei Tatevosov, Yulia Zinova; for standard Polish I would like to thank Christine Breslauer, Slawomir Kowalinski, Alice Lange-Dymarz, Marius Schafranietz, and Remigiusz Wojtyła for distributing my questionnaires and helping me to get in contact with my informants: Kinga Bienk, Dariusz Florek, Katarzyna Gasiewska, Ewelina Lamparska, Jessica and Johanna Major, Anna Michalak, Małgorzata Miśtal, Michał Piosik, Maria Przybył, Beata Rubel, Anna Świerc, Anna Wideł, Anna and Elżbieta Zamolska; for Upper Silesian Krystyna and Jerzy Chrobok, Ursula and Wilhelm Czardybon, Georg Glomb, Eugeniusz Major, Liliana Mandel, Dominika Skrzypek, Georg and Mathilde Skupinski. Furthermore, I would also like to thank the huge number of anonymous informants who filled out my questionnaires.

 Special thanks to Joanna Strzępek and Helena Zamolska for their work in my project during the past two years. You spent hours and hours answering my questions, judging hundreds of Polish sentences, and filling out numerous questionnaires. Thank you for being so patient and motivated. I will miss the productive meetings full of laughter on Monday mornings. I also thank my office mate Lei Li for the motivating talks and coffee breaks, which I enjoyed a lot and the great time we had in our office.

I owe a great deal to my friends Heiko and Sven Kluth, Laura Kles, Katharina and Marc Erdmann, Ramona Peters, Julia Schmidt, and Sarah Liebert, who supported me and distracted me if it was necessary. They reminded me that there is also a world outside my thesis.

I would also like to take this opportunity to thank my parents Wilhelm and Ursula Czardybon, my brothers Arthur and Arkadius, and my grandparents Georg and Mathilde Skupinski in Upper Silesian: Chca wom podziynkować całym sercym za miłość i za pomoc. Niy wiym, czy by mi sie udało napisać ta praca bez wos. Mom szczynście, że mom tako cudowno familia. Moje rodzice zawsze mieli czas i cierpliwość, jak żech chcioł wiedzieć coś ło ślonskij godce. Żech sie mog zawsze zapytać łobojyntnie kedy i kaj. Chioł żech wom za to piyknie podziynkować!

Finally, I want to thank Michel. Words simply cannot express my gratitude for everything you have done. You have always been so supportive and understanding, even if I was grumpy at times. You kept me motivated and reminded me to be "fleißig" even when the goal seemed so far away. Thank you for believing in me.

This thesis has been written in the framework of the project "Conceptual Shifts: Statistical Evidence", which is part of the Collaborative Research Center "The Structure of Representations in Language, Cognition, and Science" (CRC 991) financed by the German Science Foundation (DFG).

2 Theoretical basis

Section 2.1 deals with the distribution of the definite article as exemplified by German and English and serves as the basis for an evaluation of the approaches to definiteness discussed in 2.2. Any adequate and convincing theory also needs to be able to explain the distribution. Section 2.3 is dedicated to Löbner's uniqueness approach and his concept type distinction, upon which my thesis is based. The mass/count distinction, which is crucial for the discussion about aspect in chapter 4, is discussed in 2.4. The last section provides a critical overview of the definiteness strategies mentioned in the Slavistic literature.

2.1 The distribution of the definite article in English and German

Most of the contexts in which definite articles occur in German and English have already been described by authors such as Christophersen (1939) and Hawkins (1978) for English and Bisle-Müller (1991) for German. Their observations will be summarized here and missing contexts will be added.

In German, the definite article can also be found in deictic contexts, in which the referent of the definite NP is accessible to and perceivable by the discourse participants and a pointing gesture is often involved. In such contexts, the German definite article is stressed (indicated in the example by capital letters)[1] and thus functions as a demonstrative.[2] Imagine a situation in which three bottles are standing on a table. A person is pointing to one of these bottles saying the following.

---

[1] In the thesis, I use capital letters to indicate the placement of sentence stress.
[2] This is why *die* is glossed as a demonstrative 'DEM' in (1).

2 Theoretical basis

(1) Gib   mir DIE Flasche!
     give.IMP me DEM bottle
     'Give me this bottle!'

The bottle can be identified with the help of a gesture made by the speaker. If we slightly change the deictic context in (1) by assuming that only one bottle is standing on the table, then the sentence can be uttered without a gesture and we have a deictic use of the definite article, which is not stressed. These contexts are called 'visible situation use' (Hawkins 1978: 110). Another example is given in (2). Imagine a situation in which person A is in a room with only one door which is open and person A says to another person in the room:

(2) *Can you close the door?*

The definite article also occurs with NPs whose referents are not visible, but can be perceived differently (3):

(3) a. *Where does the terrible smell come from?* (Löbner 1985: 310)
     b. *Can't you stop the noise?* (Löbner 1985: 311)

In contrast to the examples (2) and (3), in which the referents of the definite NPs are perceivable, there are also examples showing that the referent need not be perceived in the speech situation, as is the case with the dog in the following example:

(4) *Beware of the dog!* (Hawkins 1978: 112)

Imagine you read this sentence written on a garden fence. Although the dog is not visible in the situation, the definite article is present, which Hawkins (1978: 111) calls 'immediate situation use' of the definite article.

The definite article is also found in contexts in which a referent is introduced into the discourse by an indefinite article and then mentioned again. The NP with the previously introduced referent occurs with the definite article. These contexts are called 'anaphors,' exemplified in (5). Same subscripts indicate coreference.

(5) *Maria bought a dog$_i$. The dog$_i$ is very young.*

In contrast to anaphors, where the previous mention is responsible for the presence of the definite article, in the examples (6) there is an article due to the following modifier. This modifier can be a relative clause, which leads to a definite interpretation of the NP *the car* in (6a). Hawkins (1978: 131) calls such relative clauses 'referent-establishing relative clauses' which "establish a definite referent" (Hawkins 1978: 140).[3] In (6a), the relative clause provides sufficient information to enable a definite interpretation of the NP *car*. Also prepositional phrases (6b) or subordinate clauses[4] (6c) can have this effect.

(6)   a.   *The car that I bought yesterday was expensive.*
       b.   *The woman from the shop next door will visit us today.*
       c.   *The possibility that John will pass the exam*

The example in (7) illustrates the occurrence of the definite article with associative anaphors, also called 'bridging' or 'indirect anaphors'. Associative anaphors are characterized by the fact that, by mentioning a referent, other associated entities are also implicitly introduced into the discourse and can then be referred to in a first mention with the definite article. In example (7), *a house* is mentioned and, along with the house itself, all its parts (*roof, windows, front door, garden*) are made available as well. It is therefore possible to use *roof* with a definite article in the next sentence without having introduced the referent previously, provided that the house has no more than one roof.

(7)   *Maria had a house, but the roof was too steep.*

The definite article is also found with NPs that are modified by adjectives of order (Löbner 2015) such as *last, former, next* (8a), superlatives (8b), and ordinal numbers (8c).

(8)   a.   *The next student will pass the exam.*
       b.   *The fastest car will win the race.*
       c.   *He won the second prize.*

---

[3] Cabredo Hofherr (2014: 184) calls such relative clauses 'functional restrictive relatives'.
[4] Examples like the one in (6b) are called 'NP-complements' by Hawkins (1978: 140).

2 Theoretical basis

The definite article can also appear with some relational nouns[5], i.e. nouns which are two- or more-place predicate terms.

(9) a. *He wanted to know the price of the house.*
　　b. *The distance from Germany to Spain is 2000 km.*

In (9a), the relational noun is *price* and its argument is realized by *the house*, while in (9b) the two arguments of *distance* are *Germany* and *Spain*. The article is also obligatory with objects that are unique in our world. They are sometimes called 'uniques' and examples are *sun, Pope, moon, US president.*

In standard German, there are some names for countries which occur with the definite article (10a) and others which do not (10b). In colloquial German, personal names (10c) may also appear with a definite article. This shows that proper names in German behave differently with respect to the distribution of the definite article.

(10) a. **(die) Schweiz*
　　　　DEF Switzerland
　　　　'Switzerland'
　　b. *(*das) Deutschland*
　　　　DEF Germany
　　　　'Germany'
　　c. *(die) Maria*
　　　　DEF Mary
　　　　'Mary'

Generic NPs[6] can occur with the definite article, too. However, they do not refer to an individual, but to an entire class or kind, as in the example (11).

(11) 　*The dolphin is a mammal.*

---

[5] Strictly speaking, the definite article is expected with functional nouns, which are discussed in section 2.3.2.
[6] The term 'genericity' is used for two distinct phenomena, kind-denoting NPs such as in (11) and characterizing sentences. For a detailed analysis see Krifka et al. (1995).

The definite article can also occur in recognitional[7] contexts in which the referent of the definite NP is identified with the help of the common knowledge of the hearer and speaker. Here, the referent is neither perceivable nor has it been previously mentioned. As Diessel (1999: 106) puts it, it is discourse-new information but old information for the discourse participants. The context is often introduced by "do you know/remember", as is illustrated by the following German example:

(12) *Weißt   du   noch, als   ich den schrecklichen Unfall*
     know.2SG.PRS you still when I   DEF terrible   accident
     hatte?
     have.PST
     'Do you remember when I had the/that terrible accident?'

In the next section, different approaches to definiteness will be discussed. A valid theory of definiteness will have to explain the distribution of the article depicted in this section.

2.2 Approaches to definiteness

There are two main approaches, namely *uniqueness* and *familiarity* which try to explain the function of the definite article and thus to capture the notion of definiteness. These two approaches will be discussed in the following two sections.

2.2.1 Familiarity

Although authors such as Christophersen (1939), Heim (1982), and Roberts (2003) can be subsumed as supporters of the familiarity approach, each of them has a different notion of 'familiarity'. Irene Heim (1982) has one of the most restrictive definitions of familiarity. In her 'File Change Semantics', the NP accompanied by an indefinite article introduces a novel referent, whereas an NP with the definite article indicates that the referent of the definite NP is familiar by virtue of a previous mention or

---

[7] The term 'recognitional' is taken from Himmelmann (2001: 833).

immediate situation (Heim 1982: 309, 369), which is the main function of the definite article (Heim 1982: 311, 314). Heim uses the metaphor of a "file" where every piece of information about the discourse referents is written on indexed file cards. She argues that the introduction of a new referent means to "start a new card", which is associated with indefiniteness, and to "update a suitable old card" means that a referent is familiar and is associated with definiteness (Heim 1982: 276, 302).

Heim's theory can be illustrated by example (5) repeated in (13), in which the referent of *dog* is introduced into the discourse for the first time and thus is new, which is indicated by the presence of the indefinite article. This means that a new card with the entry *a dog* is started. In the second sentence, *dog* is an anaphoric NP and is therefore now familiar, hence the definite article occurs. The card with the entry *a dog* can be updated, which means that all the information about the referent can be added on the card.

(13)   Maria bought a dog$_i$. The dog$_i$ is very young.

The occurrence of the definite article such as in (13) can be explained very well by her approach. Other contexts, however, seem to be problematic; for example, SNs with complements establishing uniqueness, associative anaphors, NPs with superlatives and ordinal numbers as well as uniques. Here, the referents of the definite NPs need not be mentioned previously in order to occur with the definite article. Heim (1982: 370f.) herself is aware of these problematic cases. This is why she proposes an adaptation of her theory by stating that a newly added card has some sort of "crossreference to some already-present file card(s)" (Heim 1982: 373) in order to explain the occurrence of the definite article with associative anaphors, or to link a new card to the utterance situation as in immediate situation use (Heim 1982: 374). In spite of the modification of her theory, there is still an open question as to how the other occurrences of the definite article can be explained with her approach.

Another problem the theory has to cope with is the fact that there are examples with which an indefinite article is in general not possible. This means that it is impossible to introduce new referents by an indefinite NP. This is illustrated in (14).

(14) a. *The/*a fastest car will win the race.*
b. *He spent two years in the/*a Middle East.*

NPs with superlatives (14a) and some unique names (14b) generally cannot be combined with an indefinite article, which again weakens her theory. For most theories of familiarity, the examples in (14) represent a difficulty in explaining the presence of the definite article.

The familiarity approach is also associated with Paul Christophersen. He has a much broader definition of familiarity than Heim, defining familiarity as follows:

> the speaker must always be supposed to know which individual he is thinking of; the interesting thing is that the *the*-form supposes that the hearer knows it, too (Christophersen 1939: 28).
> The article *the* brings it about that to the potential meaning (the idea) of the word is attached a certain association with previously acquired knowledge, by which it can be inferred that only one definite individual is meant. This is what is understood by *familiarity*. Now, in all strictness, this term is not always quite correct. Though the previously acquired knowledge may relate to the very individual meant, yet it is often indirectly that one is familiar with what is denoted by the word. It may be something else that one is familiar with, but between this "something" and the thing denoted there must be an unambiguous relation (Christophersen 1939: 72f.).

These often-cited text passages make clear that the referent of a definite NP must be familiar to both the speaker and addressee and that the definite article indicates this shared knowledge. Christophersen is able to account for the occurrence of the definite article with anaphoric NPs in the same way as Heim, but he also captures associative anaphors and uniques since they are familiar too. However, his approach is not able to explain the article with SNs with complements establishing uniqueness and NPs with superlatives and ordinals since they need not be familiar to or known by the hearer and speaker.

Roberts (2003), for whom Heim's definition of familiarity is also too narrow (Roberts 2003: 295), makes a distinction between two kinds of familiarity, namely strong and weak familiarity. According to Roberts (2003: 288, 297f., 304f.), strong familiarity means that a discourse referent is familiar due to a previous mention of the referent by an explicitly realized NP and that this NP is anaphoric to refer to the introduced discourse referent. Strong familiarity is similar to Heim's notion of familiarity. Weak familiarity, by contrast, means that a referent can be familiar due to other reasons, for example, perceptual accessibility to the discourse participants, global familiarity in the general culture, or "contextual existence entailments" (Roberts 2003: 304).

With the concept of weak familiarity, Roberts is able to explain more first-mention uses of the definite article than Heim's and Christophersen's theories are able to. Her notion of weak familiarity captures the occurrence of the definite article with uniques, associative anaphors, and in immediate situations. However, her approach has similar weaknesses as Christophersen's approach since the article with SNs with complements establishing uniqueness and NPs with superlatives and ordinals cannot satisfactorily be explained without accommodation (Roberts 2003: 302).

This shows that the familiarity approach – with its various definitions of the term 'familiarity' – cannot account for all article occurrences presented in 2.1. In the next section, I present the second main approach to definiteness, namely the uniqueness approach.

2.2.2 Uniqueness

For Russell (1905: 481f.), as a representative of the uniqueness account, the definite article has two functions, namely to indicate the existence and the uniqueness of the referent, which is illustrated by Russell's famous sentence *The king of France is bald*. The logical structure of a sentence like *The king of France is bald* is presented in (15)

(15) $\exists x (N(x) \& VP(x) \& \forall y(N(y) \rightarrow y=x))$ (Löbner 1985: 289)

As Löbner (1985: 290) points out, Russell's approach can be criticized since the formula given in (15) only holds for nouns which are not inherently unique. The uniqueness condition in (15), namely $\forall y(N(y) \rightarrow y=x)$, is redundant with inherently unique nouns or superlative constructions such as in (16), where there can be only one car which is the fastest.

(16)   *The fastest car will win the race.*

If the uniqueness condition is left out, (15) only consists of the existence condition, which is Russell's standard analysis of a sentence with an indefinite NP (Löbner 1985: 290). We would thus end up with the same formula for definite as well as indefinite NPs if the head noun is inherently unique, which cannot be the case.

Hawkins (1978, 1991), who extends Russell's theory by including mass and plural nouns (Hawkins 1978: 17, 159), offers a unified theory of indefiniteness and definiteness on the basis of exclusiveness and inclusiveness, respectively. He states that

> [t]he use of the definite article acts as an instruction to the hearer to locate the referent of the definite NP within one of a number of sets of objects which are pragmatically defined on the basis of different types of shared speaker-hearer knowledge and the situation of utterance. [...] The definite description refers 'inclusively' to the totality of the objects satisfying the descriptive predicate within the relevant pragmatic set (Hawkins 1978: 17).

This means that in his 'Location Theory' (1978: 17f., 109, 167f., 186f.) the referent of the definite NP is selected from a set and is made unique on the basis of shared knowledge and thus refers inclusively to all referents matching the definite description, e.g. in the case of plural or mass nouns, whereas the indefinite article requires more than one possible referent matching the indefinite description, which only refers to a subset.

Russell and Hawkins share some common ground in that they both assume that it is existence and uniqueness which is indicated by the definite article (Hawkins 1978: 89, 94). For Hawkins, the additional aspect of shared knowledge is crucial in order to single out the referent. Hawkins' approach, however, does not sufficiently explain, for example, the definite article with associative anaphors as well as counterexamples to Russell's approach.

2.3 Löbner's approach to definiteness

In this section, I present Löbner's theory and the motivation for basing this study on this theory.

2.3.1 Inherent uniqueness and inherent relationality

Löbner (1985, 2011) defines "uniqueness"[8] differently than the uniqueness approaches introduced above. Russell (1905) and Hawkins (1978) consider uniqueness as an accidental property of sortal nouns (Löbner 1985: 290f.). Depending on the situation, zero, one or more referents can match the definite description. In an example such as *woman with glasses*, the NP refers uniquely in a situation in which there is only one woman with glasses. But this is an accidental property of the NP because in another situation there might be no woman with glasses or more than one and here the NP would not refer uniquely. In contrast to this example, *sun* exemplifies a noun which is not accidentally unique, but has the property of inherent uniqueness built into its meaning. Löbner (1985, 2011) takes these nouns – which were called uniques in 2.1. – as the starting point for his approach to definiteness.

The second semantic property that is crucial in Löbner's theory is inherent relationality. This has to do with the question whether nouns are one-place or more-place predicate terms. The minimal pair *man* vs. *husband* illustrates the difference: *man* is not inherently relational since it is a one-place predicate term and thus does not require a further argument to be realized while *husband* is inherently relational since the concept of *husband* involves a further argument as in *Mary's husband*. In this example, the additional argument *Mary* is the possessor whereas *husband* is the possessee (Heine 1997: 143). The notion of inherent relationality is commonly accepted (cf. Partee 1983/1997, Barker 1995: 8; 2000: 214, Koptjevskaja-Tamm 2001a: 964, and Asudeh 2005: 399f.).

---

[8] Löbner (2011: 281, note 5) uses the term 'uniqueness' in the sense of 'non-ambiguousness' or 'non-ambiguous reference'.

Löbner proposes a classification of concept types based on the two inherent properties of uniqueness and relationality, and this is the topic of the following section.

2.3.2 Concept types

In Löbner's theory (2011), which is a refinement and extension of Löbner (1985), he distinguishes four types of nouns: sortal, relational, functional, and individual. Table 1 illustrates the resulting four noun types.

	[−U]	[+U] inherently unique
[−R]	Sortal nouns (SN): stone, book, chair	Individual nouns (IN): sun, weather, Maria
[+R] inherently relational	Relational nouns (RN): brother, hand, uncle	Functional nouns (FN): head, mother, age

Table 1: The four noun types with regard to inherent relationality and uniqueness (Löbner 2011: 307).

The four types of nouns result from the combination of the two parameters of inherent relationality [±R] and inherent uniqueness [±U]. **Sortal nouns** are one-place predicates and are thus [−R]. They are not inherently unique due to the fact that in a given context of utterance they can have one, zero or more referents. The meanings of SNs are sortal concepts (SC) (Löbner 2011: 280).

Relational nouns are inherently relational. The relation between the two entities, for example, the brother and a person he is the brother of is one-to-many and thus not unique because one can have more than one brother or none. Among others, kinship terms (*brother, uncle, grandmother*) and terms for body parts (*arm, finger, eye*) that are [−U] belong to the class of RNs. The noun for the body part *nose* does not belong to the class of RNs since it is [+U]. The meanings of RNs are relational concepts (RC) (Löbner 2011: 281).

Functional nouns are inherently unique as well as inherently relational. In contrast to RNs, FNs express a one-to-one relation between two entities because a person can only have one mother. Further examples of FNs are relational role terms such as *father, author, president*; terms for unique parts like *head, top, cover*, and terms for abstract aspects or dimensions *weight, age, price*. The meanings of FNs are functional concepts (FC) (Löbner 2011: 282).

Individual nouns are [–R], but they are inherently unique since in the context of utterance they have only one referent. Löbner (2011: 281, 284) classifies INs into subtypes such as: role terms (*king of Spain*), terms for institutions (*Catholic Church*), unique objects (*moon*), singular events (*World War II*) and terms such as *weather* and *date*. Moreover, he counts proper names and personal pronouns as INs, too. Löbner (2011: 284) emphasizes that INs have different ranges of reference due to the fact that they depend on the context of utterance for the determination of their referent which, in itself, has to do with the situational argument specifying the time and location. As Löbner (1985: 294) notes, the situational argument is usually not explicitly realized, but it can be expressed by an adverbial such as in *the weather in Germany on October 12*. Some INs, such as *pope,* have a very wide or even global range of reference because there is only one pope at the same time on earth. Other INs, such as proper names, have a small range of reference. However, the relation between an IN and its referent is unique and "in the given context of utterance there is exactly one [referent] that fits" (Löbner 2011: 284), which need not be the case with non-inherently unique nouns. Individual concepts (IC) are the meanings of INs.

Löbner (2011: 282f.) argues that the lexical type of nouns is specified in the lexicon. Uses of nouns which do not match their lexical type can be explained in terms of systematic type shifts, which will be the topic of the next section.

2.3.3 Shifts and determination

In (17), we can see that all four types of nouns can be used as one of the four concept types. This is illustrated in (17) by the underlying SN *book*, IN *pope*, FN *mother*, and RN *brother*.[9]

---

[9] I will adapt Ortmann's (2014: 295) notation differentiating between the noun's underlying type (SN, IN, FN, RN) and its actual use (SC, IC, FC, RC) at the NP level.

		SN	IN	FN	RN
(17)					
a.	SC	*a book*	*a pope*	*a mother*	*a brother*
b.	IC	*the book*	*the pope*	*the mother*	*the brother*
c.	FC	*my book*	*my pope*	*my mother*	*my brother*
d.	RC	*a book of mine*	*a pope of mine*	*a mother of mine*	*a brother of mine*

In (17a), only the SN *book* is used in accordance with its lexical type. All other NPs are shifted to SCs, which is indicated by the indefinite article. The definite article in (17b) signals the shift to an IC. The possessive pronoun *my* in (17c) shifts the NPs to an FC and in (17d) the NPs are shifted to RCs.

Löbner (2011) claims that there are modes of determination which are 'natural' with certain types of nouns. For example, the natural determination of SNs, which are inherently non-unique, is the indefinite article since there is no shift of the SN involved. The noun is used in accordance with its underlying concept type. Determination that does not cause a shift is called 'congruent' by Löbner (2011: 287). Incongruent determination causes a shift of the noun, since it is not in accordance with its underlying concept type (Löbner 2011: 306).

Table 2 shows which types of determination are (in)congruent with which types of nouns. Congruent determination is indicated by "✓" and incongruent by "→". The abbreviation "indef." stands for simple and unspecific indefinite, free choice, negative, and interrogative and "pl." for plural, numerical, and quantitative, and "dem." for demonstratives (Löbner 2011: 306):

	[–U]	[+U]
[–R]	**Sortal nouns (SN):** ✓ indef., pl., quantification, dem. → singular definite ✓ absolute → relational, possessive	**Individual nouns (IN):** → indef., pl., quantification, dem. ✓ singular definite ✓ absolute → relational, possessive

	[−U]	[+U]
[+R]	**Relational nouns (RN):** ✓ indef., pl., quantification, dem. → singular definite → absolute ✓ relational, possessive	**Functional nouns (FN):** → indef., pl., quantification, dem. ✓ singular definite → absolute ✓ relational, possessive

Table 2: Congruent and incongruent determination (Löbner 2011: 307).

The focus of this study is the question as to how unique reference is expressed in Polish and therefore I have paid particularly close attention to the shift from RN/SN to FC/IC.

2.3.4 Semantic vs. pragmatic uniqueness

For Löbner (2011: 289), "the definite article has the function to indicate that the CNP[10] is to be construed as a unique concept". If the CNP is an IN or FN, the definite article signals that they are used in accordance with their underlying unique concept type. That is why Löbner (1985: 298f.) calls them "semantic definites" since uniqueness is inherent to their semantics. Furthermore, the definite article is semantically redundant with inherently unique nouns (Löbner 1985: 311), which is reflected in languages in which the definite article is not found with lexical INs/FNs, which will be shown in the next section.

With SNs/RNs, the definite article also signals a unique concept. This is achieved by adding linguistic or extralinguistic information in order to narrow down the reference of the noun to a single entity. This can be done by using the noun anaphorically or deictically as well as by adding a uniqueness establishing relative clause. Using an SN or RN uniquely involves a shift indicated by the definite article as demonstrated in (17b). Since SNs/RNs need to be enriched by the (extra)linguistic context, Löbner calls them "pragmatic definites" (Löbner 1985: 298). As was shown in

---

[10] According to Abbott (2010: 6), a CNP or common noun phrase is "everything in the NP except the determiner".

2.3 Löbner's approach to definiteness

the previous section, Löbner (2011: 289) extends his theory to determination in general and does not restrict his theory only to the definite article.

By making a distinction between semantic and pragmatic uniqueness, Löbner is able to explain the distribution of the definite article, as shown in section 2.1.[11] The definite article with FNs/INs shows that they are used in accordance with their underlying concept type. NPs with superlatives and ordinals are unique too, since there can be only one referent matching the definite NP. The counterexamples presented for the other approaches can be explained by Löbner, since the article does not have the function to indicate existence or familiarity, but only unambiguous reference. Existence and familiarity is not necessarily presupposed by Löbner's approach.

The definite article in immediate situational use can also be explained with the notion of pragmatic uniqueness: the NP is shifted to a unique concept due to the information provided by the extralinguistic context in which the referents of the definite NPs are part of the situation and are accessible to the discourse participants (Löbner 1985: 309f., 319) such as in (18):

(18) *Can you close the door?*

Uniqueness-establishing relative clauses[12] give the linguistic context to narrow down the reference of the NP and shift it to an IC (Löbner 1985: 307f., 314f.). Löbner illustrates this shift with Hawkins' (1978: 131) example in (19):

(19) *What's wrong with Bill? Oh, the woman he went out with last night was nasty to him.*

According to Löbner (1985: 314f.), a functional link is established from the referent of the NP *Bill* to the referent of *the woman* using the relative

---

[11] Generic NPs will be excluded from the investigation to follow since Löbner's (2011: 279f.) theory is only about nouns in referential use.
[12] Löbner (1985: 314) speaks of 'endophoric DDs (definite descriptions)' which are composed of a relational or sortal head noun and an additional attribute, whereas Ortmann (2014: 311) calls them 'autophoric'.

23

clause *he went out with last night*. The situation of going out is linked to Bill and thus the referent of *the woman* is also linked indirectly. According to Löbner, the personal pronoun *he* refers to *Bill* and is also linked to the situation. The event of going out is specified or singled out by the temporal adverbial *last night* and the agent Bill. Thus, the individual event is functionally linked to Bill. There is only one person one usually goes out with for the night which here is the referent of *the woman*. Since it is not only relative clauses that can establish a unique reference, but also other subordinate clauses or prepositional phrases, I will use the term 'complements establishing uniqueness'.

The definite article with anaphoric NPs can also be explained in the same way, since the NP is shifted to a unique concept by the previous linguistic context (Löbner 1985: 309, 317f.). This is illustrated by Löbner's example in (20), in which a functional link is established from the anaphoric NP *the house* to the antecedent *a house* by using all the information which is given about the referent of *house*, namely that it is the house the door of which the ball ran right forward to.

(20)   ...*The ball ran right forward to the door of a house that stood there, and the ball went into the house and she saw it no more.*

The occurrence of the definite article with associative anaphors is covered by Löbner's theory, too. According to Löbner (1998), a definite associative anaphor (DAA) consists of a head interpreted as an FC and an antecedent (also called an 'anchor'). As Ortmann (2014: 309) states, definite associative anaphors (DAA) are semantically unique due to the FC and pragmatically unique because of the pronominal or implicit anaphoricity of the antecedent. In the example (21), *roof* is to be interpreted as the FC and *Michael's house* as the antecedent of *roof*, which is understood as *the roof of Michael's house*.

(21)   *We have seen Michael's house. The roof is yellow.*

The referent of *roof* is thus anchored by a functional link to the referent of *Michael's house*. This is why we have a definite article with *roof* although it has not been mentioned explicitly before.

With semantic as well as pragmatic uniqueness "[i]t is the CoU [context of utterance] that ultimately determines the respective referent of the definite description" (Löbner 2013: 78). This means that, in both cases of uniqueness, the context of utterance is required in order to fix the reference of the definite NP. However, in the case of pragmatic uniqueness the context is also required to achieve unique reference. The sortal noun *dog* needs additional context in order to refer uniquely, for example, a deictic context. The use of *dog* in this context also fixes its reference. By contrast, the individual noun *pope* does not need any context to refer uniquely since this is already part of its meaning. In the context of utterance, only its reference is fixed since this depends on a time index.

2.3.5 Scale of uniqueness

Using the distinction between pragmatic and semantic uniqueness, the distribution of the German and English definite articles can be mapped onto the scale of uniqueness in (22). This implicative scale is based on the scales proposed by Löbner (2011: 320), and Ortmann (2009, 2014: 314), which I have modified on the basis of a number of languages (see Czardybon 2010). Ortmann in particular provides typological evidence for the structuring of the scale. Still, the question remains whether the scale is universal and can capture the distribution of the definite articles cross-linguistically.

The scale is an attempt to arrange the occurrences of the definite article by using the property of inherent uniqueness. No inherent uniqueness and thus pragmatic uniqueness is found with the segment on the top down to SN with complements establishing uniqueness. Here, uniqueness is achieved through deictic and anaphoric use of an SN or by adding complements establishing uniqueness to an SN such as relative clauses, PPs or adverbial phrases that narrow down the number of potential referents to only one entity. Towards the bottom of the scale we find semantic uniqueness, which is found with FNs/INs. NPs with superlatives or ordinals are called complex IC. Personal pronouns as well as proper names are INs. The scale thus has a hierarchical structure with regard to inherent uniqueness.

(22) pragmatic | deictic SN <
      uniqueness | anaphoric SN <
                 | SN with complements establishing uniqueness <
                 | relational DAAs <
                 | part-whole DAAs <
                 | complex IC <
                 | lexical IN/FN <
                 | proper names <   semantic
                 | personal pronouns   uniqueness

With respect to DAAs, Schwarz (2009) proposes a subdivision. He analyses the distribution of contracted prepositions with the definite article with DAAs in German and concludes that the contracted form occurs with DAAs which exhibit a part-whole relation between the antecedent and head as in (23). In (23), *Kühlschrank* 'refrigerator' is the antecedent while *Gemüsefach* 'crisper' is the head of the DAA. The head and the antecedent have a part-whole relation. This is why the contracted form of the preposition and definite article *im* has to be used, according to Schwarz:

(23) German (West Germanic, Indo-European; Schwarz 2009: 34)
      Der Kühlschrank war so groß, dass der Kürbis
      DEF refrigerator was so big that DEF pumpkin
      problemlos   im/   #in dem Gemüsefach
      without_a_problem PREP.DEF PREP DEF crisper
      untergebracht werden konnte.
      stowed   AUX   could
      'The refrigerator was so big that the pumpkin could easily be stowed in the crisper.'

DAAs with a producer-product relationship as in (24) are called 'relational anaphora' by Schwarz (2009: 12). With relational DAAs that do not express a part-whole relation, the non-contracted form occurs, which supports the subdivision of DAAs. In (24), the author is not a part of the play; this is why the non-contracted form has to be chosen according to Schwarz:[13][14]

(24) German (Schwarz 2009: 34)
Das Theaterstück missfiel dem Kritiker so sehr, dass
DEF play displeased DEF critic so much that
er in seiner Besprechung kein gutes Haar #am/ an dem
he in his review no good hair PREP.DEF PREP DEF
Autor ließ.
author left
'The play displeased the critic so much that he tore the author to pieces in his review.'

There is further Slavic evidence for this subdivision of DAAs, which I will present in the chapter on demonstratives. Moreover, a further subdivision will be proposed.

The lower one goes on the scale the more redundant the definite article becomes, which is the case with semantic uniqueness. This is why, in most languages, the definite article is not found with all NPs that are semantically unique on the scale, but there is a cut-off point down to which the article occurs. The scale predicts that if the definite article occurs in a language, for example, with proper names, as is the case in Modern Greek, then all other NPs above also occur with the article. The cut-off points are language-specific (Löbner 2011, Ortmann 2014).

In languages with two definite articles, there is normally a strong and a weak form of the article. This situation can be found in many West Germanic languages such as Dutch (Ortmann 2014: 302f.), Fering, a North Frisian dialect (Ebert 1971), and many German dialects such as Alemannic (Studler 2004), Bavarian (Schwager 2007), and Ripuarian (Hartmann 1982). Usually the strong form is found with pragmatic uniqueness, whereas the weak article occurs with semantic uniqueness

---

[13] For further discussion on the distribution of the contracted and non-contracted forms of prepositions and definite articles in German see Löbner (2011) and in particular Cieschinger (2007).
[14] Schwarz's results seem to be only tendencies. For some native speakers of German the contracted form is also possible in (24).

(Ortmann 2014). The cut-off points from weak article to no marking on the scale is again language-specific and there is also variation across languages with respect to the cut-off point from the strong to the weak article (see Ortmann 2014). The following examples are from Fering and illustrate that the weak form a/at[15] is found with lexical INs/FNs[16] such as with *the sun* in (25b) while the strong form det/di is found with pragmatic uniqueness such as SN with complements establishing uniqueness (25a), indicating a shift to an IC.

(25) Fering (North Frisian, West Germanic; Ebert 1971: 71, 160)
    a. Det as det   (*at)   buk, wat hi tuiast
       this is DEF.strong   DEF.weak book that he at first
       skrewen hee.
       written AUX
       'This is the book that he wrote first.'
    b. A   san skiinjt.
       DEF.weak sun shine
       'The sun is shining.'

Both articles can occur with DAAs as well as complex ICs (Ebert 1971), which represent the transition from weak to strong article. There are also languages with more than two articles. Maori is such an example. It has a definite article *taua* (sg)/*aua* (pl) for anaphoric NPs and SN with complements establishing uniqueness and thus for the top-most segment on the scale, which is demonstrated in (26).

(26) Maori (Eastern Polynesian, Austronesian; Bauer 1993: 51)
    Ko aua raakau i tua-ina raa e maatou he
    TOP DEF.A tree   T/A fell-PASS DIST by 1PL.EXCL CLS

---

[15] In Fering, the weak article is not a phonologically reduced form of the strong article as in dialects of German. However, the two articles differ with respect to their phonological complexity (Ortmann 2014: 301).
[16] There are only a few names for countries such as *a Türkäi* 'Turkey' which occur with the weak definite article. In general, no article occurs with proper names (Ebert 1971: 71).

ri-riki   katoa.
DUP-small all
'The trees we cut down were all small.'

For the right end of the scale, there is a separate article *a*, occurring with proper names and personal pronouns for all persons.[17] (27) shows the definite article with the personal pronoun for the first person *au*, which is extremely rare from a typological perspective (Ortmann 2011: 297).

(27) Maori (Bauer 1993: 4)
 Kaaore koe i te riri   ki a   au, nee?
 NEG   2SG T/A angry to DEF.P 1SG Q
 'You aren't angry with me, are you?'

Furthermore, there is a default definite article *te* (sg)/*ngaa* (pl), which occurs with pragmatic uniqueness as *taua* (sg)/*aua* (pl) but also with semantic uniqueness other than proper names and personal pronouns. This means that with all stages of the scale a definite article occurs.[18]

To conclude, the (strong) article with pragmatic uniqueness indicates a shift from SN to IC, while with semantic uniqueness the article is semantically redundant and signals the congruent use. More typological evidence for the distinction between semantic and pragmatic uniqueness can be found in Gerland & Horn (2015) and in particular in Ortmann (2014).

On the basis of the implicative scale, one can systematically analyse the distribution of the article in a language. Furthermore, the scale is an instrument that enables us to compare the distribution of definite articles in different languages. The scale will also be important when dealing with the question as to when a demonstrative has fully grammaticalized

---

[17] Bauer (1993: 109f.) enumerates some factors which are responsible for the fact that the definite article *a* does not occur before proper names and personal pronouns. One factor he mentions is that *a* can only occur if preceded by the prepositions *i, ki, kei, hei* (Bauer 1993: 109).

[18] For a detailed analysis of the distribution of the definite articles in Maori see Czardybon (2010).

into a definite article. Table 3 summarizes the language-specific cut-off points discussed in this chapter:

	English	German	Fering	Maori
deictic SN	the	der/ die/ das	det/ di	taua
anaphoric SN				
SN with complements establishing uniqueness				
relational DAAs			a/ at	te
part-whole DAAs				
complex IC				
lexical IN/FN				
proper names	–		–	a
personal pronouns	–	–	–	

Table 3: Distribution of the definite articles in English, colloquial German, Fering, and Maori.

To sum up, the definiteness splits presented in this chapter can be basically explained by the notion of semantic and pragmatic uniqueness, which results from the distinction of the four concept types.

There are also other ways of classifying nouns. In the next section, the distinction between count and mass nouns will be presented, and this will play an important role in chapter 4.

2.4 Mass/count distinction

The distinction between mass and count nouns is a different classification of nouns proposed in the literature (cf. McCawley 1975, Pelletier 1975, 2010, Allan 1980, Bunt 1981, Krifka 1986, 1989, 1991, Pelletier & Schubert 2002, Wisniewski et al. 2003, Bale & Barner 2009, Rothstein 2010, Wisniewski 2010, Doetjes 2012, Massam (ed.) 2012, among others).[19] As is shown in figure 1, nouns can be divided into mass and count, while mass nouns can be further subdivided into stuff and collective nouns.

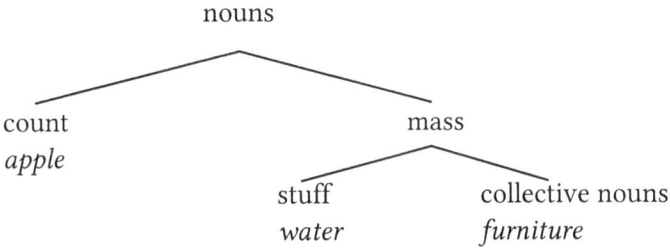

Figure 1: Mass/count distinction (based on Krifka 1991).

Mass and count nouns can be distinguished by several criteria (see also Krifka 1989: 3f., 1991, Gillon 1992, Wisniewski et al. 2003, Rothstein 2010). Only those criteria which are relevant in Polish will be discussed in the following.

There are two semantic criteria proposed in the literature. The first is cumulativity, which was introduced by Quine (1960: 91). According to Quine "[s]o-called mass terms like 'water' [...] have the semantic property of referring cumulatively: any sum of parts which are water is water" (28a). The same applies to bare plurals like *apples* (28b). In contrast, singular count nouns like *apple* are not cumulative. If one has an apple and then adds another apple to it, the sum cannot be described as *apple* but as (*two*) *apples* (28c). Mass nouns and plurals are cumulative while singular count nouns are not.

(28)   a.   water + water = water
        b.   apples + apples = apples
        c.   apple + apple ≠ apple
                 = (two) apples

---

[19] Krifka (1989: 3) uses the term "Individualnomina" ('individual nouns') in the sense of 'count nouns' and not in the sense of inherently unique nouns as Löbner (2011) does.

2 Theoretical basis

The second semantic criterion was proposed by Cheng (1973), it relates to the fact that mass nouns have distributive or divisive reference.[20] Cheng (1973: 287) calls this 'Cheng's condition' and gives the following definition: "Any part of the whole of the mass object which is *w* is *w*". Thus mass nouns and bare plurals are divisive, which means that a proper part of *water* can be denoted by *water*. This is not the case with singular count nouns since no proper part of *apple* is still an apple.[21][22]

In Polish, the distinction between mass (rzeczownik niepoliczalny) and count nouns (rzeczownik policzalny) is reflected grammatically (Piernikarski 1969: 67f., Laskowski 1998a: 204f., Bartnicka et al. 2004: 223f., Nagórko 2006: 111f.). It is often argued that there is no systematic plural form available for mass nouns. Like with English 'apple', the Polish noun *jabłko* 'apple' in (29a) has a plural form *jabłka* 'apples' and is thus a count noun while *woda* 'water' (29b) only allows for a plural in connection with shifting processes, which will be discussed later.[23] This is indicated by the hash mark.

(29) a. *jabłk-o* - *jabłk-a*   b. *wod-a* - #*wod-y*
       apple-SG   apple-PL   water-SG   water-PL
       'apple'   'apples'   'water'   '#waters'

To distinguish between mass and count nouns on the basis of an existing plural form is difficult, since due to shifting processes a plural form is also available for mass nouns. A much more convincing criterion is the

---

[20] The criterion of divisibility goes back to Aristotle and was brought into the discussion as a criterion of the semantics of mass nouns by Cheng (Krifka 1989: 39).
[21] Although the referents of stuff nouns such as *water* and collective nouns such as *furniture* are cumulative they differ with respect to the fact that stuff nouns are not atomic whereas the referents of collectives are, which is also the case with count nouns. The atoms of the collective noun *furniture* are, for example, *chairs* or *tables* not *furniture*. Collective nouns will be neglected in the following. For a detailed analysis of collectives, see Wiese (2012).
[22] See Löbner (2015) for a discussion of the semantic criterion of summativity, which includes divisibility and cumulativity.
[23] As with stuff nouns like *water*, there is no plural form available for collectives such as *rycerstwo* 'chivalry' in Polish either. In addition to collectives, there are other singularia tantum such as abstract nouns like *miłość* 'love'. On the other hand, there are also pluralia tantum such as *okulary* 'glasses', *drzwi* 'door', and *usta* 'mouth' (cf. Barticka et al. 2004: 167f., 224f.). For a detailed enumeration of pluralia tantum in Polish see Swan (2002: 122f.).

following: The quantifier *dużo* 'much/many' combines with mass nouns in the singular (30b), but not with count nouns in the singular (30a) (Witwicka-Iwanowska 2012: 181). The quantifier requires the noun to be in the genitive case, which is independent of the number of the noun. A similar situation is found with *many* in English, which also requires the plural with count nouns, while *much* requires the singular.

(30) a. *Jan kupi-ł   dużo   samochod-ów/ *samochod-u.*
         Jan buy-PST much/many car-PL.GEN/   car-SG.GEN
         'Jan bought many cars/*car.'
     b. *Jan kupi-ł   dużo   wod-y.*
         Jan buy-PST much/many water-SG.GEN
         'Jan bought much water.'

According to Pelletier (1975), shifting processes can take place between mass and count nouns.[24] One count-to-mass shift is captured by the process known as the "universal grinder":[25]

> Consider a machine, the "universal grinder". This machine is rather like a meat grinder in that one introduces something into one end, the grinder chops and grinds it up into a homogeneous mass and spews it onto the floor from its other end. The difference between the universal grinder and a meat grinder is that the universal grinder's machinery allows it to chop up any object no matter how large, no matter how small, no matter how soft, no matter how hard. (Pelletier 1975: 456)

An example of a count-to-mass shift is given in (31). The count noun *dog* is used as a mass noun, which is indicated by the lack of articles. *Dog* is treated like a homogenous mass which is on the road and not as an individual dog.

(31)   *There was dog splattered all over the road* (Bach 1986: 10)

---

[24] In Pelletier (2012), he argues that nouns are lexically unspecified with respect to mass and count.
[25] The universal grinder was suggested by David Lewis to Jeffry Pelletier (1975: 464, note 7) in 1968.

Mass-to-count shifts are captured by the process known as the "universal packager" as illustrated by the examples in (32). Mass-to-count shifts are indicated by the presence of the indefinite article or numerals and plural marking of the mass noun *beer*. In (32a), the mass noun *beer* is shifted to a count noun. Depending on the context a portion (for example *glass, bottle*) (32a) or kind reading (32b) is possible.

(32) a. *Can I have a beer/two beers please!*
→ portion
b. *We only sell one beer/two beers.*
→ kind

In articleless languages, the shift from mass to count cannot be indicated by articles. However, numerals and plurals can be used to signal a mass-to-count shift, as is demonstrated by the Polish examples in (33a). Here, the mass noun *piwa* 'beers' is shifted to a count noun with a portion reading by the presence of a numeral and plural marking while in (33b) we get a kind reading with *wina* 'wines'.

(33) a. *Kupi-ł w sklep-ie trzy piw-a.*^{C}
buy-PST in shop-LOC three beer-PL
'He bought three beers in the shop.'
b. *W sklep-ie sprzedaje się różne win-a.*
in shop-LOC sell REFL various wine-PL
'In the shop various wines are sold (= kinds of wine).'
(Bartnicka et al. 2004: 224)

The distinction into mass and count nouns presented in this section is independent of the classification proposed by Löbner (2011). In contrast to the count nouns in table 1, table 4 gives only examples of mass nouns (Löbner 2015).

	[−U]	[+U] inherently unique
[−R]	Sortal nouns (SN): *water*	Individual nouns (IN): *air*
[+R] inherently relational	Relational nouns (RN): *baggage*	Functional nouns (FN): *skin*

Table 4: The four types of nouns and the mass/count distinction (based on Löbner 2015).

In the chapter on aspect, I will discuss why the distinction of mass and count is crucial in more detail and how Löbner's approach is connected to it.

2.5 Definiteness strategies discussed in the Slavistic literature

This section will present only a brief and incomplete survey of existing studies on definiteness in Slavic. A thorough overview and critical discussion of the relevant literature, especially with regard to Polish, will be presented in detail in the corresponding chapters.

There is a large amount of literature on definiteness from a typological and theoretical point of view. The semantic approaches were discussed in section 2.2. and 2.3. Typological investigations were carried out by Krámský (1972), Himmelmann (1997, 2001), Lyons (1999), Dryer (2015a, 2015b), and Schroeder (2006), among others. Often the focus is on the morphosyntactic realization of definiteness by articles. However, recent decades have seen a great deal of growth in the investigation of articleless languages, and strategies that compensate the lack of articles. Extensive studies have been carried out, for example, on Mandarin Chinese (Li & Thompson 1975, 1981; Chen 2004), Estonian (Hiietam 2003), Finnish (Chesterman 1991), and Turkish (Dede 1986), to mention but a few.

The grammaticalization of articles has also been the focus of a number of papers. One of the best-studied cases is the development of definite articles in the Romance languages from demonstratives in Latin. Grammaticalization is also investigated in other languages, for instance, by Laury (1995, 1997), who discusses the demonstrative *se* in spoken Finnish. She comes to the conclusion that *se* grammaticalized to a marker of identifiability and thus occurs if the referent can be identified by the hearer on the basis of previous mention or cultural knowledge. A discussion of the article status of the Estonian demonstrative *see* is offered by Hiietam & Börjars (2002).

The analysis of articleless languages is often connected to the topic of bare NPs[26]. Chierchia (1998) classifies languages depending on whether they allow for bare NPs or not, using the two binary features [±pred(icative)] and [±arg(umental)]. [±arg] deals with the question whether bare nouns specify an argument of some predicate term or not and [±pred] whether bare nouns can be used as predicates or not. If the bare noun is [+arg] it is of the type <e> and can be the argument of a verb without any determiners and thus behaves like proper nouns in English. If the bare noun is [+pred] then it is of the type <e,t>, i.e. it can be used as a predicate. According to Chierchia, nouns in languages like Chinese are [+arg] and [−pred], which should explain why NPs can be bare in the argument position in Chinese. This is not the case in the Romance languages, according to Chierchia, where the bare nouns are [−arg] and [+pred] and therefore have to occur with a determiner in the argument position. The third group of languages is represented by the Germanic and Slavic languages. Here, the bare nouns are [+arg] and [+pred]. In these languages, singular count nouns behave like those in the Romance languages whereas mass and plural NPs behave like those in Chinese. However, the fact that Chierchia puts the Germanic and Slavic languages into one group, despite the fact that all Germanic languages have a grammaticalized definite article (König & van der Auwera 1994) while most Slavic languages do not and thus allow all NPs to be bare, is something that must be viewed critically. Chierchia's assumption is not applicable to the Slavic languages, which shows that his classification is too coarse. The NPs in articleless Slavic languages behave like

---

[26] Bare NPs do not contain quantifiers and determiners (articles, pronouns). However, bare NPs can have modifiers such as adjectives and relative clauses.

those in Chinese with respect to bare use. The difference between Chinese and articleless Slavic languages is of course that Slavic languages do not have a classifier system while Chinese does not have plural marking.

The lack of articles in most Slavic languages and the investigation of alternative strategies to express definiteness is a subject of interest for linguists and philologists. There is a great deal of literature on definiteness in Russian (Christian 1961, Dončeva-Mareva 1966, Gladrow 1972, Birkenmaier 1979, Chvany 1983, Hauenschild 1985, 1993, Mehlig 1988, Steube & Späth 1999, Friedrich 2009), as well as on Czech (Berger 1993, Cummins 1999, Filip 1993/1999), Serbo-Croatian (Trenkic 2002, 2004), and Polish (Błaszczak 2001, Golovačeva 1979, Mendoza 2004, Miodunka 1974, Pisarkowa 1968, 1969, Reiter 1977, Sadziński 1995/6, Szwedek 1975, 1976b, 1986, Topolińska 1976, 1981, 1984, Wierzbicka 1967, Witwicka-Iwanowska 2012). In the Slavic literature on definiteness, the following strategies for expressing definiteness are often mentioned.

Demonstratives are discussed as a strategy for expressing definiteness since they mark an NP as definite. In the Kashubian example (34), the demonstrative *na* signals definiteness for the anaphoric NP *szklónka* 'cup' and thus it is understood as coreferential with the NP *snôżą szklónkã* in the first sentence.

(34) Kashubian (West Slavic)
Jô dostôł òd Marie snôżą szklónkã$_j$. Ale wczerô na
I got from Maria nice cup but yesterday DEM
szklónka$_j$ mie sã stłëkła.
cup me REFL get_broken
'I got a nice cup from Maria. But the cup got broken yesterday.'

There is extensive literature on the Polish demonstratives, especially on the demonstrative *ten* (cf. Mendoza 2004 and the literature cited therein). A number of authors have only focused on anaphoric NPs and how coreference can be established (Szwedek 1975, 1976b, 1986, Golovačeva 1979). They analyse important factors for the occurrence of *ten* with anaphoric NPs. Other authors have investigated spoken Polish, also covering uses other than anaphoric uses (Miodunka 1974, Wróbel 1984). In chapter 3, I provide a systematic approach by investigating all important occurrences in which a demonstrative can be found and take the distinction of the four concept types into consideration; something which has not been done so far. Furthermore, I will show that there is a difference between spoken and written Polish concerning the distribution and frequency of *ten*. In the literature, most authors only concentrate on the analysis of either spoken or written Polish and those who cover both do not observe a significant difference. Another drawback of previous studies is that no convincing criteria are presented when dealing with the question as to whether *ten* is a demonstrative or a definite article. Moreover, Polish is mostly analysed in isolation without looking into the other Slavic languages.

Aspect is another strategy which can influence the definiteness of an NP. This is illustrated by the Czech examples in (35).

(35) Czech (West Slavic; Filip 1993/1999: 227)
    a.   *Ivan s-nědl^{PF} jablka.*
        Ivan S-eat.PST apple.PL.ACC
        'Ivan ate (up) (all) the apples.'
    b.   *Ivan jedl^{IMPF} jablka.*
        Ivan eat.PST apple.PL.ACC
        (i) 'Ivan ate (some/the) apples.'
        (ii) 'Ivan was eating (some/the) apples.'

In (35a), the verb *snědl* is perfective, while in (35b) we have the imperfective verb *jedl*.[27] The English equivalents show that the perfective construction leads to a definite interpretation of the direct object in contrast to the direct object in (35b) which can have a definite as well as an indefinite reading. Aspect as a definiteness strategy in Polish is also mentioned (cf. Wierzbicka 1967), although there is not much literature on this topic and often it is discussed only briefly and superficially as done, for example, by Sadziński (1982: 89, 1985: 171, 1991: 159, 1995/6: 87), who gives only one example to illustrate this strategy. In chapter 4, I will take a closer look at the conditions under which a definite reading is enforced.

---

[27] The grammatical aspect is superscripted to the verbs in (35) and not given in the glossings. The reason for doing so will be explained in chapter 4.

2.5 Definiteness strategies discussed in the Slavistic literature

For direct objects of some Russian verbs, there is an alternation available between accusative and genitive case (Dončeva-Mareva 1966: 39f., Solonicyn 1962: 96 quoted after Birkenmaier 1979: 108, Gladrow 1972: 650, Kagan 2013: 3ff.). This alternation is only observable with perfective verbs (Birkenmaier 1979: 113, Kagan 2013: 3f.). In (36a), the direct object in the accusative case in combination with a perfective verb leads to a definite reading. The genitive case in (36b) leads to an indefinite (pseudo-)partitive[28] reading of the NP *vody* 'water'.

(36) Russian
    a. *On vy-pil*^{PF} *vod-u*
        he VY-drink.PST water-ACC
        'He drank (all) the water.'
    b. *On vy-pil*^{PF} *vod-y*
        he VY-drink.PST water-GEN
        'He drank some (of the) water.'

The influence of case alternation on definiteness is also described for Polish by, for example, Reiter (1977), Sadziński (1977, 1982, 1985, 1991, 1995/96), and Witwicka-Iwanowska (2012). But it is not totally clear with which nouns and verbs a case alternation between accusative and genitive is possible. Furthermore, if an alternation is available, the question arises as to whether case correlates with (in)definiteness or with other factors. These questions will be addressed in chapter 5.

In the South Slavic languages Slovene, Serbian, and Croatian, there are two different adjectival endings, one of which can indicate definiteness. The long form is associated with definiteness and the short one with indefiniteness, which is demonstrated by the Serbian example in (37). In (37a), we have the short form of the adjective *star* 'old' and thus *kamion* 'truck' is interpreted as indefinite. By using the long adjectival form *-i* with masculine singular nouns in nominative case in (37b) a definite interpretation is achieved.

---

[28] The notion of (pseudo)partitivity will be explained in section 5.3.1.

(37) Serbian (South Slavic; Hammond 2005: 204)
    a.   *star   kamion*
          old.SHORT truck
          'an old truck'
    b.   *star-i   kamion*
          old-LONG truck
          'the old truck'

There is a debate whether the contrast described in (37) expresses definiteness or rather specificity[29]. For Trenkic (2002: 116), the difference between definiteness and specificity refers "to whom something is identifiable (*odredjen*): to both the speaker and the hearer (definite), or just to the speaker (specific)". For Trenkic (2002), it is specificity that is expressed by the different adjectival endings and not definiteness as argued by Krámský (1972: 179), Hlebec (1986: 33), Progovac (1998: 174), Leko (1999: 230), Lyons (1999: 82f.), and Mendoza (2004: 209f.). As will be shown later, this strategy is not available in Polish.

The order of constituents within the sentence is also frequently mentioned as a means to signal (in)definiteness. This is connected to information structure, which will be introduced only informally at this point. A sentence or utterance can be divided into a topic and a focus.[30] Topics, which can be defined as being under discussion and taken for granted for the speaker and the hearer (Lambrecht 1994)[31], are sentence-initial or preverbal in unmarked sentences in Slavic. Due to the fact that topics represent presupposed information, they are interpreted as definite or generic. Post-verbal NPs are part of the focus expressing the added or new proposition, which can have a definite as well as indefinite reading depending on several factors. This is illustrated with the Czech example

---

[29] Specificity is orthogonal to definiteness (Lyons 1999: 165f.) and deals with the reference to a particular entity that "the speaker has in mind" (von Heusinger 2011: 1026). A definite as well as an indefinite NP can be specific or unspecific. Von Heusinger (2002a, 2011) investigates specificity in the domain of indefinite NPs. Different types of indefinite specificity are discussed in more detail by von Heusinger (2002a, 2011).

[30] At this point, I neglect sentences without a topic which are called 'thetic' (Sasse 1987, Rosengren 1997).

[31] Lambrecht's detailed definition of the terms 'topic' and 'focus' are given in section 6.1.4.

2.5 Definiteness strategies discussed in the Slavistic literature

in (38a), in which the noun *kniha* 'book' is the topic in (38a), placed preverbally and thus resulting in a definite reading. In (38b), the noun *kniha* 'book' is placed post-verbally, and thus, is the focus, which has the effect that the NP is interpreted as indefinite, according to Krámský (1972: 42).[32]

(38) Czech (Krámský 1972: 42)
  a. *Kniha je na stole.*
     book is on table
     'The book is on the table.'
  b. *Na stole je kniha.*
     on table is book
     'On the table (there) is a book.'

Word order as a definiteness strategy in Polish is discussed by Szwedek (1974, 1975, 1976b, 1986), Sadziński (1982, 1985, 1991, 1995/6), Grzegorek (1984), Engel et al. (1999), and Mendoza (2004). These authors provide important observations regarding in which position within the sentence an NP allows for a definite or an indefinite interpretation. However, there are still a number of questions left open, for example, whether the sentence-final NP is associated with indefiniteness as claimed by Szwedek (1974: 209, 1976b: 62) or whether it also allows for a definite reading as assumed by Mendoza (2004: 217) and Błaszczak (2001: 11). The interaction of word order and definiteness will be discussed in chapter 6.

Sentence stress also correlates with information structure and can interact with definiteness. Furthermore, it can override the effect of word order as pointed out by Gladrow (1972: 648f.). As an illustration, he provides the Russian examples in (39). Sentence stress is indicated by capital letters:

(39) Russian (Pospelov 1970, quoted after Gladrow 1972: 649)
  a. *poezd PRIŠEL*
     train arrived
     'The train arrived'

---

[32] Later, I will show that postverbal NPs in Czech also allow for a definite reading and not only an indefinite one as argued by Krámský in (38b).

b. *POEZD prišel*
train   arrived
'A train arrived'
c. *prišel POEZD*
arrived train
'A train arrived'
d. *PRIŠEL poezd*
arrived train
'The train arrived'

In (39a) and (39b) we have the word order SV, while in (39c) and (39d) the order is VS. (39a) and (39b) only differ with respect to the placement of the sentence stress, which is also the case with (39c) and (39d). According to Gladrow (1972: 648f.), (39a) and (39c) represent the stylistically neutral construction in contrast to the other two which are stylistically expressive. Birkenmaier (1979: 56f.) comes to the conclusion that nouns that bear the sentence stress are interpreted as indefinite as in (39b) and (39c), while unstressed nouns are definite (39a) and (39d). It can also be observed that the effect of word order is overridden by intonation as mentioned above. Even though *poezd* 'train' is placed at the beginning of the sentence in (39b) it has an indefinite reading. The fact that this situation is more complex than shown here can be deduced from Späth's claim (2006: 59) that the sentence in (39c) can have an indefinite as well as a definite interpretation.

For Polish, there are only a few studies dealing with the topic of sentence stress and its influence on definiteness (Szwedek 1974, 1975, 1976b, 1986). The interaction of sentence stress and the definiteness of NPs will be the focus of chapter 6.

3 Demonstratives[1]

In this chapter, the discussion focuses on adnominal demonstrative pronouns, as they represent a strategy for explicitly marking an NP as definite. The focus is on the Polish determiner *ten* and not on other demonstratives since the status of *ten* as a definite article is frequently discussed in the literature (cf. Bacz 1991, Mendoza 2004: 292, Piskorz 2011). In order not to be biased during my analysis as to whether *ten* is a demonstrative or a definite article, I will speak of (and gloss) *ten* as a determiner. However, the English translation forces me to make a decision. Although I will translate *ten* as the definite article *the* in some examples this does not automatically mean that we can deduce that we have a grammaticalized definite article in Polish. Whether *ten* is a definite article or a demonstrative will be discussed at the end of this chapter. In section 3.1, I will discuss a number of criteria which will help to decide when a demonstrative is fully grammaticalized into a definite article. In section 3.2, I introduce the Polish determiners and the paradigm of *ten*. Before presenting my own analysis of the determiner *ten* in standard Polish in section 3.4, I present a survey of previous studies on Polish determiners in 3.3. In my analysis, only the adnominal use of *ten* will be taken into consideration. For an analysis of the Polish determiners in nominal use see Mendoza (2004: 292f.). In the last section 3.5, I compare the distribution of the standard Polish determiner *ten* to other Slavic languages in order to show micro-variation within this language family.

---

[1] This chapter is partially based on Czardybon (2010).

3 Demonstratives

3.1 Criteria for the grammaticalization of definite articles

Grammaticalization can be defined as the development "from a lexical to a grammatical or from a less grammatical to a more grammatical" item (Kuryłowicz 1975: 52). With respect to the grammaticalization of definite articles, Greenberg (1978) notes that they most commonly develop from demonstratives. In his approach, he distinguishes several stages in which demonstratives can develop into pure noun markers. Demonstratives are the starting point for this process representing stage 0. Stage I is characterized by definite articles, stage II by an article covering definite and non-definite specific uses, and in stage III noun markers represent the endpoint of this development.

The development from stage 0 to I is attested for a large number of languages. One of the best documented cases is represented by the Romance languages, which developed a definite article from Latin demonstratives.

However, the question arises as to when a demonstrative is fully grammaticalized into a definite article and has achieved stage I according to Greenberg. In order to answer this question, we need appropriate defining criteria. The grammaticalization path can involve a change on all levels of language structure. By analysing these changes, important criteria for the article status of a determiner can be deduced. The following changes are frequently mentioned in the literature (Diessel 1999: 117, Hopper & Traugott 1993: 87f., 145, Lehmann 1991: 493, Löbner 2011: 326, Lyons 1999: 275f., Traugott & Heine 1991: 2f.).

At the semantic level, grammaticalization can lead to a semantic bleaching of the lexical item and thus to a loss of meaning. With respect to demonstratives, this means that the distal/proximal distinction is neutralized and that demonstratives lose their deictic value when developing into definite articles (Löbner 2011: 326; Lyons 1999: 331f.). However, this does not necessarily have to be the case. This is exemplified by the South Slavic language Macedonian, which has three suffixed definite articles which show a distal/proximal distinction (Lyons 1999: 56).

At the phonological level, demonstratives can be reduced to an unstressed morpheme, can be shortened, or become a clitic or affix (Lyons 1999: 54, 116).

The obligatory occurrence is another important criterion mentioned by Christophersen (1939: 83), Krámský (1972: 33), Diessel (1999:118), and Himmelmann (2001: 832f.). However, the question arises: in which contexts does the determiner have to be obligatory? For Krámský (1972: 33, 62), a determiner is a definite article if it occurs with generic NPs. However, his view is too restrictive since with this definition many languages for which we have good reasons to assume an article would not have one. Himmelmann (1997: 41f., 2001: 833f.) makes the crosslinguistic observation that we can speak of a definite article if the determiner under investigation is found with definite associative anaphors or other semantically unique concepts because only definite articles and not a demonstrative can occur in these contexts.[2] Himmelmann (2001: 833f.) states that

> The crucial distinguishing feature, however, is that they [articles] are consistently used in some additional contexts in which demonstratives must not be used. For definite articles two contexts are of particular importance. One is **larger situation use**, the first mention of entities that are considered to be unique [...], (e.g. *the sun, the Queen, the pub*). The other is **associative-anaphoric use** [...]

Himmelmann's statement is illustrated in (1) and (2). The heads of the DAAs *bride* and *driver* can only be associative-anaphorically linked by the definite article but not by a demonstrative.

(1) Last week we were at our neighbour's wedding. The (*This) bride was beautiful.

(2) When I got onto the bus I asked the (*this) driver how much a ticket costs.

Although Himmelmann's observation is correct, the obligatory occurrence in this context is a sufficient but not a necessary condition for

---

[2] Similar statements are made by Hawkins (1978: 127) for English and Bisle-Müller (1991: 70f.) for German.

definite articles. The necessary condition is defined by Diessel (1999: 128f.), whom I follow in this study:

> The use of anaphoric demonstratives is usually confined to non-topical[3] antecedents that tend to be somewhat unexpected, contrastive or emphatic [...]. When anaphoric demonstratives develop into definite articles their use is gradually extended from non-topical antecedents to all kinds of referents in the preceding discourse. In the course of this development, demonstratives lose their deictic function and turn into formal markers of definiteness. (Diessel 1999: 128f.).

According to Diessel (1999: 118, 128f.), a determiner has grammaticalized into a definite article if it occurs obligatorily with anaphoric NPs of topical antecedents, is semantically bleached by losing the deictic value, and is not contrastive or emphatic. Another distinguishing feature of definite articles and anaphoric demonstratives is that the former is unstressed (Diessel 1999: 129, Lyons 1999: 54).[4] In the following sections, I will apply this definition to the Polish determiner *ten*.

3.2 Polish determiners and the paradigm of *ten*

There are four demonstratives in Polish, *ten*, *tamten*, *ów*, and *taki*.[5] In table 5, the paradigm of *ten* is given. Standard Polish distinguishes between two numbers (singular and plural), three genders (feminine, mas-

---

[3] A topical NP represents old or presupposed information about its referent that has to be under discussion (Lambrecht 1994). For a detailed discussion of what topics are see chapter 6 on information structure.
[4] For an overview of anaphoric articles, see Lyons (1999: 53f., 158ff.).
[5] *taki* 'such a' is also counted as a demonstrative pronoun in Polish (Bartnicka et al 2004: 305, Birnbaum & Molas 2009: 155, Engel et al. 1999: 69, 802), but it does not lead to a definite but an indefinite reading of the NP. (For more information on indefinite demonstratives see Lyons (1999: 151f.)). Indefiniteness can also be expressed explicitly by indefinite pronouns such as *jakiś* 'some', *niektóry* 'some', *niejaki* 'some', *jakikolwiek* 'any', *pewien* 'certain', and the numeral *jeden* 'one'. Since the focus is on definiteness in this study, the pronouns indicating indefiniteness will not be considered. For further literature see Pisarkowa (1968, 1969), Miodunka (1974: 53f.), Sadziński (1995/96: 93f.), and Mendoza (2004: 306f.).

culine, and neuter) and seven cases (nominative, accusative, genitive, dative, locative, instrumental, and vocative). There is no vocative form for *ten*.[6]

	singular				plural	
	masculine animate	masculine inanimate	neuter	feminine	masculine persons	others
Nom	ten	ten	to	ta	ci	te
Acc			to	tę/(tą)[7]		te
Gen	tego	tego	tego	tej	tych	tych
Dat	temu	temu	temu	tej	tym	tym
Loc	tym	tym	tym	tej	tych	tych
Ins	tym	tym	tym	tą	tymi	tymi

Table 5: Paradigm of the standard Polish determiner *ten*.

Ten is not a distal or proximal determiner, but unmarked for distance (Miodunka 1974: 51). Furthermore, it can occur in pre- and post-nominal position. Post-nominal *ten* is restricted to anaphoric NPs and is characteristic of written Polish and untypical for spoken Polish (Miodunka 1974: 82, Mendoza 2004: 289). Wróbel (1984), who investigates spoken Polish, says "no example of the postposition of *ten* could be found, so we may conclude that postposition is the characteristic feature of written texts" (Wróbel 1984: 49). The following example illustrates the use of post-nominal *ten*.

---

[6] A separate accusative form of *ten* is only available for feminine singular. For all other classes, we find a syncretism either with the nominative or genitive case. This will be discussed in more detail in chapter 5 on case alternation.

[7] In prescriptive Polish grammars (Rothstein 1993: 702; Swan 2002: 171), it is pointed out that *tę* is the only correct feminine singular accusative form. However, in spoken language the form *tą* is frequently used and accepted as correct. This is also observed by Laskowski (1998b: 359) and Nagórko (2006: 157).

(3) Wtedy spotka-ł-am   jakiegoś pan-a[8]   i   pan
     then meet-PST-1SG.F some   gentleman-ACC and gentleman
     ten pokazał mi drog-ę.
     DET show.PST me way-ACC
     'Then I met some gentleman and the gentleman showed me the way.' (Topolińska 1984: 327)

It has to be emphasized that the occurrence of post-nominal *ten* is not obligatory. According to my informants, it can be omitted in examples such as (3), where the NP *pan* 'gentleman' is still coreferential to the man previously introduced. Furthermore, post-nominal *ten* can only occur in topic position, which is the preverbal position in a sentence with an unmarked topic-focus structure[9], as in (3). In non-topic position as part of the sentence-final NP, post-nominal *ten* is ungrammatical, as is illustrated by Sadziński's example in (4). In contrast, prenominal *ten* is not restricted to anaphoric NPs and is unmarked for register, which will be shown in section 3.4.

(4) *Chłopiec kupi-ł   książk-ę tę.
     boy.NOM buy-PST   book-ACC DET
     (Sadziński 1982: 86)

The determiner *ów* represents a stylistic variant of the anaphoric post-nominal *ten* (Topolińska 1976: 59, Mendoza 2004: 302)[10] occurring in written Polish of high register (Pisarkowa 1969: 50). Miodunka (1974: 37), for example, points out that it seldom if ever appears in spoken Polish. In (5), the anaphoric NP *wąż* 'snake' is found with *ów*, however, *ów* is not obligatory. In most cases, the anaphoric NP need not be marked by a determiner in written Polish to be interpreted as coreferential.

---

[8] For masculine nouns, there is a syncretism of the genitive and accusative case. In this example, the suffix -*a* functions as an accusative. Such syncretisms are discussed in more detail in chapter 5.
[9] The notion of topic and focus is explained in detail in chapter 6.
[10] According to Mendoza (2004: 302), *ów* also appears in recognitional uses.

(5)   [...] o   psie   co   zobaczy-ł węża   w ogrodzie
about dog.LOC REL see-PST   snake.ACC in garden.LOC
gdy   pasterz-e   spa-li,   ów   wąż   zatru-ł   mleko
when shepherd-PL sleep-PST.PL DET snake poison-PST milk
w mis-ie^C
in bowl-LOC
'about a dog that saw a snake in the garden when the shepherds were sleeping, this snake poisoned the milk in the bowl'

In Polish, there is also a distal demonstrative *tamten* available. It is formed by adding the prefix *tam-* 'there' to *ten*.[11] It mainly appears in deictic contexts.[12] In the following, I will only investigate the distribution of prenominal *ten* since it is not restricted to a certain register or a certain linguistic context as is the case with *tamten*, *ów*, and post-nominal *ten*. Although *ów* and post-nominal *ten* are found with anaphoric NPs, they are not obligatory. This shows that they cannot be regarded as definite articles, but represent anaphoric demonstratives. Furthermore, prenominal *ten* is the most frequent pronoun according to Miodunka's (1974: 44) study, which reveals that *ten* occurs in 42.1 % of all NPs with pronouns in spoken standard Polish, while *tamten* only occurs with 1 %. Furthermore, quoting Zarębina, Miodunka (1974: 86) shows that *ten* is third on the list of the most frequent words in spoken standard Polish and the fourth position in written standard Polish.

3.3 Previous studies on demonstratives in Polish

A number of authors have focused exclusively on anaphoric NPs. Szwedek (1974, 1975, 1976b, 1986) is one of them, discussing several strategies such as sentence stress, word order, and pronouns like *ten* in order to express coreferentiality in Polish. For him, for example, word order has an influence on the occurrence of *ten* with anaphoric NPs. He

---

[11] For feminine accusative, only the form *tamtą* and not *tamtę* exists.
[12] For a detailed investigation of the distribution of *tamten* see Mendoza (2004: 297ff.) and the literature therein.

states that *ten* is obligatory with NPs in sentence-final position in order to achieve a coreferential reading (Szwedek 1975: 125, 1976b: 99). He demonstrates this by the following example:

(6) *Widzia-ł-em jak do pokoj-u wchodzi-ł mężczyzna. Kiedy*
 see-PST-1SG how in room-LOC enter-PST man when
 wszedł-em zobaczy-ł-em, że przy okn-ie stoi
 enter.PST-1SG see-PST-1SG that at window-LOC stand.PRS
 ten mężczyzna.
 DET man
 'I saw a man go into the room. When I entered I saw that the man was standing at the window'
 (Szwedek 1975: 122f., 1976b: 96f.)

Without *ten* in the second sentence, the sentence-final NP would be interpreted as indefinite and thus would not be coreferential to the NP *mężczyzna* 'man' in the first sentence, as Szwedek claims. In these contexts, *ten* is obligatory to indicate coreferentiality (Szwedek 1975: 121f.). For NPs in sentence-initial position, he reports that *ten* is optional (Szwedek 1975: 125). Szwedek's observations are only partially correct since the omission of *ten* in (6) would not automatically lead to an indefinite reading of the sentence-final NP *mężczyzna* 'man', but also allows for a definite interpretation in an appropriate context.

Sadziński (1977, 1982, 1985, 1991, 1995/6), who works on the Polish equivalent of the German article, comes to a similar partially incorrect conclusion as Szwedek, stating that with anaphoric NPs prenominal *ten* is obligatory in sentence-final position while it is optional in sentence-initial position (Sadziński 1982: 86f., 1985: 168f., 1995/6: 85f.). In his study, he also includes associative anaphors claiming that *ten* is ungrammatical with part-whole DAAs, which is illustrated by him in (7) (Sadziński 1995/6: 121f.). However, it has to be stressed that (7) does not represent a part-whole DAA since the referent of the DAA head *kościelny* 'verger' is not a part of the referent of the antecedent *katedra* 'cathedral'. However, Sadziński is right claiming that *ten* is normally not found with part-whole DAAs, which I will discuss in more detail in section 3.4.2.1.

(7) Katedra   hucza-ł-a. [...]   Rozległ   się głos   (*tego)
     cathedral reverberate-PST-F   boom.PST REFL voice DET
     kościelnego.
     verger
     'The cathedral reverberated. The voice of the verger boomed.'
     (Sadziński 1995/6: 121)

The studies by Wróbel (1984) and Miodunka (1974) both only investigate the distribution of *ten* in spoken Polish. In contrast to the authors mentioned before, they also include other than anaphoric uses of *ten*.

Wróbel (1984: 41f.) looks at spoken standard Polish and distinguishes between three contexts in which *ten* occurs. The first context is represented by what Wróbel (1984: 42f.) calls "deixis in praesentia". These are deictic contexts in which the referent is present and visible to the discourse participants. Deixis in absentia is the second context in which *ten* occurs. Under this point, he subsumes (i) the recognitional use, (ii) "NP including a predicative expression", e.g. a restrictive relative clause, and (iii) a context which is quite vaguely described. What he probably has in mind is associative anaphors defining the context as "the reproduction of a certain state of affairs in the framework of the general subject matter due to which both objects and events involved become specified for the sender and receiver" (Wróbel 1984: 48). The third context is the anaphoric use of *ten* (Wróbel 1984: 45, 48). Concerning the question of optionality or obligatoriness of *ten*, Wróbel makes some important observations. According to him, *ten* is "regularly" used in all cases of deixis in praesentia and anaphors, regardless of the position of the anaphoric NP within the sentence. One of the anaphoric examples Wróbel discusses is given for illustration purposes in (8). The anaphoric NP *deskach* 'board' is determined by the determiner *ten*.

(8) tam były desk-i   poukładane a   na tych desk-ach
     there were board-PL   put   and on DET board-LOC.PL
     były szczebel-k-i   poprzybijane
     were rung-DIM-PL   nailed
     'there were some boards put there and there were small rungs nailed on the boards' (Wróbel 1984: 45)

3 Demonstratives

Ten also regularly occurs with restrictive relative clauses (Wróbel 1984: 49). Wróbel's observation concerning the occurrence of the determiner *ten* with anaphors is in contrast to Szwedek's and Sadziński's claims. I will show later that the different observations can be attributed to a difference between spoken and written Polish.

In contrast to Wróbel, Miodunka (1974) analyses the pronouns *ten*, *taki* 'such a', and *jakiś* 'some' in the spoken varieties of Polish (spoken standard, colloquial, and dialectal[13] Polish). He observes that *ten* occurs in the following contexts: demonstratio ad oculos, anaphoric, cataphoric, deixis am Phantasma, and emphatic contexts (Miodunka 1974: 45f.). He calls the first context "demonstratio ad oculos", which corresponds to deictic uses. "Cataphoric" means *ten* with complements establishing uniqueness and "deixis am Phantasma" corresponds to the recognitional uses in which shared knowledge is crucial. Miodunka (1974: 60f.) argues that the emphatic or emotional use of *ten* is only its secondary function and is needed for the special intonation pattern. The results concerning the investigated dialect are interesting. He states that *ten* has the highest frequency of all pronouns in spoken standard and colloquial Polish at 42.1 % and even reaching as high as 56.1 % in dialectal Polish. He also shows that among the first ten most frequent words, *ten* is in fourth position in written standard Polish, in third position in spoken standard Polish, and in first position in dialectal Polish. Quoting Mistrika, he compares this picture with the ten most frequent words in article languages such as French and German, where the most frequent word is the definite article. This is why one can conclude that *ten* functions as an article in dialectal Polish due to its high frequency (Miodunka 1974: 90). This shows that standard Polish and Polish dialects differ with respect to the occurrence of the determiner *ten*. This will also be further exemplified in section 3.5.1 by means of an examination of the Polish dialect Upper Silesian, which crucially differs from standard Polish.

One drawback of Miodunka's study is that he does not distinguish sufficiently between the different varieties of spoken Polish in his analy-

---

[13] He collected his dialectal material in the area of the cities of Cracow/Rzeszów, where the Lesser Polish dialect (dialect małopolski) is spoken (Miodunka 1974: 34, 97).

sis. This is also reflected by the mixture of standard Polish and dialectal examples which he gives for illustration. No distinction is made: they are treated alike in the analysis.

Mendoza's (2004) habilitation thesis is about nominal determination in Polish and focuses on the demonstratives *ten, tamten, ów* as well as indefinite pronouns in adjectival and nominal function and not on other strategies such as case alternation or grammatical aspect. Her investigation is based on a corpus consisting of spoken and written material as well as work with Polish informants (Mendoza 2004: 3).

Analysing different contexts, she makes the observation that *ten* does not occur with generic NPs, proper names, and absolute and relative uniques such as *sun* and *bathroom* (Mendoza 2004: 85, 130f., 274, 278, 290). In deictic contexts, *ten* cannot be omitted and it is almost obligatory in recognitional uses (Mendoza 2004: 278, 279). With respect to relative clauses, Mendoza (2004: 224) points out that there are different means of indicating if it is a restrictive or non-restrictive relative clause. *Ten* can signal that it is a restrictive one. However, she does not mention if *ten* is obligatory or optional.

Part-whole DAAs are counted by Mendoza as relational uniques and she calls other than part-whole DAAs 'implicit anaphors'. *Ten* is not found with part-whole DAAs, while it is optional with non-part-whole DAAs in colloquial Polish, as she states (Mendoza 2004: 122, 130, 283). Her claim about non-part-whole DAAs, however, is too general and thus only partially correct. In section 3.4.2, I will analyse the different types of DAAs in more detail as well as the acceptability of *ten*.

Regarding the article status of *ten*, she writes that one can speak of a developed definite article if it is found regularly in contexts in which it is redundant. The anaphoric use would be the beginning of this development. She concludes that *ten* cannot be regarded as a definite article since it does not occur regularly with anaphoric NPs and is only obligatory in some cases (Mendoza 2004: 142, 166, 292). Her observation is in contrast to Wróbel's, which can be attributed to the fact that Mendoza uses written and spoken material whereas Wróbel only makes use of spoken material.

Piskorz (2011) is particularly interested in the article status of *ten* in spoken Polish. She claims that *ten* functions as an article when found in anaphoric, generic, individuating, recognitional, and expressive contexts (Piskorz 2011: 164f.). By individuating, Piskorz (2011: 166) means that the NP is not interpreted as generic but as referential, which is illustrated by (9). In the absence of the determiner *ten*, the NP *czerwonej sukienki* 'red dress' could be interpreted as generic.

(9) *Nie powinnaś nosić tej czerwonej sukienki.*
 NEG should.2SG wear DET red dress
 'You should not wear the red dress.' (Piskorz 2011: 166)

Piskorz's (2011: 167f.) conclusion is that *ten* cannot be regarded as a full equivalent of the German definite article, but is on its way to becoming one due to its occurrence in the contexts mentioned above. She draws a parallel to Old High German in which the demonstrative also began to occur with anaphoric NPs. This is also the case in Polish, especially in the post-verbal position to mark an NP as definite.

However, she also discusses arguments against the article status of *ten*: *ten* is optional in many contexts and it is difficult to distinguish between the deictic and the anaphoric function. Furthermore, *ten* is not found with generic expressions in general but only in generic comparisons such as in (10). As a final argument, no new demonstrative is developing as was the case in Old High German (Piskorz 2011: 168).

(10) *Pracuje jak ten wół!*
 work.3SG.PRS like DET ox
 'He is working like an (lit. the) ox.' (Mendoza 2004: 272)

This discussion of the literature on the determiner *ten* reveals that the various authors have significantly contributed to our understanding of the occurrence of *ten* in its various contexts. However, there are still a number of questions to be answered. The authors do not present a systematic approach that includes all possible occurrences of a determiner, and the distinction of the four concept types has still not been taken into consideration. Most authors only concentrate on the analysis of either spoken or written Polish and those who do include both do not observe a striking difference. Moreover, Polish is usually analysed in isolation without comparison with the other Slavic languages. My own analysis will try to compensate for these shortcomings.

3.4 My analysis of *ten*

This section presents the results of my questionnaire on the distribution of *ten*, the work with my informants and the analysis of parts of the Polish National Corpus "NKJP", the Polish translation of Orwell's novel *1984*, as well as spoken material published in Pisarkowa (1975) and Lubaś (1978). In the following sections, I investigate the distribution of *ten* with pragmatic and semantic uniqueness as structured on the scale, starting with pragmatic uniqueness in section 3.4.1. Since DAAs have a special status – being semantically and pragmatically unique – they are placed between sections 3.4.2 and semantic uniqueness in 3.4.3. Finally, certain factors which trigger the presence of *ten* with semantically unique NPs are discussed in 3.4.4.

3.4.1 The occurrence of *ten* with pragmatic uniqueness

3.4.1.1 Deictic SNs
One has to distinguish between two types of deictic contexts which differ in the occurrence of the determiner *ten* in Polish. There are deictic contexts in which more than one potential referent can fit the definite NP. In such a context, the determiner *ten* cannot be omitted and has to be stressed. Furthermore, a pointing gesture is required in order to achieve unique reference. Imagine a situation in which several cars are parked in front of the speaker and the speaker utters the sentence in (11). The only way of establishing unique reference would be by means of a gesture, for example pointing to one of the cars.

(11)   TEN samochód jest mój.
        DET car   COP my
        'This/That car is mine.'

3 Demonstratives

The second type of deictic contexts is characterized by the fact that there is accidentally only one referent in the context that fits the definite NP. In such a context, the determiner *ten* is optional and unstressed. Moreover, a pointing gesture is not required to achieve a unique reference because unique reference is already created by the context itself. Imagine a situation in which two people are sitting in a room with only one door that is open. One person utters the sentence in (12) to the other. It is obvious from the context which door is meant, namely the only open one in the room.

(12) *Zamknij (te) drzwi!*
close.IMP DET door
'Close the door!'

In both types of deictic contexts, the referent of the definite NP is perceivable[14] by the discourse participants. According to Bacz (1991: 5), *ten* is stressed in deictic contexts. As I have shown, this is not necessarily the case in contexts where only one referent can fit the definite NP as in (12). In this section, I also discuss recognitional contexts[15] in which the referent is neither perceivable – as with the deictic contexts so far – nor was previously mentioned. In such contexts, the referent of the definite NP is only present in the minds of the discourse participants and is identified on the basis of the shared knowledge of hearer and speaker (cf. Wróbel 1984: 43f., Topolińska 1984: 312). The context is often indicated with the help of the phrase "do you know/remember (...)". As Diessel (1999: 106) points out, the referent of the definite NP is discourse-new information, but for the hearer it is old information. (13) is given for illustration:

(13) *Anula zawsze wlewa-ł-a ją do tej jasn-ej*
Anula always pour-PST-F it into DET bright-GEN

---

[14] The referent need not be visible, but can also be perceived olfactorily or acoustically.
[15] The term 'recognitional' is taken from Himmelmann (2001: 833), whereas other authors such as Berger (1993: 297) call such uses 'pseudo-anaphoric'.

waz-y,   pamięta-sz?^{C}
vase-GEN remember-2SG
'Anula always poured it into this bright vase, do you remember?'

In (13), the whole NP with the SN *waza* 'vase' is shifted to [+U] due to the determiner *ten*. Although the vase is not present and perceivable in this situation, the NP refers to a vase which is made unique due to the common knowledge of the participants. According to my informants, *ten* is obligatory and unstressed in (13).

3.4.1.2 Anaphoric SNs

In Polish, the presence of *ten* with SNs as anaphoric NPs is influenced by several factors such as register (spoken vs. written), information structure, and the exclusion of generic readings of NPs.

In section 3.2, I have already shown that anaphoric NPs in written Polish (e.g. in novels and newspapers) need not be accompanied by a determiner. In a sentence with an unmarked topic-focus structure with a preverbal topical anaphoric NP, *ten* is optional. This can be explained by the fact that topical NPs contain information that is taken as given and thus the topical NP is interpreted as definite.[16] This is why *ten* is not necessary to indicate unique reference. Example (14) is taken from a daily newspaper showing that the anaphoric NP *mężczyzna* 'man' in preverbal position is bare. The placement of the NP at the beginning of the sentence indicates that it is definite and thus most probably coreferential to the NP *mężczyzna* 'man' introduced before. The occurrence of *ten* in this position is a question of style. My informants report that they would avoid it in written Polish to achieve a better style.

(14) [...] do   kabin-y   wszedł... obcy   mężczyzna. Mężczyzna
       into cabin-GEN enter.PST foreign man   man
       o   nic   nie pytał, po prostu wszedł.^{C}
       for nothing NEG ask.PST simply   enter.PST
       'A foreign man entered the cabin. The man did not ask for anything, he simply entered.'

---

[16] Topical NPs can also be generic or partitive, which is neglected at this point, but will be discussed in more detail in chapter 6 on information structure.

3 Demonstratives

Bare post-verbal focal NPs can also serve as anaphoric NPs showing that this position allows a definite or indefinite interpretation, contrary to Szwedek (1974). This is demonstrated by example (15), in which the anaphoric NP *mężczyznę* 'man' is post-verbal and part of the focus in this sentence and is still interpreted as coreferential to the referent of *rowerzysta* 'cyclist' in the first sentence.

(15) *Dość   nietypowo zareagował na widok radiowoz-u*
rather untypical react.PST   on view police_car-GEN
straży miejskiej   rowerzysta [...]. Strażnicy złapali
police municipal cyclist   policemen catch.PST
mężczyzn-ę,^{C}
man-ACC
'A cyclist reacted rather untypically upon seeing a car belonging to the municipal police. The policemen caught the man.'

However, there are examples in which the determiner is preferred in order to explicitly indicate the definiteness of the post-verbal focal NP (16).

(16) *Widzia-ł-em jak   do pokoj-u   wchodzi-ł mężczyzna. Kiedy*
see-PST-1SG how in room-LOC enter-PST man   when
wszedł-em   zobaczy-ł-em, że przy okn-ie
enter.PST-1SG see-PST-1SG that at   window-LOC
stoi   ten mężczyzna.
stand.PRS DET man
'I saw a man go into the room. When I entered I saw that the man was standing at the window' (Szwedek 1976b: 96f.)

Assuming an unmarked topic-focus structure in (16), the anaphoric NP *mężczyzna* 'man' is in sentence-final position and thus a focal NP. The omission of the determiner *ten* would cause the NP *mężczyzna* to allow for a definite and indefinite reading and not simply indefinite, as claimed by Szwedek (1976b). In such a context, one simply does not know whether it is the same man or a different one. To signal that we are referring to the same man we just mentioned, *ten* is used.

3.4 My analysis of ten

To see how frequently anaphoric NPs are accompanied by determiners, I checked the first 479 sentences of the Polish translation of George Orwell's novel *1984*. Although the text sample is relatively small, the results given in table 6 show a clear tendency. There are a total of 154 anaphoric NPs. Only 20 are marked by a determiner, whereas 134 are undetermined. This shows that 87 % and thus the vast majority of anaphoric NPs are bare. The anaphoric demonstrative *ów* is found only once in this text sample and the anaphoric post-nominal *ten* is also rare – only 8 occurrences and always with preverbal anaphoric NPs. Prenominal *ten* only occurs 11 times with no preference between preverbal or post-verbal anaphoric NPs. This result substantiates the claim made above that, in written Polish, using *ten* to mark anaphoric NPs as definite is avoided.

	Preverbal NP	Post-verbal NP
No determiner	46	88
Post-nominal *ten*	8	0
Prenominal *ten*	6	5
ów	0	1

Table 6: The frequency of the determiners with anaphoric NPs in written Polish.

Ten also occurs with anaphoric NPs in order to exclude the possibility of a generic interpretation (Fontański 1986: 143f.). This is sometimes necessary since topical NPs can be interpreted as either generic or definite. This is exactly what would happen if *ten* were to be absent in (17). The presence of the determiner means that only a definite interpretation is possible and not a generic one.

(17)   *Ten lekarz leczy   chore osoby.*
       DET doctor treat.PRS.3SG sick   people
       'The doctor treats sick people.'

Spoken Polish differs from written Polish with respect to the occurrence of *ten* with anaphoric NPs. The first observation that spoken Polish differs from written Polish is made by Wróbel (1984), who is interested in the functions of *ten* in spoken standard Polish. According to him, *ten* "appears regularly [...] in all cases of anaphora" (Wróbel 1984: 49).[17] For written Polish, we have seen that this is not the case. I checked parts of the recorded conversations published in Lubaś (1978)[18] and telephone calls in Pisarkowa (1975) and I came across numerous anaphoric NPs which were accompanied by the determiner *ten*. The example in (18) is a small part of a conversation between an engineer (P) and a master craftsman (J) during a meeting recorded in the city of Dąbrowa Górnicza in 1976 (Lubaś 1978: 331).[19]

(18) P ale **te śruby** zostały ścinte
         but DET screws AUX   sawed_off
         'but the screws were sawed off'
      J ale o **tych śrubach** myżeśmy jeszcze cały
         but about DET screws   we   still   all
         czas fcale nie wiedzieli
         time at_all NEG knew
         'but we still didn't know at all about the screws all the time'
      P no   a puźniéj okazało sie bo   wzieli
         PART and later turned_out REFL because took.3PL
         je   do analizy że **te śruby** były jusz
         them to analysis that DET screws AUX already
         fcześniej zerwane
         earlier   torn_off
         'well, and later it turned out because they analysed them that the screws had already been torn off earlier'
         (Lubaś 1978: 332)

---

[17] For Miodunka (1974: 87), who analyses among others the determiner *ten* in all spoken varieties of Polish, *ten* is not obligatory in the contexts he investigates such as cataphoric, recognitional, deictic, and anaphoric contexts.
[18] Lubaś (1978) recorded the conversations in Upper Silesian cities. Only the data was considered which was free of dialectal elements and represented standard Polish.
[19] The texts by Lubaś (1978) are written in a simplified phonetic transcription to capture at least some phonetic phenomena (e.g. assimilation), which are not captured by the standard orthography (Lubaś 1978: 351).

In the first sentence, the NP *śruby* 'screws' is already definite due to the context and is marked by the determiner *ten*. In this sentence, the NP *śruby* 'screws' is topical because the NP's referents are given information. In the second sentence uttered by speaker J, the NP *tych śrubach* is anaphoric to the topical preceding NP *śruby* 'screws' in the first sentence. Another anaphoric NP accompanied by *ten* and referring to the screws is found in the last sentence. We have two anaphoric NPs which are determined by *ten* and refer to a topical antecedent. Both anaphoric NPs are placed preverbally.

Another example of the anaphoric use of *ten* is found in (19), which is part of an interview of a pensioner telling stories about her past work as a librarian. This interview was recorded in the city of Czeladź in 1976 (Lubaś 1978: 293).

(19) muwiłam pszynieście **dzieci** troche **ziemniakuf** to
said.1SG bring.2PL.IMP children some potatoes PART
każdy przyniuz w reŋku aa ponieważ było
everyone brought.3SG in hand and since was.3SG.N
tag dużo dzieci to z s **tych ziemniakuf**
so many children PART from DET potatoes
urosło asz puł metra to puźniej żeśmy tak
grew until half meter PART later we so
dzieci objerały **te ziémniaki** tarły na tarce
children peeled DET potatoes grated on grater
nieras sobje palce utarły że kref do **tych**
quite_often REFL fingers grated that blood to DET
ziemniakuf tam yy y zleciała
potatoes there and fell
'I said, children bring some potatoes, so they all brought some in their hands and since there were so many children, the pile of potatoes grew up to half a meter and then we so [≈ did the following:] the children peeled the potatoes, grated them on a grater, quite often they hurt their fingers on the grater so that blood fell into the potatoes' (Lubaś 1978: 297)

3 Demonstratives

The NPs *ziemniaki* 'potatoes' are of interest for us. They are introduced in the first line. What can be observed is that the *ziemniaki* 'potatoes' are mentioned later three times as anaphoric NPs and all of these are found with the determiner *ten* independently of whether the anaphoric NPs are placed in preverbal or post-verbal position. From this observation alone, one could generalize that *ten* occurs with all anaphoric NPs. And this is indeed the case with many anaphoric NPs in spoken Polish. However, I also came across anaphoric NPs in spoken Polish which were not accompanied by *ten*. The NP *dzieci* 'children' in (19) occurs once as an anaphoric NP which is bare. This counterexample shows that it is only a very strong tendency and not a rule to mark anaphoric NPs with *ten*. From this observation it can be deduced that *ten* cannot be regarded as obligatory.

To get a better picture of how frequently the determiner *ten* appears with anaphoric NPs in spoken Polish, I chose some text samples of spoken Polish from Pisarkowa (1975) and Lubaś (1978) and checked all anaphoric NPs to see whether they are accompanied by the determiner *ten* or not. The results in table 7 show that there is a strong tendency in spoken Polish to use *ten* with anaphoric NPs, namely in 75 % of all anaphoric NPs. No post-nominal *ten* and no occurrences of *ów* were found in the investigated sample. Furthermore, there is no tendency for bare anaphoric NPs to be placed pre- or post-verbally. The results in table 7 clearly show that spoken Polish and written Polish differ strongly in the frequency of determiners with anaphoric NPs.

	Preverbal NP	Post-verbal NP
No determiner	19	26
Prenominal *ten*	54	79
Post-nominal *ten*	0	0
ów	0	0

Table 7: The frequency of determiners with anaphoric NPs in spoken Polish.

This result is also supported by my informants who prefer *ten* with anaphoric NPs in spoken Polish. However, according to them, *ten* is not obligatory since omission does not lead to an ungrammatical sentence. The bare anaphoric NP is still interpreted as coreferential. In cases where the anaphoric NP is marked by *ten*, the determiner is unstressed, which is also observed by Bacz (1991: 5).

3.4.1.3 SNs with complements establishing uniqueness

Complements establishing uniqueness can be relative clauses and prepositional phrases. According to Ortmann (2014: 311), establishing relative clauses can be dependent on the context of utterance or not. In (20), the reference of *book* depends on the context, while in (21) this is not the case since there is only one book which the person read first in his/her life.

(20) The book I am looking for is expensive.
(21) The book I read first in my life was interesting.

In Polish, no difference is made between these two kinds of relative clauses, as is shown by the following two examples:

(22) Nie zna-m   (tego) numer-u,   którego
      NEG know-1SG.PRS   DET   number-GEN   REL
      szuka-sz.
      look_for-2SG.PRS
      'I do not know the number you are looking for.'

(23) Jak nazywa się   (ten) mężczyzna, który jako pierwszy
      how call.3SG REFL DET   man   REL   as   first
      zdoby-ł   Mount Everest?
      climb-PST Mount Everest
      'What is the name of the man who was the first to climb Mount Everest?'

In (22), the relative clause is context-dependent since one only knows which phone number the person is looking for in a certain context. In (23), no context is needed since there is only one man who was the first to climb Mount Everest.

3 Demonstratives

Ten is optional with all uniqueness-establishing relative clauses. This optionality can be explained due to register differences between spoken and written Polish. For written Polish, informants report that *ten* is rather dispreferred, as in (24), which is taken from a written source. However, this does not mean that the determiner is generally excluded in this context in written Polish:

(24) [...] *ponieważ kobieta, któr-ą kochał, od kilk-u*
because woman REL-ACC love.PST since some-DAT
lat nie żyje.[C]
year.PL NEG live.3SG
'[...] because the woman he loved has been dead for a number of years.'

(24) provides an example of a context-dependent relative clause. Here, the reference of *kobieta* 'woman' is narrowed down due to the relative clause and thus shifted to an IC. The shift need not be marked explicitly by the presence of *ten*. In contrast to (24), the following example is taken from spoken Polish in which the determiner occurs with *kobieta* 'woman', but is optional according to my informants.

(25) *to jest ta kobieta która robi-ł-a nam problem-y*
DEM COP DET woman REL make-PST-F us problem-PL
z tym biznesow-ym angielsk-im[C]
with DET business.ADJ-INS English-INS
'this is the woman who caused us problems with the business English'

A similar situation is found with prepositional phrases which can also narrow down the reference of the NP to a single entity. Here, too, *ten* is optional but influenced by register (spoken vs. written Polish).

(26) *(Te) meble w mieszkani-u są od mo-ich*
DET furniture in flat-LOC are from my-GEN
rodzic-ów.
parents-GEN
'The furniture in my flat is from my parents.'

3.4 My analysis of ten

What is important is that the sentence in (26) is not uttered in a deictic situation, since then the reference of the NP *meble* is changed depending on the presence or absence of *ten*. Without *ten*, the NP refers to all furniture which is in the flat, while with deictic *ten* it would refer only to a part, namely to those items which the person is pointing to.

I checked the frequency of the determiner *ten* with NPs combined with complements establishing uniqueness in written Polish and spoken Polish. The text sample for written Polish was again the first 479 sentences of the Polish translation of Orwell's novel *1984*, whereas for spoken Polish I made use of parts of the transcribed conversations in Lubaś (1978) and telephone calls found in Pisarkowa (1975). The results are given in table 8.

	No determiner	Determined by *ten*
Spoken Polish	9	22
Written Polish	28	1

Table 8: The frequency of *ten* with NPs combined with complements establishing uniqueness in Polish.

The quantitative analysis shows that in spoken Polish the majority of NPs with complements establishing uniqueness occur with *ten*, namely 71 %, whereas in written Polish there is a very strong tendency to avoid *ten* with only one example where *ten* is found.

3.4.2 Definite associative anaphors

DAAs consist of an antecedent and a head. In the following example, *car* is the antecedent while *engine* is the head of the DAA. By introducing the antecedent, all entities which are associated with the antecedent are also accessible.

(27) *When I was sitting in my car I started the engine.*

According to Ortmann (2014: 309), DAAs are pragmatically and semantically unique and thus have a special status. The heads of DAAs are interpreted as FCs which represent the semantically unique component. In

(27), *engine* is inherently unique since cars normally have only one engine, and relational since *engine* is understood as *engine of the car*. On the other hand, DAAs are pragmatically unique due to the fact that the antecedent is left anaphorically implicit. It is not necessary to mention the car in (27) again by saying *the engine of the car*.

DAAs can be subdivided depending on the relation between the antecedent and the head of the DAA. According to Schwarz (2009), relational and part-whole DAAs can be distinguished. In (27), an example of a part-whole DAA is given. These DAAs are characterized by the fact that the referent of the head is a part of the referent of the antecedent, which is the case in (27) since an engine is a unique part of a car. On the other hand, there are DAAs which are not based on a part-whole relation, but are also relational as in (28). In (28), the head *author* is relational, but is not a part of *book*.

(28) *John bought an interesting book. I met the author in Germany last year.*

Both types of DAAs have in common that the head of the DAA is represented by an inherently relational noun. According to Löbner (p.c.), there are DAAs with a [+R] noun as head (27, 28) and 'situational DAAs' with a [−R] noun as head. In (29), an example of a situational DAA is given in which *kitchen* is the antecedent and the sortal noun *refrigerator* the head.

(29) *When I came into the kitchen, I noticed that the refrigerator was broken.*

It is also important to note that the heads of DAAs are definite, either due to the semantics of the noun such as in (27) and (28) with the underlying FNs *author* and *engine* or due to a shift as in (29) with refrigerator which is shifted from [−U] to [+U], since we usually have only one refrigerator in the kitchen. If the head is not definite but indefinite, we get an indefinite associative anaphor as in (30). The antecedent is *car* whereas the indefinite head is *window*. Since cars have more than one window, we do not have unique reference and thus an indefinite associative anaphor.

(30) *When I was sitting in my car I opened a window.*

In the following, I will show that in Polish there are five possibilities for establishing a link between the head and its antecedent, namely with (i) a determiner, (ii) a possessive pronoun, (iii) an adverbial, (iv) the repetition of the antecedent, or (v) no marking at all. I will also investigate whether the Polish data support Schwarz's subdivision of the DAAs.

3.4.2.1 Part-whole DAAs

(31) and (32) represent two examples of part-whole DAAs. In (31), the handle is a part of the cup and in (32) the sole a part of the shoes. *Ten* does not occur with part-whole DAAs, as is illustrated by the following examples.[20] However, a possessive pronoun can be used optionally. Furthermore, it is also possible to repeat the antecedent and realize it as a genitive attribute. For (31), this would be *ucho (tej) filiżanki* 'handle DET cup.GEN'.

(31) *Ma-m   ładn-ą   filiżank-ę. Ale (#to)/ (jej)*
      have-1SG.PRS nice-ACC cup-ACC   but   DET POSS.PRON
      ucho   się   ułamało.
      handle REFL break_off.PST
      'I have a nice cup. But the (lit. 'its') handle broke off.'

(32) *W zeszłym tygodniu kupi-ł   nowe but-y, a*
      in last   week.LOC buy-PST new shoe-PL and
      (#ta) (ich)   podeszwa już   się   rozpad-ł-a.
       DET   POSS.PRON sole   already REFL fall_apart-PST-F
      'Last week he bought new shoes and the (lit. their) sole has already fallen apart.'

In the next two examples of DAAs, the referents of the antecedents are people and the DAAs denote a body part. Possessive pronouns occur with such part-whole DAAs. This is shown by the DAA example in (33),

---

[20] Instead of an asterisk in (31) with *ten*, I make use of a hash. The motivation for doing this is that the determiner in (31) is not ungrammatical, but its occurrence requires a different context, for example, having mentioned the handle before and thus as an anaphoric NP it could be marked by *ten*.

in which the referent of the NP *Pomstyl* is a person and the head of the DAA is *głowa* 'head'. The possessive pronoun is regarded as obligatory by my informants.

(33)   *mruczał   Pomstyl, a   jego   głowa pochyla-ł-a*
       murmur.PST Pomstyl and POSS.PRON head bow-PST-F
       się   coraz niżej^C
       REFL lower and lower
       'Pomstyl murmured, and his head bowed lower and lower'

In contrast to (33), in (34) a possessive pronoun is not present with the head of the DAA *głowa* 'head'. This can be explained by Löbner (2011: 301) since *to raise the head* is a fixed construction where it is not necessary to use a possessive pronoun. In (34), we have a second DAA *twarz* 'face' that is marked by a possessive pronoun *swoją*, which is considered as obligatory. According to my informants, it would be unclear whose face it is if the possessive pronoun would be left out.

(34)   *Murek podniósł głow-ę   i   w lustrze   na ścian-ie*
       Murek raise.PST head-ACC and in mirror.LOC on wall-LOC
       zobaczy-ł swoją   twarz [...]^C
       see-PST   POSS.PRON face.ACC
       'Murek raised his head and saw his face in the mirror on the wall'

3.4.2.2 Relational DAAs

In this section, I discuss DAAs that consist of an inherently relational noun but do not express a part-whole relation. With this type of DAA, *ten* does not occur in written standard Polish. However, in spoken Polish *ten* can occur optionally with some relational DAAs. Although there is, however, interspeaker variation with respect to the occurrence of *ten*; for the following examples, the majority of my informants accept *ten* with *autor* 'author':

(35)   *Anna czyta   interesując-ą książk-ę   o   zwierzętach.*
       Anna read.3SG nice-ACC   book-ACC about animal.PL.LOC
       Czyta   ją przez cały   dzień, ponieważ (ten) autor
       read.3SG it for   whole day   because   DET author

napisa-ł ją tak pięknie.
write-PST it so nice
'Anna reads a nice book about animals. She reads the whole day because the author has written it so nicely.'

Mendoza (2004: 122, 130, 283) also analyses the distribution of *ten* with DAAs. She claims that *ten* is optional with other than part-whole DAAs in spoken Polish. However, she does not observe that this is not the case for all such DAAs. *Ten* is not possible with the inherently relational noun *kierowca* 'driver' in (36).

(36) *Samochód staje.   Kierowca wyłącza   silnik.*
car   stand.3SG driver   turn_off.3SG.PRS engine
Radio milknie.[C]
radio fall_silent.3SG
'The car is stopping. The driver is turning off the engine. The radio is falling silent.'

Example (37) and (38) illustrate that a possessive pronoun can sometimes be used with relational DAAs, as was the case with part-whole DAAs. In (37), the head of the DAA is *koszty* 'costs' (37) and in (38) *cena* 'price':

(37) *Trzy lata   budowa-ła Maria swój dom. (Jego) koszty*
three year.PL build-PST Maria her house   its   cost.PL
by-ł-y   wyższe   niż myśla-ł-a.
COP-PST-PL high.COMP than think-PST-F
'Maria spent three years building her house. The (lit. Its) costs were higher than she expected.'

(38) *Po   obejrzeniu mieszkani-a chcie-li   rozmawiać z*
after seeing   flat-GEN   want-PL.PST talk   with
właściciel-em o   (jego)   cenie (tego mieszkani-a).
owner-INS   about POSS.PRON price DET flat-GEN
'After seeing the flat, they wanted to talk with the owner about the price (of the flat).'

3 Demonstratives

The example (38) demonstrates that there is always the option of establishing a link between the antecedent and head of the DAA by mentioning the antecedent explicitly as a genitive attribute. It must, however, be emphasized that either the possessive pronoun or the genitive attribute can be used but not both at the same time. The following examples show the same possibilities. In contrast to the previous examples, the presence of a possessor is obligatory. It still remains open as to why the nouns in (37) and (38) do not necessarily require the expression of a possessor, while in (39) and (40) this is required; although inherently relational nouns are involved in each case.

(39) *Gdy   staliśmy   przed   Empire State Building,*
when stand.PST.1PL in_front_of E. S. B.
*wysokość *(budynku)   robi-ła   wrażenie.*
height   building.GEN make-PST impression
'When we stood in front of the Empire State Building, the height (of the building) was impressive.'

(40) *Przy   pracach wykopaliskowych w Rzymie zostały*
during excavation   in Rome   AUX.PST
*znalezione złote   monet-y. Wiek *(monet)   jest*
found   golden coin-PL age   coin.GEN.PL COP
szacowany na 2000 lat.
estimate   at 2000 years
'During an excavation in Rome, golden coins were found. The age of the coins is estimated at 2000 years.'

In (39) and (40), the possessor is expressed via a genitive attribute. Alternatively, a possessive pronoun can be used (*jego* in (39) and *ich* in (40)). One conclusion can be drawn by the two previous examples. If a possessor has to be obligatorily expressed, then this is the case with inherently relational nouns. A prediction into the opposite direction cannot be made. Not all inherently relational nouns have to have an explicit possessor.

3.4.2.3 Situational DAAs

The heads of situational DAAs are not inherently relational. They can be represented by underlyingly sortal concepts such as *film* in (41). Within the scenario of going to the cinema, the NP *film* is shifted to [+U] because one normally watches only one film in the cinema. This can be indicated by the presence of *ten* in spoken Polish whereas in written Polish no marking is found.

(41)　Po　　wizycie w kinie　　rozmawia-li jeszcze o
　　　 after visit　in cinema　talk-PST　　still　about
　　　 (tym) film-ie.　(Ci) aktorzy im　　się　podoba-li.
　　　 DET　film-LOC　DET actor.PL them REFL please-PST
　　　 'After the cinema they carried on talking about the film. They liked the actors.'

In contrast to (41), the determiner is excluded in (42) – even in spoken Polish. In the situation of a church, the service and the priest are shifted to [+U].

(42)　*Gdy Jan wszedł　do kościoła,　(#ta)　msza　już*
　　　 when Jan enter.PST to church.GEN　DET service already
　　　 się　zaczęła.　(#Ten) ksiądz odmawia-ł właśnie
　　　 REFL begin.PST　DET priest say-PST　　just
　　　 "Ojcze Nasz".
　　　 Lord's Prayer
　　　 'When Jan entered the church, the service had already started. The priest was saying the Lord's Prayer.'

In other examples of situational DAAs, adverbs (*tam* 'there') can be added to the head of the DAA to establish a link between the anchor and the head (43).

(43)   *By-ł-am   w sobotę   we francusk-iej restauracj-i.*
be-PST-1SG.F in Saturday in French-LOC restaurant-LOC
Jedzenie (tam) mi bardzo smakowało.[21]
food   there me very   taste.PST
'I was in a French restaurant on Saturday. I liked the food (there) a lot.'

It can be summarized that no marking is required with most DAAs to indicate the link between the anchor and the head. If a marker occurs, then this is often optional. The expression of the possessor – such as a possessive pronoun or the repetition of the antecedent – is only obligatory with some relational and part-whole DAAs. The repetition of the antecedent is always possible. The determiner *ten* does not occur with part-whole DAAs, whereas with some non-part-whole DAAs it is optional in spoken Polish. This shows that *ten* can be used in a domain which is typical of definite articles and where demonstratives are not possible.

3.4.3 The occurrence of *ten* with semantic uniqueness

In this section, the examples are taken from a non-emotional context and the NPs under investigation are not used contrastively. Why these conditions are important will be discussed in section 3.4.4.

3.4.3.1 Complex ICs

NPs which are composed of a superlative or ordinal number and a noun are regarded as complex ICs. According to my informants, *ten* does not occur with ordinal (44) and superlative constructions (45):

(44)   [...] *że   pierwszy samochód zatrzyma-ł się   przy nas.*[C]
that first   car   stop-PST REFL near us
'[...] that the first car stopped near us.'

---

[21] In this example, there are a few informants for whom *ten* is acceptable. For the majority it is not.

(45) że to prawdopodobnie naj-droższy film w
that DEM probably SPL-expensive.COMP film in
histori-i kin-a.^C
history-LOC cinema-GEN
'that this is probably the most expensive film in the history of cinema.'

Adjectives of order such as *ostatni* 'last' and *następny, kolejny* 'next', which are semantically unique, lead to complex ICs, too. They are semantically unique since, as in (46), there can be only one referent which is the next stop. Again, *ten* does not occur in such contexts.

(46) *Wysiadł na następnym przystanku.*^C
get_off.PST PREP next.LOC stop.LOC
'He got off at the next stop.'

In (47), it can be seen that there are adjectives such as *ostatni* 'last', which lead to a definite interpretation of an NP. The NP with the adjective *ostatni* 'last' can only have a definite interpretation while the NP with *czerwony* 'red' can be definite or indefinite depending on the context. To enforce a definite reading of the NP in (47b) a determiner can be used.

(47) a, *Sprzeda-ł-em ostatni telewizor*
sell-PST-1SG last TV
'I sold the/(*a) last TV.'
b. *Sprzeda-ł-em czerwony telewizor*
sell-PST-1SG red TV
'I sold a/the red TV.'

3.4.3.2 Lexical INs/FNs

In written and spoken Polish, lexical INs such as *słońce* 'sun' (48) and *papież* 'Pope' (49) do not occur with *ten*.

(48) *Akurat słońce zachodzi-ł-o nad morz-em [...]*^C
just sun set-PST-N above sea-INS
'The sun was just setting above the sea.'

(49) papież jest głow-ą państw-a watykańsk-iego^C
 Pope COP head-INS state-GEN Vatican-GEN
 'The Pope is the head of the Vatican state.'

This is also the case with lexical FNs such as *początek* 'beginning' (50) and *wiek* 'age' (51) which are not found with *ten* in Polish. This can be explained by the fact that they are inherently unique and definiteness marking is semantically redundant.

(50) I to jest początek dnia [...]^C
 and DEM COP beginning day.GEN
 'And this is the beginning of the day.'

(51) Chodzi   o   wiek Marysi?^C
 concern.3SG.PRS about age Marysia.GEN
 'Is it about Marysia's age?'

The FNs *beginning* and *age* are two-place predicates in contrast to the FNs *różnica* 'difference' in (52) and *odległość* 'distance' in (53), which are more-place predicates. Here again, *ten* does not occur.

(52) jaka jest różnica   między pedagog-iem   a
 what COP difference between educationalist-INS and
 pedofil-em^C
 paedophile-INS
 'what is the difference between an educationalist and a paedophile'

(53) [...] odległość od sufit-u   do podłog-i wynosi
    distance from ceiling-GEN to floor-GEN amount.3SG.PRS
 2,85 metra^C
 2.85 meter
 'the distance from the ceiling to the floor amounts to 2.85 meters'

3.4.3.3 Proper names and personal pronouns

Personal names (54), dates (55), and toponyms (54, 55) belong to the group of proper names. In (54), the personal name *Maria* and the toponym *America* do not occur with *ten*. The city name *Kraków* and the date in (55) also remain unmarked by *ten*. Personal pronouns, which are usually omitted as subjects (Swan 2002: 155ff.; Bartnicka 2004: 291), do not occur with *ten* either.

(54) *Ale Maria fatalnie czu-ł-a   się   w Ameryce.*^C
but Maria awful   feel-PST-F REFL in America.LOC
'But Maria felt awful in America.'

(55) *zosta-li   aresztowani pierwsz-ego lipca   1948 rok-u*
AUX-PST.PL arrested   first-GEN   July.GEN 1948 year-GEN
w Krakowie^C
in Cracow.LOC
'they were arrested in Cracow on the first of July 1948.'

3.4.4 Factors which enable the presence of *ten* with [+U] nominals

So far, it has been claimed that *ten* does not occur, for example, with lexical INs. However, it has to be emphasized that *ten* is not ungrammatical in these contexts. In the following, I will discuss factors which can enable the presence of *ten* and illustrate these with examples.

The first reason for the occurrence of *ten* in cases of semantic uniqueness is when the speaker is emotionally affected. This can be a positive or negative emotion such as happiness or anger. In such an emotional context, *ten* can occur regardless of the concept type since *ten* functions to indicate emotional involvement and not unique reference. In (56), the IN *Polska* 'Poland' is found with the determiner *to* express a positive attitude of the speaker in (56a) and a negative one in (56b).

(56) a. [...] *jak   ta   Polska jest piękna   i   bogata!*^C
how DET Poland COP beautiful and rich
'how beautiful and rich Poland is!'

3 Demonstratives

b. *Że   jednak ta   Polska taka pojebana.*^C
    that still   DET Poland so   damned
    'That Poland is still so damned/fucked.'

The determiner *ten* also occurs in contrastive use. This is illustrated by (57), in which the Pope is introduced in the first sentence by his name *Benedykt XVI* and in the second sentence the Pope is mentioned again, however, this time not by his name but by the NP *papież* 'Pope' which is marked by the determiner *ten*. According to my informants, *ten* in (57) would be stressed in spoken Polish and leads to a contrastive interpretation of the NP *papież* 'Pope' so that the present Pope is compared to other future or past Popes.

(57) *Czy   Benedykt XVI podjemie   pielgrzymk-i w   inne*
      whether Benedict XVI make.3SG.PRS   pilgrimage-PL in other
      newralgiczne rejon-y   świat-a? [...] *ale wydaje   mi się,*
      trouble   area-PL   world-GEN   but seem.3SG   me REFL
      że   ten papież jeszcze Moskw-y   nie odwiedzi.^C
      that DET Pope   yet   Moskow-GEN NEG visit.3SG.PRS
      'Whether Benedict XVI will make pilgrimages into other troubled areas of the world? But it seems to me that this Pope will not visit Moscow yet.'

Inherently unique nouns can occur with *ten* if combined with a complement establishing uniqueness, too. This has to do with the fact that complements establishing uniqueness require a [−U] noun. This is why first we have a shift from [+U] to [−U]. After that, due to the complement establishing uniqueness, the NP is shifted again to [+U]. In (58), *papież* 'Pope' is an IN and thus inherently unique. By the modification of a uniqueness-establishing relative clause, it is shifted to an SC. This is the case, because over the course of time there have been a number of popes. With the uniqueness-establishing relative clause, the Pope is selected who was silent during the war. This relative clause shifts the NP to an IC.

(58) *przeszedł do histori-i   jako ten papież, który*
      go.PST   to history-GEN as   DET Pope   REL
      milczał   w czas-ie   wojn-y.^{C}
      be_silent.PST in time-LOC war-GEN
      'he went down in history as the Pope who was silent during the war.'

What has been illustrated in (58) with relative clauses can also be achieved by prepositional phrases as in (59). Here, the same shift can be observed. In (59), the reference of the personal name *Jan* is made unique by the addition of the PP *z Galilei*.

(59) *czy   to   był   ten Jan z   Galile-i*^{C}
      whether DET COP.PST DET Jan from Galilee-GEN
      'if this was the Jan from Galilee'

In all the examples given in this section, we have a normal use of *ten* as a demonstrative. Either it occurs in emotional contexts or it has as an input requirement [–U], which involves a shift from [+U] to [–U].

3.4.5 Summary

In this chapter, I have investigated the distribution of the determiner *ten* with the help of the scale of uniqueness, which enables us to systematically investigate the occurrences of a determiner. The analysis of the Polish determiner *ten* in Polish shows that there is a difference between spoken and written Polish with respect to the occurrence of *ten*. *Ten* is not frequently used in written Polish and is restricted to pragmatic uniqueness, whereas in spoken Polish it is quite frequent and also extended to some relational and situational DAAs. This is why the two types of DAAs are put together at one level of the scale. The cut-off points for written and spoken Polish are illustrated in (60).

(60)   deictic SN <
　　　　anaphoric SN <
　　　　　SN with complements establishing uniqueness <
　　　　　───────────────────────────────── written Polish
　　　　　　　relational/situational DAAs <
　　　　　───────────────────────────────── spoken Polish
　　　　　　　　part-whole DAAs <
　　　　　　　　complex IC <
　　　　　　　　lexical IN/FN <
　　　　　　　　proper names <
　　　　　　　　personal pronouns

The rest of the scale remains undetermined in Polish. In 3.4.4, I presented a number of factors that can trigger the occurrence of *ten* with semantic uniques, but this either involves a shift from [+U] to [−U] or is the effect of emotional involvement, which has nothing to do with definiteness.

What about the article status of *ten* in Polish? To repeat, possible contexts of demonstratives are deictic SNs and anaphoric SNs which represent a topic shift. All other contexts of the scale are typical of definite articles. Thus the anaphoric contexts are the first step on the scale at which we can speak of a determiner morphing into a definite article. We can now apply Diessel's definition of definite articles to the Polish determiner *ten*. *Ten* partially fulfils Diessel's criteria of a definite article. It is unstressed with anaphoric SNs and also occurs with topical antecedents regardless of the syntactic position of the anaphoric NP. However, even though *ten* is frequently found with anaphoric NPs, what is still missing for a finished grammaticalization into a definite article is the obligatory occurrence. This is why the final step of the grammaticalization path is not achieved. For written Polish, a definite article is not attested since anaphoric NPs are bare in most cases.

After having examined the Polish determiner *ten*, one could ask: what about the other Slavic languages and their determiners? In the next section, I provide a Slavic comparison.

3.5 Slavic comparison

For this comparison, I present each of the three Slavic branches. Russian represents the East Slavic, Czech the West Slavic, and Croatian the South Slavic branch. Since the focus is on West Slavic, two varieties of two West Slavic languages are also included in addition to the three standard Slavic languages, namely Upper Silesian, which is a Polish dialect, and a variety of Upper Sorbian. For the last two varieties, a definite article is attested (cf. Breu (2004) and Scholze (2008) for the Upper Sorbian variety, Czardybon (2010) for Upper Silesian). Bulgarian will also be mentioned as a Slavic language which has developed a definite article. For a detailed analysis of the definite article, see Scatton (1984: 165f., 314f.; 1993: 234), Radeva et al. (2003: 233ff.), Sussex & Cubberley (2006: 235), Topolinjska (2009: 179), and in particular Sachliyan (in prep.), who investigates the distribution of the Bulgarian and Macedonian articles in the theoretical framework of CTD.

The data for this comparison has been collected with the help of translations and cloze tests. For the following Slavic languages, a smaller set of sentences was tested with a lower number of informants than in Polish. Literature on the distribution of the corresponding demonstratives and definite articles was included where available. This was the case for the Upper Sorbian variety, which has been analysed by Breu (2004) and Scholze (2008). However, an exhaustive discussion of the literature on the demonstratives – especially in Czech and Russian – is not possible here. For a detailed discussion see Birkenmaier (1979) for Russian and Berger (1993) for Czech and the literature cited therein. All examples which are taken from languages with a Cyrillic alphabet have been transliterated according to the guidelines provided by Comrie & Corbett (1993: 832).

As a Polish dialect, Upper Silesian has a special status in this comparison. Furthermore, it is underrepresented and little investigated and crucially differs from standard Polish with regard to definiteness marking. This is why it is discussed first in a section of its own.

3.5.1 Upper Silesian *tyn*[22]

Upper Silesian is spoken in the south-western part of Poland in the two provinces of Opole and Śląsk (Województwo opolskie and śląskie). According to the 2011 census, there were 509,000 Upper Silesian speakers in Poland (Adach-Stankiewicz et al. 2012: 108).

Upper Silesian can be divided into three subdialects whose centres are the cities of Opole in the province of Opole, Cieszyn in the south of the province of Śląsk, and Katowice (Skudrzykowa et al. 2001: 39). The latter subdialect in and around Katowice will be called 'Central Upper Silesian' and my Upper Silesian data are from this subdialect.

The Upper Silesian determiner *tyn* is a cognate of the standard Polish determiner *ten* and is stressed if used in deictic contexts. Imagine a situation in which more than one bottle is standing in front of the speakers and one speaker utters the sentence in (61). Unique reference can only be established by means of a gesture; for example, pointing to one of the bottles.

(61)   *Dej   mi TA flaszka*
       give.IMP me DET bottle
       'Give me that bottle'

With anaphoric NPs, *tyn* is unstressed and obligatory with all anaphoric NPs regardless of the syntactic position of the anaphoric NP or whether there is a topical or non-topical antecedent (Czardybon 2010: 22ff.). To illustrate this, we need a longer example with more preceding context such as in (62), which is taken from the data I collected. In this example, I am focusing on the two referents of *sklep* 'shop' and *lalka* 'doll'. They are introduced into the discourse for the first time in the first sentence. In the following sentence, the referent of the shop is mentioned again by the anaphoric NP *tego sklepu*. The shop is mentioned a third time in the following discourse and is also determined by *tyn*. Both anaphoric NPs are in post-verbal position. Concerning the doll, there are two anaphoric NPs which are both preverbal and accompanied by *tyn*. Furthermore, they represent topical NPs because they are given and under discussion.

---

[22] This section is partially based on Czardybon (2010).

3.5 Slavic comparison

This is why the last anaphoric NP has a topical antecedent and is a topical NP as well. We have no topic shift, rather the topic 'doll' continues to be the topic in the discourse. This is in contrast to the non-topical antecedent of the second mention of the doll.

(62) *Jak [Stefan] dojechoł do Warszaw-y, to boł już*
when Stefan arrived in Warsaw-GEN PART was already
wieczor a wypaczył **we sklepie** *w szałfynstrze* **gryfno**
evening and spotted in shop in shop_window nice
lalka *i chcioł jom kupić swoi cerze. Toż zaczon*
doll and wanted it buy his daughter PART started
klupać do **tego sklepu***, żyd co tam sprzedowoł niy*
knock to DET shop Jew REL there sold NEG
chcioł już łotworzyć, ale go prosiył, że rano
wanted already open but him asked that morning
mo pociong do dom i łon łotwar **tyn sklep** *i*
has train to house and he opened DET shop and
mu **ta lalka** *sprzedoł. Jak prziszed do dom jego*
him DET doll sold when came to house his
cera [...] *ty piykny lalki niy chciała*
daughter DET beautiful doll NEG wanted
'When Stefan arrived in Warsaw it was already evening and he spotted a nice doll in the window of a shop and wanted to buy it for his daughter. So he started knocking at the shop. A Jew selling there did not want to open the shop. But he told him that he was going home the next morning by train and so the guy opened the shop and sold him the doll. When he arrived home his daughter did not want the beautiful doll.'

Tyn differs from *ten* in the occurrence with complements establishing uniqueness since *tyn* is obligatory here, as in (63):

(63) *Piykne dziynki za tyn gyszynk, kery-ś mi posłoł.*
nice thanks for DET present REL-2SG me send.PST
'Thanks a lot for the present you sent me.'

3 Demonstratives

Tyn also differs from *ten* with respect to DAAs. Since the distribution of *tyn* is quite complicated with DAAs, only a brief overview can be given here. A detailed analysis of *tyn* with DAAs can be found in Czardybon (2010). There is a subset of relational (64) and situational (65) DAAs with which *tyn* is obligatory.

(64) *Anna czyto   fajn-o ksionżk-a   o   zwierzynt-ach.*
Anna read.3SG.PRS nice-F book-F.ACC about animal-PL.LOC
Czyto   cały dziyń, bo   tyn pisorz tak fajnie
read.3SG.PRS whole day   because DET author so nice.ADV
pisz-e.
write-3SG.PRS
'Anna is reading a nice book about animals. She reads the whole day because the author writes so nicely.'

(65) *Wczoraj boł żech   w kin-ie.   Ale tyn film boł*
yesterday was 1SG.PST in cinema-LOC but DET film was
nudny.
boring
'I went to the cinema yesterday. But the film was boring.'

With other relational (66) and situational DAAs (67), *tyn* is optional or not used:

(66) *Jak   żech   wloz   do autobus-u, to-ch   sie*
when 1SG.PST get_in.PST to bus-GEN   PART-1SG.PST REFL
pytoł   (#tego) szofer-a   wiela   kosztuje bilet.
ask.PST DET   driver-ACC how much cost.3SG.PRS ticket
'When I got onto the bus, I asked the driver how much a ticket costs.'

(67) *Jak   żech   wloz   do kuchni,   to-ch   widzioł,*
when 1SG.PST enter.PST to kitchen.GEN PART-1SG.PST see.PST
że (#ta)   lodówka   jes zepsuto.
that DET refrigerator COP broken
'When I came into the kitchen, I saw that the refrigerator was broken.'

Part-whole DAAs do not occur with *tyn*. In (68), most of my informants would not use it with the head *chynkel* 'handle'.

(68) *Jo mo-m   fajn-o   szklonk-a. Ale (#tyn) chynkel*
     I have-1SG.PRS nice-ACC cup-ACC   but DET handle
     jest   uloman-y.
     COP.PRS broken-M
     'I have a nice cup, but the handle is broken.'

Upper Silesian also differs from standard Polish in the distribution of determiners with complex ICs. Here, in contrast to *ten*, which is impossible, *tyn* is optionally possible, as in (69).

(69) *Jak boł-a   (ta) piyrszo szychta?*
     how COP.PST-F DET first   shift
     'How was the first shift?'

Lexical INs/FNs, proper names, and personal pronouns are not used with the determiner *tyn*. According to Diessel's definition of definite articles, unstressed *tyn* has achieved the status as an article, since it is obligatory with anaphoric NPs. Furthermore, it is also obligatory with a subset of non-part-whole DAAs and thus with semantic uniqueness. The function of *tyn* as an article and demonstrative can also be distinguished prosodically. As a demonstrative, *tyn* is stressed with deictic SNs while in the rest of the scale it is unstressed and thus functions as an article.

Before presenting the distribution of the determiners in the other investigated languages, a survey of available determiners is given in the next section.

3.5.2 Paradigms of the determiners in the investigated languages

In general, languages can be classified with respect to how many adnominal demonstratives they possess (cf. Diessel 2012). Some languages have a three-way and others a two-way distinction. As was presented in the previous chapter, Polish has an unmarked demonstrative *ten* and a distal one *tamten*, which results in a two-way distinction. A similar distinction can be observed in Upper Silesian. Here a distal demonstrative *tamtyn* as well as a neutral demonstrative *tyn* can be found, which can function as a definite article.

In the Upper Sorbian variety, Breu (2004) and Scholze (2008) argue for the article status of *tón*. This determiner can also function as a demonstrative if it is stressed, similar to the Upper Silesian *tyn*. Furthermore, there is the demonstrative *tóne* which is proximal (Breu 2004: 14).

In Russian, we also find a two-member system with *ètot* as the proximal and *tot* as the distal demonstrative (Isačenko 1962: 505, Topolińska 1981: 40, Timberlake 2004: 118).

Czech has a huge number of demonstratives which are derived by affixes. According to Topolińska (1981: 39/40) and Short (1993: 472), Czech has a three-member distinction with *ten* as the unmarked form, *tento* the proximal, and *tamten* the distal demonstrative. Krámský (1972: 61, 157) classifies the Czech system of demonstratives differently. For him, the three demonstratives are *ten, tento* (proximal), and *onen* (distal). According to Krámský (1972: 61), *ten* is also a demonstrative, but it has a lot in common with a definite article. As Janda & Townsend (2000: 29) argue, the suffix *–hle* 'look' is emphatic and can be added to the stem resulting in forms such as *tenhle* (proximal/distal) and *tamhleten* (distal).

A three-way system is represented by Croatian with *ovaj* the proximal demonstrative and *onaj* as distal demonstrative. *Taj*, the third member, is described as being unmarked for distance (Topolińska 1981: 40). A summary of the systems and their demonstratives is shown in table 9:

	unmarked	distal	proximal
Polish	ten	tamten	
Upper Silesian	tyn	tamtyn	
Upper Sorbian variety	tón		tóne
Russian		tot	ètot
Czech	ten	tamten/onen	tento
Croatian	taj	onaj	ovaj

Table 9: Determiners in the investigated Slavic languages.

3.5 Slavic comparison

Not all of the determiners presented here will be looked at in comparison with the Polish determiner *ten*. For the non-West Slavic languages Croatian and Russian, I will analyse the distribution of all determiners. For the West Slavic languages and varieties, only the cognates of standard Polish *ten* are included.

3.5.3 The occurrence of the determiners with pragmatic uniqueness[23]

All of the determiners mentioned in the previous section can occur in deictic contexts. However, for the Czech determiner *ten*, Berger (1993: 463) writes that it would not have a deictic function. This may be why many of my informants prefer other demonstratives such as *tohle* instead of *ten* in the context described in (70) in which two people are standing in front of cars and one person is pointing to one of them uttering the sentence in (70).

(70) Czech
 To   auto je   hezké.
 DET car   COP nice
 'This car is nice.'

With anaphoric NPs, the distribution of the determiners is influenced by information structure. The Russian *ètot* and the Croatian *taj*[24] are optional with anaphoric NPs in preverbal position. In post-verbal position, they are preferred by the majority of my Russian and Croatian informants. This is illustrated by the Russian examples in (71).

---

[23] Only a small part of my collected data can be presented in this chapter. I have checked the distribution of the determiners for the whole scale of uniqueness in Russian, Croatian, and Czech. The entire data can be found in the appendix.

[24] Trenkic (2004: 1408) mentions that in Bosnian/Croatian/Serbian the demonstratives "are restricted to the immediate situation and anaphoric uses". However, he does not go into the details for which of the three determiners this is true. Furthermore, he does not observe that information structure plays a role and that in Croatian the determiner *onaj* can occur with uniqueness establishing relative clauses too.

3 Demonstratives

(71) Russian
   a. *On kupil mašin-u$_j$, no (èta) mašina$_j$ byla očen'*
      he bought car-ACC but DET car was very
      dorogoj.
      expensive
      'He bought a car, but the car was very expensive.'
   b. *Pered domom naxoditcja mašina$_j$. Ja uže*
      in_front_of house.INS be.3SG.PRS car I already
      včera videl ètu mašin-u$_j$
      yesterday saw DET car-ACC
      'There is a car in front of the house. I already saw the car yesterday.'

For Russian, Birkenmaier (1979: 89ff.) also mentions that the determiner can optionally occur in anaphoric contexts. However, the influence of information structure is not observed by him.

Berger (1993) analyses the complex system of demonstratives in Czech. According to him, the distribution of anaphoric *ten* is determined by register. *Ten* occurs very rarely in written Czech (specialist texts such as administrative and journalistic texts). Instead, the determiner *tento* is used, which is in competition with *ten* (Berger 1993: 373f., 395). In spoken Czech, *ten* is the normal case with anaphoric NPs (Berger 1993: 450). In my study, the Czech informants strongly preferred *ten* with anaphoric NPs, but it is not regarded as obligatory. Furthermore, most of my Czech informants regard anaphoric NPs in the post-verbal position as odd and prefer them in preverbal position. The sentence in (72a), in which a book is introduced into the discourse, can perfectly be followed by (72b), in which the second mention of the book is placed preverbally in contrast to the sentence-final position of the anaphoric NP *tu knihu* 'this book' in (72c).

(72) Czech
   a. *Jan si   včera   koupil knih-u.   Když začal*
      Jan REFL yesterday buy.PST book-ACC when begin.PST
      číst, vsiml   si,
      read notice.PST REFL
      'Jan bought a book yesterday. When he began to read it he noticed,'
   b. *že   už   tu knih-u   četl.*
      that already DET book-ACC read.PST
      'that he had already read this book.'
   c. ?*že   už   četl   tu knih-u.*
      that already read.PST DET book-ACC
      'that he had already read this book.'

The Upper Sorbian variety (73) is similar to Upper Silesian since the determiner is obligatory with anaphoric NPs and information structure is not relevant.

(73) Upper Sorbian variety (Breu 2004: 19)
   Wón sej šitko   na jenu   cedlku   napisa.
   he REFL everything on INDEF slip_of_paper write.3SG.PRS
   Ha potom wón tón cedlku   tóm pólicajej
   and then he DET slip_of_paper DEF policeman
   před   nosom dźerži.
   in_front_of nose hold.3SG.PRS
   'He writes everything on a slip of paper. And then he holds the slip of paper in front of the policeman's nose.'

With SNs with complements establishing uniqueness, it is the distal determiner, which occurs optionally in Russian (74a)[25] and Croatian (74b) in contrast to the unmarked demonstrative in Polish. For these two languages, SNs with complements establishing uniqueness also represent the language-specific cut-off point up to which the determiner occurs.

---

[25] A similar observation is made by Birkenmaier for Russian (1979: 93ff.).

(74) a. Russian (East Slavic)
          Kak nazyvaetsja (ta)   ptica, kotoraja voruet?
          how call.3SG.REFL DET.DIST bird   REL   steal.3SG
      b. Croatian (South Slavic)
          Kako se   zove   (ona)   ptica koja krade?
          how REFL call.3SG   DET.DIST bird REL steal.3SG
          'What is the name of the bird that steals?'

Ten in Czech seems to be optional with NPs modified by context-independent relative clauses such as in (75). With context-dependent relative clauses, *ten* is preferred as in (76a) or there is interspeaker variation between preferred and optional use (76b). Furthermore, my informants mention that in those cases in which *ten* is optional, the presence or absence is dependent on the difference between spoken and written Czech. It rather shows up in spoken Czech while it rather does not in written Czech.

(75) Czech
      Jak se   jmenuje (ten) pták, který krade?
      how REFL call.3SG DET bird REL   steal.3SG
      'What is the name of the bird that steals?'

(76) Czech
      a. *Znáte, doufám, toho učitele, co má   chatu   a*
          know hope.1SG DET teacher REL have.3SG house and
          auto?[26]
          car
          'I hope you know the teacher who has a weekend home and a car?'
      b. *To je   ten/(ten) člověk, o   kterém jsme*
          DEM COP DET   man   about REL   AUX
          mluvili.[27]
          talk.PST
          'This is the man we talked about.'

---

[26] This example is taken from Berger (1993: 153).
[27] Ibid (1993: 148).

In the article-languages Upper Sorbian variety (77) and Bulgarian[28] (78), the determiner is obligatory.

(77) Upper Sorbian variety
Štó ha bě tón muž, kiž jo će čora
who PART was DET man REL.PRON AUX you yesterday
zawoła-ł?
call-PST
'Who was the man who called you yesterday?' (Breu 2004: 22)

(78) Bulgarian
Kak se kazva ptica-ta, kojato krade.
what REFL call bird-DET REL steals
'What is the name of the bird that steals.'

In Russian, part-whole DAAs remain unmarked. This is also the case in Croatian and Czech. However, possessive pronouns can occur, for example, in Russian (79a)[29], Croatian (79b), and Czech (79c) as is shown by the following examples. This is similar to what has been shown for Polish.

(79) a. Russian
U menja est' krasivaja čaška, no eë ručka
at me is nice cup but POSS.PRON handle
slomana.
broken

b. Croatian
Imam lijepu šalicu. Ali ručka joj
have.1SG.PRS nice cup but handle POSS.PRON
je otpala.
COP broken

---

28 The Bulgarian data were provided by Syuzan Sachliyan and Ekaterina Gabrovska.
29 Birkenmaier (1979: 93) makes a short comment concerning the absence of demonstratives with DAAs in Russian.

c. Czech
    Mám   hezký hrnek, ale jeho   ucho   je
    have.1SG.PRS nice cup   but POSS.PRON handle COP
    ulomené.
    broken
    'I have a nice cup, but the handle is broken.'

For the majority of my Russian, Czech, and Croatian informants, determiners do not occur with relational DAAs either, as is illustrated by the following Croatian example.

(80) Croatian
    Kad   sam ušao   u autobus pitao   sam vozača
    when AUX enter.PST in bus   ask.PST AUX driver
    koliko   stoji   karta.
    how_much cost.3SG ticket
    'When I got onto the bus I asked the driver how much a ticket costs.'

Contrary to Cummins (1999: 184n), who claims that *ten* never occurs with DAAs in Czech, I observe that with some situational DAAs *ten* is regarded as optional – as in (81). For (81), it is reported that, especially in spoken colloquial Czech, *ten* can occur while it is avoided in written language. The Czech data shows that situational DAAs can be considered as a separate class of DAAs since only here do we find the possibility of the presence of *ten* in contrast to part-whole and relational DAAs with which *ten* is absent in Czech.

(81) Czech
    Po   kině   se   ještě bavili o   (tom) filmu.
    after cinema REFL still talk.PST about DET film
    (Ti) herci   se   jim   líbili.
    DET actor.PL REFL them please.PST
    'After the cinema we talked about the film. We liked the actors.'

3.5 *Slavic comparison*

In Russian and Croatian, the determiners do not occur with relational DAAs, as illustrated by the Russian example (82).

(82)   Russian
       Posle osmotra kvartiry oni   xoteli   pogovorit' s
       after seeing flat   they want.PST talk   with
       xozjainom o   cene.
       owner   about price
       'After seeing the flat, they wanted to talk with the owner about the price.'

In the Upper Sorbian variety, *tón* is obligatory with all DAAs for the younger generation. The older generation regards the article with part-whole DAAs as optional (83) (Breu 2004: 41).

(83)   Upper Sorbian variety (West Slavic; Breu 2004: 41)
   a. *Moje nowo awto jo   dórbjało do reparatur-y, (tón)*
       my   new car   AUX must.PST to repair-GEN   DET
       motor bě   kaput.
       engine was   broken
       'My new car had to be repaired; the engine was broken.'
   b. *Naš wučor   jo   nam jenu   kniu pokaza-ł. Tón to*
       our teacher AUX us   INDEF book show-PST   he DET
       awtora wosobinsce znaje.
       author personally know
       'Our teacher showed us a book. He knows the author personally.'

3.5.4 The occurrence of the determiners with semantic uniqueness

With respect to complex ICs, no determiner is found in Russian and Croatian. This is demonstrated by the Croatian example in (84).

(84) Croatian
 Živim u najljepšem gradu u zemlji
 live.1SG in most_beautiful city in country
 'I'm living in the most beautiful city in the country.'

In Czech, the determiner can be used optionally with NPs with ordinal numbers and superlatives (85). However, this has the function to indicate emotional affectedness, similarly to standard Polish. If the referent has not been mentioned before and the sentence is uttered in an emotionally neutral context, *ten* does not normally occur with superlatives and ordinals. The occurrence of *ten* with superlatives in Czech has also been observed by authors such as Zubatý (1916), Mathesius (1926), and Bauernöppel et al. (1970). For Zubatý, *ten* is used incorrectly with complex ICs (Zubatý 1916, quoted after Krámský 1972: 188) while for Bauernöppel et al. (1970: 75) *ten* is used for emphasis. Eckert (1993: 117) points out that *ten* is not obligatory with superlative constructions, but "it is very typical of spoken Czech" (Eckert 1993: 117), which is confirmed by my Czech informants.

(85) Czech
 Máme na skladě (ty) nejnovější vzorky.[30]
 have.3PL.PRS on warehouse DET SPL.late sample.PL
 'We have the latest samples in stock.'

Breu (2004) observes that in the Upper Sorbian variety *tón* is optional if the complex IC is part of the topic (86a) while it is obligatory as part of the focus (86b).

---

[30] Taken from Zubatý (1916, quoted after Krámský 1972: 188). The example has slightly been modified in that the determiner is put in brackets in order to indicate its optionality.

(86) Upper Sorbian variety (Scholze 2008: 169)
 a. *Tón/Ø prejni wesnanosta po přewróće*
  DET first mayor after collapse of the GDR
  bě knez Ryćer.
  COP mister R.
  'The first mayor after the collapse of the GDR was Mr Ryćer.'
 b. *Knez Ryćer bě tón prejni wesnanosta po*
  mister Ryćer COP DET first mayor after
  přewróće.
  collapse of the GDR
  'Mr Ryćer was the first mayor after the collapse of the GDR.'

In the Upper Sorbian variety, lexical INs/FNs, proper names, and personal pronouns do not occur with the determiner. In Bulgarian, the definite article is even found with lexical INs such as *sun* in (87).

(87) Bulgarian (South Slavic)
 Slănce-to gree.
 sun-DET shine.3SG
 'The sun is shining.'

3.6 Conclusion

The scale of uniqueness has been a helpful instrument for capturing and comparing the distribution of the different determiners analysed in the previous section. On the basis of the Slavic data, the scale can be modified given in (88). In (88), no distinction is made between an obligatory or possible occurrence of the determiners.

(88) deictic SN <
　　　anaphoric SN <
　　　SNs with complements
　　　　establishing uniqueness <

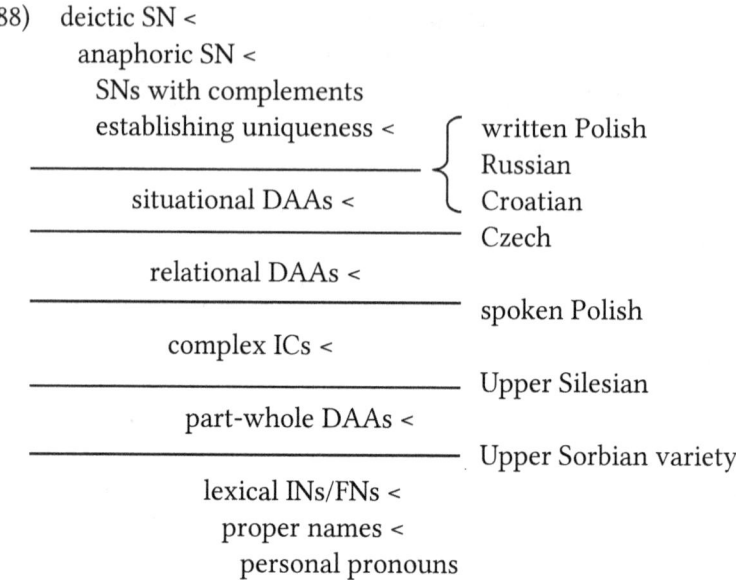

In the course of the investigation, it became apparent that the position of the DAAs and complex ICs has to be questioned. To capture the distribution of the determiners in these two levels of the scale, the scale had to be modified by changing the position of part-whole DAAs and complex ICs, resulting in the scale in (88).

The languages not only differ with respect to the cut-off points, but also with respect to the optional and obligatory occurrences of their determiners, which cannot be depicted on the scale. Table 10 provides a better overview of the optional, obligatory, or non-use of the determiners with DAAs and complex ICs ('–' stands for no use, '+' for obligatory, and '(+)' for optional).

	Czech	Spoken Polish	Upper Silesian	Upper Sorbian variety
Situational DAAs	−, (+)	−, (+)	−, (+), +	+
Relational DAAs	−	−, (+)	−, +	+
Complex ICs	−	−	(+)	(+), +
Part-whole DAAs	−	−	−	(+), +

Table 10: Distribution of the investigated West Slavic determiners with DAAs and complex ICs.

One interesting observation is that the determiners of the West Slavic languages have developed much further than the investigated non-West Slavic ones with Bulgarian as an exception. A possible reason for this could be the influence of German, which is attested for these languages.

For the West Slavic languages in particular, the question then arises as to whether they have developed a definite article. In section 3.1, I introduced a criterion that is repeated here. The determiner has only achieved the status of an article indicating unique reference if the determiner is obligatory with all anaphoric NPs (also covering topical antecedents). This criterion applied to Upper Silesian and the Upper Sorbian variety results in a positive answer. For Czech, Berger (1993: 462f., 510) comes to the conclusion that it has no definite article since *ten* is not obligatory with anaphoric NPs. This is also the finding of my study.

For Russian and Croatian, the determiners have not developed into articles since they do not accompany anaphoric NPs systematically. This leads to the following question: If definiteness in most Slavic languages is not always expressed explicitly by an article or demonstrative, how is definiteness then indicated? The answer to this question will be given in the chapters on aspect, case alternation, and information structure.

4 Aspect

The focus of this chapter is the interaction of aspect with definiteness. Before discussing this, I will provide a short introduction to the semantics of aspect and how it is morphologically expressed in Polish in 4.1 and 4.2, respectively. In order to account for the data presented in section 4.3, I will discuss the notion of incremental theme verbs in 4.4 and in 4.5 I will look at additional Polish data to investigate further criteria that influence definiteness. Section 4.6 focuses on the connection between aspect, definiteness, and the concept type approach by Löbner.

4.1 The semantics of aspect

First of all, grammatical aspect has to be distinguished from lexical aspect (Filip 1993/1999, Borik 2006: 21f., Richardson 2007: 5, 9f., Gvozdanović 2012: 781f.). 'Lexical aspect' is an inherent property of verbs and has to be distinguished from aspectual classes which also include verb phrases and sentences according to Filip (2012: 725):

> Although "lexical aspect" is also used to refer to the aspectual class of verb phrases (cf. e.g., van Hout, 2003) and sentences, this use is, strictly speaking, incorrect and should be avoided. The notion of aspectual class is a wider notion than that of lexical aspect, subsuming lexical aspect as a special case when just verbs, taken as lexical items, are at stake. Aspectual *class* is to be distinguished from aspectual *form* (see also Dowty, 1979, p. 52, following Johnson, 1977), whereby the latter concerns the expression of grammatical aspect. In contrast to aspectual form (grammatical aspect), aspectual class need have no overt marker and may remain as an intrinsic semantic property of verbs, verb phrases and sentences. (Filip 2012: 725)

4 Aspect

The term 'lexical aspect' is often (and misleadingly) used for Vendler's (1957) four-way distinction between states (*know, love*), activities (*rain, run*), achievements (*arrive, burst*)[1], and accomplishments (*build a house, run a kilometre*). As the examples show, what we have are aspectual classes since VPs are involved. A fifth class, namely semelfactives, may also be added (Smith 1991: 28). These five classes can be distinguished by the following three semantic properties: 'dynamicity' means that a change is involved, 'durativity' that the event is temporally extended, and 'telicity'[2] means that there is an inherent endpoint that is reached (Comrie 1976, chapter 2; Fleischhauer 2016: 68f.).[3] Table 11 illustrates the semantic features and the five verb classes:

Verb classes	dynamic	durative	telic
State	no	yes	no
Activity	yes	yes	no
Achievement	yes	no	yes
Accomplishment	yes	yes	yes
Semelfactives	yes	no	no

Table 11: Verb classes and their distinguishing properties (Fleischhauer 2016: 68).

What states and activities have in common is that they are not telic, in contrast to achievements and accomplishments. States can be distinguished from activities since they are not dynamic. Finally, achievements differ from accomplishments in that they are not durative but punctual. Semelfactives[4] such as *knock* differ from activity verbs only in

---

[1] Verbs such as *burst* and *explode* are not given by Vendler (1957) as examples of achievements, but they are counted here as achievements, too.
[2] The telic/atelic distinction was coined by Garey (1957: 106).
[3] Beside the endpoint approach to telicity, there is also another notion of telicity, namely the homogeneity approach. In this approach, predicates are telic if they "refer to eventualities which are not viewed as having subparts" (Borik 2006: 37). For a detailed discussion of the two approaches see Borik (2006).
[4] As Filip (2012: 727) notes "drawing the lines between aspectual classes is controversial". Semelfactives are atelic for Smith (1991: 28, 55ff.) but telic for Mourelatos (1978).

that they are punctual.[5] Tests are proposed in the literature to distinguish between the different aspectual classes, see Dowty (1979: 55f.) for a summary of the tests.[6] Since the distinction between telic and atelic predicates will be important in this chapter, one very common test will be discussed here.[7] If atelic predicates are combined with time span adverbials such as *in an hour* they can only have the reading that the event starts in an hour. This ingressive reading is also available with telic predicates. However, telic predicates also allow for an egressive reading, i.e. that the event is finished within an hour. In (1a), the time span adverbial can be added to express that the car was fixed after working on it for one hour, which shows that this predication is telic while in (1b) such an interpretation is not possible showing that (1b) is atelic.

(1)   a.   *Mary repaired the car in an hour.*
       b.   *Mary watched TV in an hour.*

Grammatical aspect, in contrast to lexical aspect, is a grammatical category which expresses the opposition between perfective and imperfective. Grammatical aspect has to do with the "different ways of viewing the internal constituency of a situation" (Comrie 1976: 3). This means that grammatical aspect is about how we look at situations, which is not the case with lexical aspect. Let me first present Comrie's classification of grammatical aspect shown in figure 2 and then present a critical evaluation of its weaknesses.

---

[5] Fleischhauer (2016: 69) points out that verbs such as *knock* "are ambiguous between a semelfactive – single event reading – and an activity reading. In their activity reading these verbs denote an iteration of single events".
[6] Vendler's tests are based on the question whether the verbs can be used in the progressive as well as the possible combination with *for-*, *in-*, and, *at-*adverbials.
[7] A summary of the telicity tests mentioned in the literature is given in Filip (1993/1999: 19f.).

4 Aspect

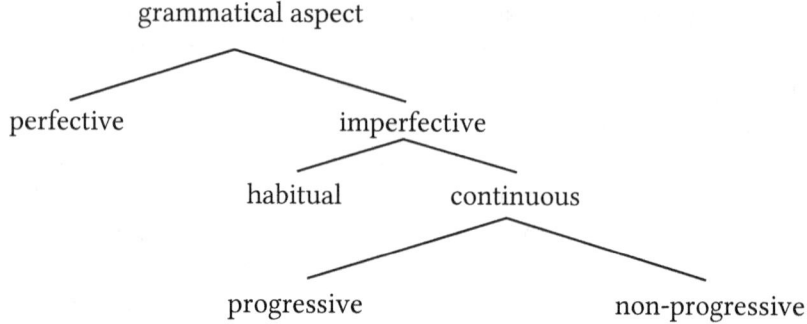

Figure 2: Subdivision of grammatical aspect (Comrie 1976: 25).

Grammatical aspect is subdivided into perfective and imperfective aspect. Perfective means that "the situation is presented as a single unanalysable whole" and that "no attempt is made to divide this situation up into the various individual phases" (Comrie 1976: 3). Thus, perfective aspect denotes a complete event. To illustrate this, a Polish example is given in (2).[8] By using the perfective verb *kupił* the speaker expresses that the action of buying the/a book is viewed as a completed event.

(2) On kupi-ł^{PF} książk-ę.
     he buy-PST book-ACC
     'He bought a/the book.'

The habitual aspect, subsumed by Comrie under imperfective aspect, describes a situation "which is characteristic of an extended period of time, so extended in fact that the situation referred to is viewed not as an incidental property of the moment but, precisely, as a characteristic feature of a whole period" (Comrie 1976: 27f.), which can be expressed in English by the construction '*used to* + infinitive' as in (3).

(3) *He used to play football.*

Filip & Carlson (1997: 98f.) argue that the habitual (or generic) aspect should be regarded as independent of aspect and thus should not be clas-

---

[8] The grammatical aspect is superscripted to the verb in (2) and not given in the glossing. The reason for doing so will be explained in section 4.2.

sified as a special case of imperfective aspect. One argument they present is that perfective verbs can also express habituality/genericity, which they illustrate by Czech and Russian examples. The Polish example in (4) demonstrates the same point. Although we have the perfective verb *przepalić* 'smoke', habituality is expressed, which is enforced by the presence of the adverbial *codziennie* 'every day'.

(4)   *Ja codziennie prze-pal-ę^{PF} 20 papieros-ów.*
       I   every_day PRZE-smoke-1SG.PRS 20 cigarette-PL.GEN
       'I smoke 20 cigarettes every day.' (Lenga 1976: 46)

The perfective verb *przepalić* in (4) can be replaced by the imperfective verb *przepalać* without changing the habitual reading in (4). This shows that habituality can be expressed by perfective and imperfective verbs and that "habituality and aspect, perfective and imperfective, are notionally orthogonal to each other" according to Filip & Carlson (1997: 99).

In contrast to perfective aspect, the imperfective aspect has an "explicit reference to the internal temporal constituency of the situation" (Comrie 1976: 4) and the situation is looked at from within. Imperfective aspect is a cover term for the continuous and habitual aspect according to Comrie. The continuous aspect is defined by Comrie (1976: 26) negatively as "imperfectivity that is not habituality". Filip & Carlson (1997: 100) argue that the continuous node is gratuitous in Comrie's figure. According to them, imperfective verbs with a progressive or non-progressive reading also allow for a habitual interpretation. This is why there is no language that has a notional or formal category of continuous aspect. According to Comrie, the continuous aspect subsumes the progressive and non-progressive aspect. With the progressive aspect, the situation is described as ongoing; in contrast to the non-progressive aspect which describes situations as non-dynamic. (5) is an example of progressive aspect in English and (6) exemplifies non-progressive aspect. (5) also shows that progressive aspect is grammaticalized in English since the construction '*be* + verb-*ing*' has to be used.

(5)   *He is eating an apple.*
(6)   *He lives in London.*

4 Aspect

Filip (2001: 468) shows that an imperfective verb can have several readings. She illustrates this with a Russian example, but her observation also applies to Polish:

(7) Russian (Filip 2001: 468)
    Ivan jel^{IMPF} jábloko.
    Ivan eat.PST apple.SG.ACC
    (i) 'Ivan was eating an/some/the apple.' (progressive reading)
    (ii) 'Ivan ate at an/some/the apple.' (partitive reading)
    (iii) 'Ivan ate all the apple/the whole apple.'(completive reading)
    (iv) 'Ivan ate an/some/the apple.' [and did (not) finish eating it] (general factual reading)
    (v) 'Ivan repeatedly ate an/some apple.' (iterative reading)
    (vi) 'Ivan used to eat an/some apple.' (generic/habitual reading)

Imperfective verbs with a completive reading overlap with the function of the perfective verb and as Filip (2001) points out "[i]n such cases, it may be preferable to use the corresponding perfective verb forms in both Russian and Polish" (Filip 2001: 469, footnote 17). The general factual reading (also called 'simple denotative') is used if "the speaker is simply interested in expressing the bare fact that such and such an event did take place, without any further implications, and in particular without any implication of progressive or habitual meaning" (Comrie 1976: 113).

According to Borik (2006: 202ff.), the imperfective aspect in Russian also corresponds to the present perfect in English. There are different types of perfect (for a detailed discussion see Comrie 1976, chapter 3). One type is the perfect of result, which is expressed by the present perfect in English (Borik 2006: 202). Here, the present situation is the result of a past event (Comrie 1976: 56). In Polish too, the imperfective verb can express the perfect of result as in (8). The present situation, namely that the person stinks out of his/her mouth, results from eating garlic in the past. The perfect of result can be expressed with the imperfective verb *jeść* 'eat'.

(8) Cuchnie ci z ust. Jadłeś^{IMPF}
stink.3SG.PRS PRON.2SG.DAT from mouth.PL.GEN eat.2SG.PST
czosnek?
garlic
'Your breath stinks. Have you eaten garlic?'

In (8), the perfective verb *zjeść* 'eat' can also be used for a perfect reading. However, the imperfective verb is preferred. In the following, the perfect reading of perfective and imperfective verbs in Polish will not be considered. Furthermore, I will only give the progressive and general factual reading of imperfective verbs in the English translations and neglect the other possible readings.

4.2 Morphological realization of grammatical aspect in Polish

There is a lot of literature on grammatical aspect in Polish, in Slavic, and in general (Isačenko 1962, Forsyth 1970, Czochralski 1975, Comrie 1976, Filip 1993/1999, Dickey 2000, Borik 2006, Gvozdanović 2012, among many others). Simplex verbs, i.e. verbs with no affixes, can be either perfective or imperfective in Polish.[9] There are several tests which can be applied to determine whether a verb is perfective or imperfective (cf. Filip 1993/1999: 178f.).

Phase verbs like *(s)kończyć* 'to finish', *zaczynać^{IMPF}/zacząć^{PF}* 'to begin' or *przestawać^{IMPF}/przestać^{PF}* 'to stop' can only be combined with imperfective verbs in Polish. The combination with perfective verbs is ungrammatical as in (9).

---

[9] There is only a small number of Polish verbs that are biaspectual. Depending on the context they are imperfective or perfective. Verbs such as *pitrasić* 'cook (coll.)', *potrafić* 'be able, manage', *powozić* 'drive (horse-drawn vehicle)' belong to this class according to Swan (2002: 280). The biaspectual status of, for example, *pitrasić* 'cook (coll.)' is, however, questionable since applying the tests given in (9) – (11) it is imperfective. Furthermore, there is a prefixed perfective counterpart *upitrasić*. Loan words of the kind *kategoryzować* 'categorize' and *organizować* 'organize' are imperfective in Polish and can be perfectivized by the prefixes *s-* and *z-*, respectively.

4 Aspect

(9) Jan skończy-ł^{PF} jeść^{IMPF}/*zjeść^{PF}.
    Jan finish-PST eat
    'Jan finished eating.'

The second test which can be applied has to do with the fact that, in Polish, only imperfective verbs can be combined with the analytic future form consisting of the auxiliary *być* 'to be' and the infinitive (10):

(10) Jan będzie jeść^{IMPF}/*zjeść^{PF}.
     Jan AUX   eat
     'Jan will eat.'

The third test is connected to the second one since perfective verbs in the present tense do not have a present, but a future time reading while imperfective verbs have a present time reading (11).

(11) a. Jan z-je^{PF} jabłk-o.
        Jan Z-eat.3SG.PRS apple-ACC
        'Jan will eat the/an apple.'
     b. Jan je^{IMPF} jabłk-o.
        Jan eat.3SG.PRS apple-ACC
        'Jan is eating the/an apple.'

The three tests, which are summarized in table 12, reveal that the verb *zjeść* 'to eat' is perfective while *jeść* 'to eat' is imperfective.

test	perfective	imperfective
Combination with phase verbs	no	yes
Combination with the future auxiliary *być* 'be'	no	yes
Present tense allows only a future time reading	yes	no

Table 12: Summary of the tests to determine the (im)perfectivity of verbs.

There is a strategy of imperfectivizing perfective verbs by adding the suffix *-(i/y)wa*, which only changes the grammatical aspect (12). This process is called 'secondary imperfectivization'. The suffix can be added to a perfective simplex verb (12a) or to a verb which is perfective due to a prefix such as *pod-* in (12b). (12c) shows that secondary imperfectivization is not possible with all Polish perfective verbs.

(12) a. *kupić*^{PF} - *kupować*^{IMPF} 'buy'
    b. *pod-pisać*^{PF} - *pod-pisywać*^{IMPF} 'sign'
    c. *na-pisać*^{PF} - **na-pisywać* 'write'

Other aspectual pairs are formed by suppletive forms (13):[10]

(13) a. *brać*^{IMPF} - *wziąć*^{PF} 'take'
    b. *mówić*^{IMPF} - *powiedzieć*^{PF} 'speak'

In Polish and in other Slavic languages, imperfective verbs can be perfectivized by the use of prefixes. Wróbel (1998: 539) gives a list of all prefixes in Polish (14):

(14) *do-, na-, nad(e)-, o-/ob(e)-, od(e)-, po-, pod(e)-, prze-, przy-, roz(e)-, u-, w(e)-, w(e)z-/w(e)s-, współ-, wy-, z(e)-/s-/ś-, za-*.

In (15), three imperfective verbs are given which are perfectivized by the prefixes *na-, prze-,* and *z-* (15). In (15), the verbs only differ in the verbal aspect and not in their meaning.

(15) a. *pisać*^{IMPF} - **na***pisać*^{PF} 'write'
    b. *czytać*^{IMPF} - **prze***czytać*^{PF} 'read'
    c. *jeść*^{IMPF} - **z***jeść*^{PF} 'eat'

Verbal prefixes can also be combined with already prefixed verbs and thus prefix stacking is possible.[11] This is illustrated in (16), where the distributive *po-* can be prefixed to an already prefixed verb adding the meaning 'one by one'.

---

[10] There are imperfectives with no perfective counterpart such as *mieć* 'have', *należeć* 'belong to', *umieć* 'know' and perfective verbs such as *ujrzeć* 'see, behold', *zdołać* 'manage to do sth', *zaniemówić* 'be speechless' that do not have an imperfective counterpart (Bartnicka et al. 2004: 403).
[11] Bulgarian allows up to seven prefixes to be attached to the verb at the same time (Istratkova 2004: 309).

(16) Po-roz-rzucała^{PF} wszystkie koszule na podłodze.
      DISTR-ROZ-threw all   shirts   on floor
      'She threw each and every one of the shirts on the floor.'
      (Swan 2002: 289)

I follow Filip (1993/1999: 9, 13, 200), for whom the verbal prefixes are derivational since they not only perfectivize an imperfective verb, but often have a semantic effect on the verb and thus derive new (perfective) verbs. Authors also distinguish between empty, lexical, and superlexical prefixes (cf. Richardson 2007: 53, Gehrke 2008a, 2008b: 161f., Gvozdanović 2012: 782f.). In (17a), the addition of the prefix *na-* does not change the meaning of the imperfective verb *pisać*, but only renders the verb perfective. This is why some prefixes are sometimes called 'empty prefixes'[12] in the combination with certain verbs with which only the aspect is changed (Młynarczyk 2004). In contrast, the prefix *pod-* in (17b) has an effect on the meaning of the verb *pisać* 'to write' in addition to the change of grammatical aspect. Such prefixes are called 'internal' or 'lexical prefixes' due to the fact that they derive new verbs. Gehrke (2008a, 2008b: 171), among others, argues that internal prefixes induce telicity, whereas external (also called 'superlexical') prefixes are orthogonal to telicity. External prefixes specify the action of the verb concerning time and intensity. For example, the delimitative prefix *po-* in (17c) adds the information that the writing event takes place for a while.[13]

(17)   *pisać*^{IMPF} 'write'
    a.   *napisać*^{PF} 'write'
    b.   *podpisać*^{PF} 'sign'
    c.   *popisać*^{PF} 'write for a while'

---

[12] They are also called 'perfectivizing prefixes' (Richardson 2007: 52).
[13] Among others, Gehrke (2008a: 1668f., 2008b: 161f.) provides four criteria to distinguish internal from external prefixes. First, internal prefixes can effect the argument structure of the verb such as the addition or deletion of an argument, which is not the case with external prefixes. Second, internal prefixes allow secondary imperfectivization, whereas external prefixes do not. Third, verbs with internal prefixes can derive complex event nominal, while this is not possible with externally prefixed verbs. Fourth, only external prefixes can be attached to already prefixed verbs.

Consequently, prefixes are not in general markers of perfectivity. The only true aspectual marker is –*(i/y)wa*, which marks imperfectivity. Due to the reasons mentioned above, the grammatical aspect of the verbs will be indicated by superscripts and not in the glossings.

4.3 The interaction of aspect and definiteness

For Russian, it is well known that aspect can have an influence on the definiteness of the direct object (cf. Forsyth 1970: 91f., Birkenmaier 1979: 112f., Chvany 1983: 71, Filip 1993/1999: 11, 233, Leiss 2000). In (18a), the verb is perfective while in (18b) we have an imperfective verb. The direct object has only a definite reading in (18a), in contrast to the definite or indefinite interpretation in (18b).

(18) Russian
    a.   *On s''-el^{PF} jablok-i*
        he S-eat.PST apple-ACC.PL
        'He ate the apples.'
    b.   *On el^{IMPF} jablok-i*
        he eat.PST apple-ACC.PL
        'He ate/was eating (the) apples.'

On the basis of Slavic data such as in (18), some authors – such as Leiss (2000) and Borer (2005) – argue that articleless languages, like the majority of the Slavic languages, express definiteness with the perfective/imperfective distinction while in Germanic this is expressed by the definite and indefinite article. Leiss (2000) explicitly claims that the perfective aspect and the definite article express the same grammatical category on the verb in Slavic languages and inside the object NP in the Germanic languages. Arguments against this view will be presented in this chapter.

    Wierzbicka (1967) was one of the first to describe the interaction of grammatical aspect with definiteness of the direct object in Polish. Wierzbicka (1967: 2237f.) argues that due to the perfective verb in (19a) the direct object is best translated with a definite article in contrast to (19b), where only an indefinite reading is possible for Wierzbicka.

(19) a. *On wy-pił*^{PF} *wod-ę*
he WY-drink.PST water-ACC
'He drank (all) the water'
b. *On pił*^{IMPF} *wod-ę*
he drink.PST water-ACC
'He was drinking water'
(Wierzbicka 1967: 2237)

Wierzbicka contributes to the discussion on aspect and definiteness by showing that for perfective verbs a definite direct object is only enforced with bare plural and mass nouns, but not with count nouns. Krifka (1989: 186) formulates this condition explicitly on the basis of Wierzbicka's research on Polish, Birkenmaier's (1979) research on Russian, and Filip's (1985) research on Czech. The bare singular count noun *truskawka* 'strawberry' combined with a perfective verb as in (20a) can have a definite or indefinite reading. If the direct object is not bare, but used with, for example, the quantifier *kilka* 'a few'[14] (20b) the direct object is not definite.

(20) a. *Jan z-jadł*^{PF} *truskawk-ę.*
Jan Z-eat.PST strawberry-SG.ACC
'Jan ate a/the strawberry.'
b. *Jan z-jadł*^{PF} *kilka truskawek.*
Jan Z-eat.PST a few strawberry.PL.GEN
'Jan ate a few strawberries.'

For Krifka (1989: 186) as well as Wierzbicka (1967), the direct object of an imperfective verb can only have an indefinite interpretation. Filip (1992, 1993/1999: 10, and elsewhere) points out that in examples like (19b), the bare mass noun *woda* 'water' can be definite or indefinite. She shows that the imperfective aspect cannot automatically be associated with

---

[14] The quantifier *kilka* requires the direct object to be in the genitive case.

4.3 The interaction of aspect and definiteness

indefiniteness. Filip gives a fully fledged account of this phenomenon, which will be discussed in detail in the next section.

So far, it has been shown that there are perfective verbs which enforce definiteness of a bare plural or mass noun as direct object. However, the question is whether this effect is observable with all perfective verbs. For Polish, Piñón (2001) states "[i]f a verb is perfective, then it cannot have a syntactically bare plural or singular mass noun phrase argument that receives a bare plural or bare singular mass interpretation" (Piñón 2001: 399) but is only "acceptable if the bare noun phrase is understood to be definite" (Piñón 2001: 398). Nevertheless, at the end of his article he admits "that not all perfective verbs in Polish exhibit the restriction [...]. This is imaginable, even if clear counterexamples are rather hard to detect" (Piñón 2001: 414). (21a) shows that in Polish the perfective verb *zjeść* 'eat' also only allows for a definite reading of the direct object *truskawki* 'strawberries'. However, (21b) illustrates that this is not the case with all perfective verbs since the direct object *truskawki* can also have an indefinite reading with the perfective verb *kupić* 'buy'.

(21)   a.   *On z-jadł^{PF} truskawk-i.*
           he Z-eat.PST strawberry-PL.ACC
           'He ate (all) the strawberries.' (Wierzbicka 1967: 2238)
     b.   *On kupi-ł^{PF} truskawk-i.*
           he buy-PST strawberry-PL.ACC
           'He bought (the) strawberries.'

The context may enforce the definite or indefinite reading of the direct object in (21b). The same holds for singular count nouns as direct objects or direct objects of imperfective verbs. Other strategies such as information structure can be used in order to indicate that the direct object is definite. This is shown by example (22a), in which the singular count noun *truskawka* 'strawberry' is the unstressed preverbal direct object and only allows for a definite interpretation due to the fact that it is the topic of the sentence.[15] The same applies to the plural noun *truskawki* 'strawberries' as the direct object of an imperfective verb (22b).

---

[15] Information structure will be discussed in detail in chapter 6.

4 Aspect

(22) a. *Truskawk-ę   z-jadł^{PF} JAN.*
strawberry-SG.ACC Z-eat.PST Jan
'Jan ate the strawberry.'
b. *Truskawk-i   jadł^{IMPF} JAN.*
strawberry-PL.ACC eat.PST Jan
'Jan ate/was eating the strawberries.'

The definite interpretation can also be enforced by a determiner (23):

(23) a. *Jan z-jadł^{PF} tę   truskawk-ę.*
Jan Z-eat.PST DEM strawberry-SG.ACC
'Jan ate this strawberry.'
b. *Jan jadł^{IMPF} te   truskawk-i.*
Jan eat.PST DEM strawberry-PL.ACC
'Jan ate/was eating these strawberries.'

My own observation shows that there are also other verbs than *wypić*^{PF} 'drink' and *zjeść*^{PF} 'eat' with which this definiteness enforcement persists, such as the Polish verb *skosić* 'mow'. The following examples show that we get a definite reading with the perfective verb *skosić* while a definite or indefinite reading is possible with the imperfective verb *kosić*.

(24) a. *Jan s-kosi-ł^{PF} traw-ę.*
Jan S-mow-PST grass-ACC
'Jan mowed the grass.'
b. *Jan kosi-ł^{IMPF} traw-ę.*
Jan mow-PST grass-ACC
'Jan mowed/was mowing (the) grass.'

The question now arises under which conditions and with which verbs perfective aspect has an effect like in (24a). The verbs *eat, drink, mow* which were discussed in this section are all incremental theme verbs. With these verbs, only a definite interpretation of the bare cumulative direct object argument can be found. We do not see the effect of aspect with the verb *buy* in (21b). Since incremental theme verbs seem to be an explanatory factor, it will be the topic of the next section.

4.4 Incrementality

4.4.1 Incremental theme verbs

The notion of incremental theme verbs such as *eat, drink, mow* was introduced by Krifka (1986, 1989: 158f., 1992, 1998). Krifka differentiates between "Sukzessiv-Patiens" and "Simultan-Patiens" in order to distinguish the semantic relations of the object of the German verbs *sehen* 'see' and *trinken* 'drink'. He defines the two relations as follows:

> Bei *trinken* wird das Objektdenotat nach und nach dem Ereignis unterzogen; ich nenne die Relation daher **Sukzessiv-Patiens** [...]. Bei *sehen* ist es hingegen möglich, daß das Objektsdenotat simultan dem Verbereignis unterzogen wird; ich nenne es daher **Simultan-Patiens** (Krifka 1989: 161)

> [With *drink*, the object referent is gradually subjected to the event; this is why I call this relation the gradual patient [...]. With *see*, however, it is possible that the object referent is simultaneously subjected to the event; this is why I call it the simultaneous patient]

What Krifka calls 'Sukzessiv-Patiens' was later called 'incremental' by Dowty (1991: 567). With incremental theme verbs, the referential properties of the direct object have an influence on the telicity of the whole predication. There are three types of incremental theme verbs: (i) verbs of consumption (*eat, drink, smoke*), (ii) verbs of creation/destruction (*build, write, burn, destroy*), and (iii) verbs of performance (*sing, read*) (Krifka 1989: 158f., Dowty 1991: 568f.).

Incremental theme verbs provide a homomorphic mapping between the incremental theme argument and the event. The mapping to subevents and mapping to sub-objects are two requirements for the definition of the homomorphism (Krifka 1998: 211f.). Taking an example such as *Mary ate a tomato*, these two requirements ensure that every proper part of the tomato which is consumed is mapped to a part of the eating event and every part of the eating event is mapped to a proper part of the tomato.

4 Aspect

The progress of the eating event is measured out by the incremental theme argument.[16] When half of the tomato is consumed, half of the event is over. When the entire tomato is eaten, then the event is finished. And vice versa, i.e. when half of the eating event is over, then half of the tomato is eaten and when the whole event is over, the tomato is completely consumed.

For the definition of strictly incremental theme verbs such as *eat* and *drink* the uniqueness of the events and the uniqueness of the objects have to be fulfilled (Krifka 1998: 212). These conditions ensure that there is exactly one event to which the object is mapped and that there is only one object the event is mapped to.

Given the introduction of all four conditions for strict incrementality by Krifka (1998), it becomes obvious that only verbs of consumption (*eat, drink, smoke*) and verbs of creation/destruction (*build, write, burn, destroy*) fulfil all of them. Verbs of performance (*sing, read*) do not since despite the fact that they express a gradual change of state, two distinct subevents of, for example, reading can be mapped to the same object, which means that a book can be read more than once in contrast to writing a book, which is (usually) written only once (Filip 2007: 220). The same holds for verbs like *wash* and *copy*, which do not fulfil the condition of the uniqueness of events (Filip 1993/1999: 93). The uniqueness of events can be tested by checking whether the verb can be combined with *twice, three times* etc. The verb *read* in (25) can be combined with *twice* while the verb *eat* in (26) cannot. Therefore, *eat* fulfils the condition that we have a unique event and *read* does not.[17]

(25) Mary read this book twice.
(26) #Mary ate this bread twice.

---

[16] See Tenny (1994) for the 'measuring-out' of direct internal arguments and her Aspectual Interface Hypothesis. The incremental theme relation is also called the 'ADD TO' relation by Verkuyl (1972, 1993, 1999, 2005), and 'structure-preserving binding' by Jackendoff (1996).
[17] A 'kind' reading for the example in (26) in which Mary ate this kind of bread twice has to be excluded.

4.4.2 Aspectual composition

As already mentioned, the direct object influences the (a)telicity of the whole predication with incremental verbs, which is demonstrated with the verb *eat* in (27):

(27) a. *Mary ate a/the tomato in ten minutes.*
 b. *#Mary ate tomatoes in ten minutes.*
 c. *#Mary ate soup in ten minutes.*

A telic predication is achieved only in (27a). In (27b, c), we get an atelic predication due to the fact that the incremental theme argument in (27b) is a bare plural and in (27c) a bare mass noun. This can be explained in terms of aspectual composition as in (28):

(28) **Aspectual composition of incremental theme predications**: An incremental theme verb combined with a quantized incremental theme argument yields a telic predication whereas combined with a cumulative incremental theme argument it yields an atelic predication. (based on Krifka 1986, 1989: 158, 1992: 31, 1998; Filip 1993/1999, 2001).

There are several means available which give rise to the quantization of a mass or plural object. In (29a), the definite and indefinite article leads to quantization while the same is achieved in (29b) by a numeral construction or a container construction in (29c).

(29) a. *Mary ate the tomatoes/a soup in ten minutes.*
 b. *Mary ate five tomatoes in ten minutes.*
 c. *Mary ate a plateful of tomatoes in ten minutes.*

Since most Slavic languages do not have articles, they cannot use this quantization strategy (29a) and allow for bare singular count nouns. In contrast to the Germanic languages, the Slavic languages have a grammaticalized aspectual system as was presented for Polish. In Slavic languages, the telicity of incremental theme verbs is dependent on the perfective/imperfective distinction of the verb. With perfective verbs, a telic incremental theme predication is achieved. The examples in (30) differ only with respect to the grammatical aspect of the verb. In (30a), the perfective incremental theme verb is combined with a bare count noun which yields a telic predication indicated by the time span adverbial *w godzinę* 'in an hour'. In contrast to (30a), the predication with an imperfective verb in (30b) is atelic.[18]

(30) a. *Maria z-jadł-a^{PF} jabłko w godzinę.*
Maria Z-eat.PST-F apple in hour
'Maria ate the/an apple in an hour.'
b. *Maria jadł-a^{IMPF} jabłko (*w godzinę).*
Maria eat.PST-F apple in hour
'Maria ate/was eating the/an apple.'

4.4.3 Filip's approach

Filip (1993/1999: 3f.) focuses on the interaction of the nominal and the verbal domain and their contribution for achieving a telic predication.[19] She investigates the impact of the perfective and imperfective aspect as well as verbal affixes on the (in)definite reading of bare noun phrases in the articleless Slavic languages with special emphasis on Czech, but also on Russian (Filip 2005b). She analyses the factors under which a definite interpretation is enforced. As has been shown in section 4.3, a perfective verb by itself does not enforce a definite reading. Filip focuses on perfective and strictly incremental theme verbs and argues that with such verbs definiteness of the direct object is enforced. This is why the concept of incrementality was introduced in the previous section. Before touching on the different factors she proposes, I will present Filip's approach to the perfective aspect. Filip (2005a: 134) analyses the perfective aspect as a totality operator (TOT):

> [t]he effect of *TOT(P)* is to individuate atomic events in the denotation of a perfective verb, given that it is required that no two events in the denotation set of a given predicate *P* overlap.

---

[18] Imperfective incremental theme verbs can also lead to a telic predication. See Filip (2004: 105, 109) for the discussion of Russian data and Czardybon & Fleischhauer (2016) for Polish.
[19] Filip (2004: 93f.) defines the notion of telicity semantically, by assuming that telic verbs have the property of denoting atomic events.

Intuitively, *TOT(P)* denotes events each of which is conceived as 'a single whole without distinction of the various phases that make up that situation' (Comrie 1976, p. 16).

The perfective aspect thus expresses single events which are taken as a whole. Given the homomorphism between the event and object for incremental theme verbs and the fact that the perfective aspect expresses total events, Filip (2005a: 134f.) concludes that "the Incremental Theme argument must refer to totalities of objects falling under its description." Totality of objects means that the incremental theme argument has to have a quantized reference, which is the case with singular count nouns. However, with bare mass nouns and bare plurals we have cumulative reference and thus "they do not match the '[TOT+]' requirement imposed on the Incremental Theme argument by a perfective verb" (Filip 1993/1999: 251, 2001: 487). In such cases, the event cannot be delimited by the incremental theme verb and this is why bare plurals and mass nouns are shifted by the totality operator to a totality interpretation, i.e. to the maximal quantity of a mass predicate or the maximal group of a plural predicate (Filip 1993/1999: 247f.) and "[s]uch maximal objects are unique, therefore, anchoring bare plurals and bare mass terms to such maximal objects in the domain of discourse amounts to their having the definite referential interpretation" (Filip 2005a: 136). This shifting leads to a definite interpretation of the direct object, which is, however, only a side effect. With singular count nouns, which are inherently quantized, this shifting is not necessary. This also explains why singular count incremental theme arguments do not necessarily have to be interpreted as definite (Filip 1993/1999: 253) while cumulatively referring direct objects of strictly incremental theme verbs do. This captures the empirical observations made so far very well.

Filip mentions a further factor: definiteness is only enforced if the incremental theme arguments "are not in the scope of other quantificational elements" (Filip 1993/1999: 243). This point is crucial in order to explain sentences such as (31a), a Czech example taken from Filip (1993/1999: 239). In spite of a perfective and strictly incremental theme verb, the direct object has an indefinite reading due to the presence of the accumulative prefix *na-*, which perfectivizes the verb, but also adds the quantificational meaning 'a lot of' and requires a "non-specific indefinite interpretation [of the direct object], regardless whether the verb they form is perfective or imperfective" (Filip 2005b: 231).[20] The same is true for the equivalent Polish sentence in (31b).[21] This example only differs in the case marking of the direct object. In Polish, verbs with the accumulative *na-* require the direct object to be in genitive case while in Czech the accusative or the genitive case can be used.[22]

(31) a. Czech (Filip 1993/1999: 239)
Na-tkala^{PF} jsem plátno.
ACM-weave.PST AUX cloth.SG.ACC
'I weaved a lot of cloth.'
b. Polish
Na-tka-ł-em^{PF} tkanin-y   /*tkanin-ę.
ACM-weave-PST-1SG cloth-SG.GEN / cloth-SG.ACC
'I weaved a lot of cloth.'

Filip (1993/1999, 2001) shows that aspect as a definiteness strategy has been over-estimated because not every perfective verb automatically leads to a definite reading of the direct object. The definite interpretation is a side effect of the totality operator of perfective aspect; equating the function of the definite article for object NPs and perfective aspect is inadequate.

4.4.4 Evidence against the equation of definiteness and perfectivity

Empirical support against equating definiteness and perfective aspect is furthermore offered by Czardybon & Fleischhauer (2014), who investigate Bulgarian and the Polish dialect Upper Silesian. These two lan-

---

[20] The accumulative *na-* and delimitative *po-* are called measure prefixes by Filip (2005b).
[21] For a detailed analysis of the accumulative prefix *na-* in Polish see Piernikarski (1969: 94) and in particular Piñón (1994), for Czech see Filip (1993/1999: 229f., 261f., 2005b), and for Russian see Birkenmaier (1977: 402f.).
[22] Filip (1993/1999: 266, note 6) stresses that in Czech the accusative is preferred especially by younger speakers and that the genitive is regarded as archaic.

guages have a grammaticalized aspectual system, like the other Slavic languages, but they also have a grammaticalized definite article like the Germanic languages. The authors analyse the strategies that achieve a telic incremental theme predication. They show that with perfective strictly incremental theme verbs, cumulative objects have to be explicitly quantized, for example, by a definite article, to yield a telic predication. This is shown by the Upper Silesian example (32d) and Bulgarian example in (33d). Otherwise, the constructions only allow for a kind reading and are atelic (32c)/(33c). The imperfective verb only leads to an atelic predication, irrespectively of the presence (32b)/(33b) or absence of the definite article (32a)/(33a).

(32) Upper Silesian (Czardybon & Fleischhauer 2014: 388–389)
   a. *Łon jod^{IMPF} jabk-o   (*za godzina).*
      he eat.PST apple-ACC.SG (in hour)
      'He ate/was eating an apple.'
   b. *Łon jod^{IMPF} te jabk-o   (*za godzina).*
      he eat.PST DEF apple-ACC.SG (in hour)
      'He ate/was eating the apple.'
   c. *#Łon z-jod^{PF} jabk-a.*
      he Z-eat.PST apple-ACC.PL
      'He ate [some plurality of the kind] apples.'
   d. *Łon z-jod^{PF} te jabk-a   za godzina*
      he Z-eat.PST DEF apple-ACC.PL in hour
      'He ate the apples in an hour.'

(33) Bulgarian (Czardybon & Fleischhauer 2014: 388–389)
   a. *Marija jade^{IMPF} jabălka/ jabălki/ kaša (*za edin čas).*
      Maria ate   apple.SG/ apple.PL/ mash in one hour
      'Maria ate/was eating an apple/apples/mash.'
   b. *Marija jade^{IMPF} jabălka-ta (*za edin čas).*
      Maria ate   apple.SG-DEF in one hour
      'Maria ate/was eating the apple.'
   c. *#Marija iz-jade^{PF} jabălki.*
      Maria IZ-ate   apple.PL
      'Maria ate [some plurality of the kind] apples.'

d. *Marija iz-jade^{PF} jabǎlki-te za edin čas.*
   Maria IZ-ate apple.PL-DEF in one hour
   'Maria ate the apples in one hour.'

The examples in (32) and (33) show that in Upper Silesian and Bulgarian the definite article alone is not sufficient to yield a telic predication, and thus differs from the Germanic languages. However, Upper Silesian is not like the articleless Slavic languages either since the combination of a perfective incremental verb and a bare mass noun does not yield a telic interpretation. On the basis of these data, Czardybon & Fleischhauer (2014) provide arguments against the assumption that the perfective aspect and the definite article have the same semantic functions and that they do not mark the same, as is claimed by Abraham (1997: 60) for Bulgarian.

4.5 Definiteness conditions – Polish data and analysis

So far, Filip's approach accounts for the definiteness enforcement with strictly incremental theme verbs. Her analysis also holds for the Polish strictly incremental theme verbs given in section 4.3. In the following, two major questions will be discussed. First, is Filip's generalization true of all strictly incremental theme verbs of Polish (section 4.5.1)? Second, do we find non-strictly incremental theme verbs with which definiteness of the direct object is also enforced (4.5.2)? Filip only focuses on strictly incremental theme verbs and allows for the possibility that there are further factors that may contribute to the definite interpretation of NPs with other classes of verbs.

4.5.1 Strictly incremental theme verbs

If one looks for the combination of a perfective and strictly incremental theme verb combined with a bare mass NP in the National Corpus of Polish, one comes across examples in which the direct object is interpreted as indefinite. This is especially the case with the mass nouns *piwo*

4.5 Definiteness conditions – Polish data and analysis

'beer', *kawa* 'coffee', *herbata* 'tea', and *zupa* 'soup', less so with *miód* 'honey', *mięso* 'meat', and *cukier* 'sugar'. This is illustrated by the following example in which the perfective and strictly incremental theme verb *wypić* 'drink' is combined with the bare mass noun *piwo* 'beer'. The noun does not have a definite reading as would be expected, but rather an indefinite reading. The preceding context of the sentence is that a man is stopped by the police.

(34) *Wykazało 0,6 promila   w wydychanym przez niego*
proved   0.6 alcohol level in exhaled   by   him
powietrzu. Mieszkaniec Rzecht-y   miał przyznać
air   inhabitant   Rzechta-GEN had admit
policjant-om,   że   wy-pi-ł^{PF} piwo i   sto
policemen-DAT that WY-drink-PST beer and hundred
gram-ów   wódk-i.^{C}
gram-GEN vodka-GEN
'An alcohol level of 0.6 in his exhaled air was proven. The inhabitant of Rzechta admitted to the policemen that he had drunk some (delimited quantity of) beer and a hundred grams of vodka.'

How can this indefinite reading be explained? According to Filip (p.c.), the interpretation of *wypił piwo* in the above context involves an implicit nominal measure phrase "a delimited quantity of beer", and what the quantity might be here capitalizes on our knowledge that beer is drunk in certain well-known conventional portions like glasses or bottles. *Wódka* 'vodka' in (34) occurs in a nominal measure construction with the measure phrase *sto gramów* 'hundred grams'. So the parallel to the explicit nominal measure phrase *hundred grams* may also be seen as supporting the presence of an implicit nominal measure phrase "[a delimited quantity of] beer". The presence of this implicit nominal measure phrase makes the interpretation of *beer* quantized, and hence exempt from further quantization stemming from the perfective aspect of the verb. With a quantized reference, they match the totality requirement imposed by the perfective aspect just like singular count nouns. Thus, they also allow for an indefinite interpretation which explains the data presented above.

4 Aspect

What still needs to be done is to check strictly incremental perfective theme verbs other than *drink* and *eat* in Polish such as *wypalić* 'smoke', *napisać* 'write', *stworzyć* 'create', and *spalić* 'burn', and see if a definite interpretation is achieved. In (35), the bare plural *papierosy* 'cigarettes' only allows for a definite interpretation with the perfective and strictly incremental theme verb *wypalić* 'smoke'. The same is true for the mass noun *mięso* 'meat' with the perfective verb *zjeść* 'eat'.

(35) Brakowa-ł-o   tylko konserw-y   i   paczk-i
     be_missing-PST-N only canned_food-PL and packet-PL
     papieros-ów.   Z-jadłem^{PF} mięso, a   papieros-y
     cigarette-PL.GEN Z-eat.PST.1SG meat and cigarette-PL
     wy-pali-ł-em^{PF}.^{C}
     WY-smoke-PST-1SG
     'Only canned food and cigarette packets were missing. I had eaten the meat and smoked the cigarettes.'

Another example of a strictly incremental theme verb is *spalić* 'burn'. The perfective verb *spalić* combined with the plural noun *listy* 'letters' leads to a definite interpretation of the direct object, while the imperfective equivalent allows for a definite as well as an indefinite reading of the direct object, depending on the context.

(36) a. Jan s-pali-ł^{PF} list-y.
        Jan S-burn-PST letter-PL.ACC
        'Jan burnt the letters.'
     b. Jan pali-ł^{IMPF} list-y.
        Jan burn-PST letter-PL.ACC
        'Jan burnt/was burning (the) letters.'

This shows that bare plurals and mass nouns also enforce definiteness with other strictly incremental theme verbs.

In the following, I will discuss how the addition of different prefixes to a strictly incremental theme verb affects the (in)definite interpretation

4.5 Definiteness conditions – Polish data and analysis

of the incremental theme argument.[23] The addition of the terminative prefix *do-* to the strictly incremental theme verbs *pić* 'drink' and *jeść* 'eat' also gives rise to a definite reading of the direct object. The bare plural *truskawki* 'strawberries' (37a) and mass nouns *zupa* 'soup' (37a) and *herbata* 'tea' (37b) only allow for a definite reading.

(37) a. *Do-jadł-em^{PF} zup-ę/   truskawk-i.*
    DO-eat.PST-1SG soup-SG.ACC strawberry-PL.ACC
    'I finished eating the soup/the strawberries.'
   b. *Do-pi-ł-em^{PF} herbat-ę.*
    DO-drink-PST-1SG tea-SG.ACC
    'I finished drinking the tea.'

The prefix *wy-* in combination with *jeść* 'eat' also leads to a definite reading of the direct object. However, there is a restriction with respect to the direct object: a singular count noun cannot be combined with this prefix and verb form since a cumulatively referring NP is required. This is not the case with singular count nouns.

(38) *Wyjadłem^{PF} truskawk-i/   śmietan-ę/ *truskawk-ę*
    pick_out.1SG strawberry-PL.ACC cream-ACC   strawberry-SG.ACC
    z   tort-u
    from cake-GEN
    'I picked out and ate (all) the strawberries/the cream from the cake.'

Focusing on Russian, Filip (2005b: 229, 242, 270) shows that measure prefixes such as the delimitative *po-* and accumulative *na-* induce an indefinite and require a cumulative incremental theme argument. Thus, Filip demonstrates that not all prefixes that are combined with strictly incremental theme verbs such as *eat* and *drink* lead to a definite interpretation of the direct object. The Polish example in (39) is taken from Fleischhauer & Czardybon (2016), who investigate the role of Polish verbal prefixes and German particles in aspectual composition. The delimi-

---

[23] Filip (1992: 142f.) shows that there are prefixes that lead to an indefinite interpretation of direct objects with strictly incremental theme verbs. She gives Czech examples and claims that this is also the case in other Slavic languages.

tative prefix *po-* perfectivizes the verb and adds the meaning that the event took place for a while. Filip's (2005b) observation explains the Polish data in (39). (39a) is grammatical because the direct object is cumulative, whereas (39b) is ungrammatical due to the quantized direct object resulting from a container construction (Filip 1992).[24]

(39)   a.   *Po-pi-ł-em*^{PF} *herbat-y.*
           DEL-drink-PST-1SG tea-GEN
           'I drank tea for a while.'
     b.   **Po-pi-ł-em*^{PF} *szklank-ę herbat-y.*
           DEL-drink-PST-1SG glass-ACC tea-GEN
           (Fleischhauer & Czardybon 2016)

(39b) shows that the delimitative prefix is not compatible with a direct object that is quantized due to the container construction *szklanka* 'glass'. Fleischhauer & Czardybon (2016) explain the data in (39) by arguing that delimitative *po-* individuates the event by measuring the running time and not the quantity of the incremental theme argument as is the case with *wypić* and *zjeść*. With the perfective verb *popić*, the event is regarded as total with respect to the temporal duration. This is sufficient for the individuation of the event, and the total consumption of the direct object is not required, which explains why *popić* allows a cumulative direct object.

This shows that the semantic content of the prefix influences the (in)definite reading of the direct object, and not every prefix leads to a perfective strictly incremental theme verb which requires a definite reading of the bare plural or mass noun as direct object.

---

[24] *Popić* can also have other meanings. Without a direct object *popić* means 'to get drunk'. With a direct object in the accusative case, it means 'to swallow (down)' as in (i).

(i)   *Jan po-pił*^{PF} *tabletk-ę wod-ą.*
      Jan PO-drank pill-ACC water-INS
      'Jan swallowed (down) the pill with water.'

4.5.2 Incremental and non-incremental theme verbs

In this section, I want to focus on incremental and non-incremental verbs and investigate whether they enforce definiteness. The difference between strictly incremental and incremental theme verbs is that with the latter the referent of the incremental theme argument can be affected more than once. An apple can only be eaten once, but a book can be read more than once. This is why the verb *eat* is strictly incremental while *read* is only incremental. For Polish, it seems that with all incremental theme verbs the direct object is also interpreted as definite. The example in (40) is taken from Piñón (2001: 397), who shows that with the perfective verb *przeczytać* 'read' in (40b) only a definite reading of the incremental theme argument *artykuły* 'articles' is possible, which is also confirmed by my informants. For the direct object of the imperfective verb in (40a), he gives only an indefinite reading as a possible interpretation while according to my informants a definite interpretation is also possible, which has been added in the translation.

(40) a. *Basia czyta-ł-a^{IMPF} artykuł-y.*
        Basia read-PST-F article-PL.ACC
        'Basia read (the) articles.'
     b. *Basia prze-czyta-ł-a^{PF} artykuł-y.*
        Basia PRZE-read-PST-F article-PL.ACC
        'Basia read the articles.'
        (after Piñón 2001: 397)

This example demonstrates that definiteness can also be enforced with incremental theme verbs, but only if the incremental theme argument is cumulative as in (40). With singular count nouns, a definite as well as indefinite interpretation is possible (41), just like with strictly incremental theme verbs:

(41) *Jan prze-czyta-ł^{PF} list.*
     Jan PRZE-read-PST letter.SG.ACC
     'Jan read a/the letter.'

4 Aspect

The same effect can be observed with other incremental theme verbs such as *skopiować* 'to Xerox/photocopy'. A possible explanation of why a definite interpretation of the incremental theme argument is enforced with such verbs, too, is that the individuation of the event is achieved by measuring the quantity of the incremental theme argument. Here, too, a quantized incremental theme argument is required to individuate the event. In case of a cumulative noun, the event cannot be individuated, which leads to the quantization of the direct object. As a side effect, the direct object gets a definite interpretation. We are dealing with the same situation as with strictly incremental theme verbs.

I would now like to discuss verbs which are not incremental. The difference between incremental and non-incremental theme verbs is that incremental theme verbs provide a homomorphism between the event and the incremental theme argument. This is not the case with non-incremental theme verbs such as *bring an apple*. If half of the bringing event is over this does not mean that half of the apple is brought.

I divide the non-incremental theme verbs into two groups. One group of verbs enforces the definite reading of the direct object and the other does not. In the following, I will investigate these two groups and will try to find the factors that are responsible for their different behaviour.

The perfective verbs in (42) *kupić* 'buy' and *znaleźć* 'find' are not incremental and do not enforce a definite reading of bare mass nouns (42a), bare plurals (42b), or bare singular count nouns (42c). In all three examples, the direct objects can be interpreted as definite or indefinite, which is dependent on the context.

(42)   a.   *Jan kupi-ł^{PF} mlek-o.*
              Jan buy-PST milk-ACC
              'Jan bought (the) milk.'
      b.   *Jan znalazł^{PF} w plecak-u cukierki.*
              Jan find.PST in backpack-LOC sweet.PL.ACC
              'Jan found (the) sweets in the backpack.'
      c.   *Jan kupi-ł^{PF} jabłk-o.*
              Jan buy-PST apple-SG.ACC
              'Jan bought the/an apple.'

4.5 Definiteness conditions – Polish data and analysis

There are many other perfective non-incremental theme verbs which do not enforce definiteness of their direct objects, e.g. *dać* 'give', *poczuć* 'smell', *przynieść* 'bring', *usłyszeć* 'hear', *wygrać* 'win', *wziąć* 'take', *zamówić* 'order', *zauważyć* 'notice', to mention only a few. Among these verbs we find many verbs of perception and verbs which are found in Levin's (1993:138) class called 'Verbs of Change of Possession'.

The second group of verbs imposes definiteness on the direct object. An example is given in (43)[25]. In (43b), only a definite reading of the bare plural *ziemniaki* is possible, whereas in (43a) the direct object also allows for a definite reading rather than only indefinite as claimed by Sadziński. The verb in (43b) is combined with the distributive prefix *po-*, which has the meaning 'one by one'.

(43) a. *Waży-ł-em*^{IMPF} *ziemniak-i.*
weigh-PST-1SG potato-PL.ACC
'I weighed/was weighing (the) potatoes.'
b. *Po-waży-ł-em*^{PF} *ziemniak-i.*
DISTR-weigh-PST-1SG potato-PL.ACC
'I weighed the potatoes one by one.'

Here again one could ask why only a definite reading is available in (43b). Is this due to the verb or due to the distributive prefix *po-*? It was shown above that the prefixes have an influence on the direct object. In (44), the most neutral prefix for the verb *ważyć* 'weigh' was chosen. What can be observed is that the change of the prefix does not change the fact that the direct object only allows for a definite reading.

(44) *Z-waży-ł-em*^{PF} *ziemniak-i.*
Z-weigh-PST-1SG potato-PL.ACC
'I weighed the potatoes.'

There are also other perfective non-incremental theme verbs which enforce the definiteness of the direct object. The same effect can be observed with the following verbs: *otworzyć* 'open', *udowodnić* 'prove', *włączyć* 'turn on', *zarezerwować* 'reserve', *zorganizować* 'organize',

---

[25] This example is taken from Sadziński (1995/6: 87), but the translation was changed.

among many others. Here, too, definiteness is only imposed if the direct object is a bare plural (45a) or mass noun. Otherwise it can have an indefinite reading (45b).

(45) a. Artur otworzy-ł^{PF} okn-a.
Artur open-PST window-PL.ACC
'Artur opened the windows.'
b. Artur otworzy-ł^{PF} okn-o.
Artur open-PST window-SG.ACC
'Artur opened a/the window.'

It seems to be the case that with verbs such as in (45a) the individuation of the total event is achieved by measuring out the referent of the direct object. This is why the direct object is quantized and, as a side effect, achieves definiteness. With other verbs such as those given in (42) this is not the case. However, it is difficult to find a feature which would predict which verbs enforce the definiteness of the direct object and which do not.

4.6 Aspect, definiteness, and concept types

In this section, I want to discuss the question whether the concept type approach by Löbner (1985, 2011) is relevant for aspect. This is, in turn, linked to the question whether his noun classification plays a role for the definite or indefinite interpretation of the direct object. As shown in this chapter, the mass/count distinction is of crucial importance. According to Löbner (2015), the properties of inherent relationality and inherent uniqueness are independent of the mass/count distinction illustrated in the following table:

	SN	RN	IN	FN
Mass noun	water	*baggage*	air	*skin*
Count noun	book	*brother*	sun	*mother*

Table 13: Classification of nouns based on Löbner (2015).

If we assume that there are mass nouns which are inherently unique, as claimed by Löbner (2015), then the concept type distinction would play a role. We should avoid them in this analysis since they are definite due to their semantics and independent of the factors which enforce the definiteness of the direct object. Only underlyingly [−U] mass nouns should be used as direct objects in order not to blur the picture as to which conditions have to be fulfilled for the enforcement of definiteness. However, this problem may not actually arise, as authors such as Gamerschlag & Ortmann (2007) argue that there are no underlying non-shifted [+U] mass nouns. In order to determine the underlying concept type of a noun in Polish, Czardybon & Horn (2015) make use of the test given in (46).

(46)   To   jest 'x' i   to   jest też 'x'
       DEM COP x   and DEM COP also x
       'This is x and this is also x' (Czardybon & Horn, 2015)

The question is whether the two equal NPs that replace the two 'x' in (46) can refer to two distinct referents. If this is possible, then the noun is not an underlying [+U] concept type. For instance, if we insert the noun *samochód* 'car' in (46), the two NPs *samochód* can only refer to two distinct cars. This is not possible if we use the noun *słońce* 'sun', since we only have one sun we can refer to, leading to the result that *słońce* 'sun' is [+U]. This test works perfectly for count nouns. However, the underlying concept type of mass nouns cannot be determined by the test. If we use the mass noun *powietrze* 'air', it is unclear whether we can refer to two distinct referents or not, because 'air' does not have boundaries. This is why it seems not to be possible to test whether there are underlying [+U] mass nouns in Polish.

4.7 Conclusion

This chapter has shown that not every perfective verb automatically leads to a definite reading of the direct object in Polish, rather that there are special conditions which have to be fulfilled. First, the definiteness enforcement is only observable if the direct object is cumulative (cf. Wierzbicka 1967, Krifka 1989, Filip 1993/1999) and is not interpreted as an implicit measure phrase (Filip, p.c.). Second, the definiteness effect is also dependent on the verb itself, such as with incremental theme verbs. Even with some non-incremental theme verbs definiteness is enforced. However, it was not possible to find an explanation why some non-incremental theme verbs have this effect on the direct object and others do not. Third, the semantic content of the prefixes which perfectivize the verb is crucial. Some prefixes such as the accumulative *na-* or delimitative *po-* do not enforce a definite reading of the direct object (cf. Filip 1992, 2005b).

5 Differential object marking and case alternation

The aim of this chapter is to discuss differential object marking and case alternation in Polish and the factors underlying them. In the first section, I will introduce the notion of differential object marking and what kinds of patterns we find cross-linguistically. The following two sections deal with differential object marking in Polish. Section 5.2 looks at split case alternation and section 5.3 deals with fluid case alternation. In these sections, I will focus on the question whether definiteness is responsible for the case alternation. Furthermore, I will only investigate bare NPs.

5.1 Differential object marking

This section on differential object marking is based on Aissen (2003) and de Swart (2007), who analyse this phenomenon cross-linguistically. To illustrate the phenomenon, de Swart starts by giving the following examples from Malayalam, a Dravidian language spoken in India:

(1) Malayalam (Dravidian; Asher & Kumari 1997: 203, quoted after de Swart 2007: 1)
    a. *Avan oru paʃuvin-e vaɲɲi.*
        he   INDEF cow-ACC buy.PST
        'He bought a cow.'
    b. *ɲaan teeɲɲa vaɲɲi.*
        I   coconut buy.PST
        'I bought a coconut.'

As de Swart (2007: 1) observes, the sentences in (1) differ in that in (1a) the direct object *paʃuvine* 'cow' is marked by accusative case while there is no case marking in (1b) with *teeɲɲa* 'coconut'. The different case marking of the two direct objects is motivated by the fact that the referent of the direct object in (1a) is animate whereas in (1b) it is inanimate. Only direct objects with animate referents are marked by the accusative case, but direct objects with inanimate ones are not.[1] Thus the animacy of the object plays a role in Malayalam and leads to differential object marking. This case marking alternation prevents syntactic ambiguities since referents of subject arguments tend to be animate. In the case of two arguments that have animate referents and no case marking on the direct object and subject, it would be unclear which one of the two arguments is the subject (de Swart 2007: 3f., 73f.).

In Turkish, the specificity of the direct object has an influence on case marking. In (2a), the direct object is marked with the accusative case as specific while in (2b) there is no marking, which results in an unspecific direct object.[2] As noted by de Swart (2007: 5), the differential object marking in Turkish cannot be attributed to the avoidance of ambiguities, but to the marking of prominent objects.[3]

(2) Turkish (Turkic; Kornfilt 2003: 127, quoted after de Swart 2007: 5)
  a. *Ahmet dün akşam pasta-yı ye-di.*
     Ahmet yesterday evening cake-ACC eat-PST
     'Yesterday evening, Ahmet ate the cake.'
  b. *Ahmet dün akşam pasta ye-di.*
     Ahmet yesterday evening cake eat-PST
     'Yesterday evening, Ahmet ate cake.'

---

[1] Later on, de Swart (2007: 88f.) shows that, in certain contexts, direct objects with inanimate referents can be marked by the accusative case in Malayalam in order to avoid misinterpretations.
[2] The accusative case only marks the direct object as specific if it directly precedes the verb as in (2). In other syntactic positions, the direct object must be marked by the accusative case and does not necessarily lead to a specific interpretation (Heusinger & Kornfilt 2005: 11f.).
[3] The English translations of the Turkish examples (2) given by Kornfilt (2003: 127) are misleading by using the definite article in (2a) vs. no article in (2b). They suggest that the Turkish sentences differ with respect to definiteness and not specificity.

A similar situation can be found in Hebrew, where only definite direct objects are marked by the accusative case *'et* (3a) while indefinite ones are unmarked (3b) (Aissen 2003: 453; de Swart 2007: 17f.).

(3) Hebrew (Semitic; Aissen 2003: 453)
    a. *Ha-seret her'a 'et-ha-milxama.*
        DEF-movie showed ACC-DEF-war
        'The movie showed the war.'
    b. *Ha-seret her'a (*'et-)milxama.*
        DEF-movie showed   ACC-war
        'The movie showed a war.'

On the basis of the given examples, de Swart (2007: 5f.) argues that differential object marking can be explained as a means of avoiding ambiguities – as in Malayalam – or by the prominence of the direct object – as in Hebrew and Turkish. Furthermore, he states "that animacy can only *trigger* the occurrence of overt case marking. Definiteness/specificity, on the other hand, can itself be determined by the occurrence of overt case marking" (de Swart 2007: 5f.). This again has to do with the fact that "[a]nimacy is an inherent (lexical) feature of noun phrases which cannot be altered by case (or any other) marking. Nouns are, by contrast, not inherently specified for definiteness or specificity, but can be marked as such by means of articles or case marking" (de Swart 2007: 6).

Spanish is an example of a language that shows an interaction of animacy and definiteness/specificity. The preposition *a* is found with definite direct objects which have an animate referent. In (4a) and (4b), the direct objects are definite and their referents are animate and this is why the presence of *a* is required whereas in (4c) the referent of the direct object is inanimate and thus the NP *la mesa* 'the table' does not allow for the combination with *a* (Bleam 2005: 3f., de Swart 2007: 128f., 189f.).[4]

---

[4] Direct objects referring to inanimate entities can occur with *a* in contexts in which syntactic ambiguities could arise as is emphasized by de Swart (2007: 129f.).

(4) Spanish (Romance, Indo-European)
 a. *Mari vió a la mujer.*
  Mari saw A DEF woman
  'Mari saw the woman.' (Bleam 2005: 3)
 b. *Mari vió a-l gato.*
  Mari saw A-DEF cat
  'Mari saw the cat.' (Bleam 2005: 4)
 c. *Mari vió (*a) la mesa.*
  Mari saw A DEF table
  'Mari saw the table.' (based on Bleam 2005: 4)

In the case of an animate referent of an indefinite direct object NP, *a* marks the NP *una mujer* 'a woman' as specific (5).

(5) Spanish (Bleam 2005: 5)
 Mari vió (a) una mujer.
 Mari saw A INDEF woman
 'Mari saw a woman.'

This shows that with definite objects animacy triggers the occurrence of *a* whereas in the domain of indefinite objects of animate referents specificity is determined by the presence of *a*.

For the following, it is crucial to distinguish between split and fluid case alternation (cf. Dixon 1979). Fluid case alternation means that "[w]ithin one linguistic context the same noun can either be marked or not with a concomitant change in meaning" (de Swart 2007: 186). The Turkish accusative marking on direct objects represents a fluid case alternation where only specific objects are marked. The differential object marking in Malayalam which is due to animacy is an example of split case alternation since "within one linguistic context, i.e., animate nouns, case marking is obligatory, whereas it is not in another linguistic context, i.e., inanimate nouns" (de Swart 2007: 185). In the next section, two cases of split case alternation will be presented before discussing fluid case alternation in Polish in section 5.3.

5.2 Split case alternation

In this section, I discuss two cases in which split case alternation is found in Polish. I will start by giving a brief overview of the Polish case system with special emphasis on the occurrence of the accusative and genitive case, referring especially to Tokarski (2001: 71f. [1973]) and Skibicki (2007: 31f.). This section also provides the basis for the discussion of information structure in chapter 6.

5.2.1 The Polish case system and animacy

In Polish, we find a rich case system. Polish has seven cases, which are illustrated with the feminine noun *kobieta* 'woman' in table 14:

	kobieta 'woman'	
	singular	plural
NOM	*kobieta*	*kobiety*
ACC	*kobietę*	
GEN	*kobiety*	*kobiet*
DAT	*kobiecie*	*kobiet**om***
LOC		*kobiet**ach***
VOC	*kobieto*	*kobiety*
INS	*kobietą*	*kobiet**ami***

Table 14: Case endings of feminine nouns like *kobieta* 'woman' in Polish.

Feminine nouns ending in *-a* which have inanimate referents, such as *lampa* 'lamp', follow the same paradigm as given in table 14 for the noun *kobieta* 'woman'. In contrast to English, for instance, the word order in Polish is flexible. This is shown by (6a) and (6b), in which it is not word order, as in English, but rather case marking that is responsible for indicating which NP is the subject and which is the direct object of the sentence in Polish. Although in both examples the noun *Maria* is at the beginning of the sentence, in (6a) it is the subject marked with nominative case whereas in (6b) it is marked with accusative case and is thus the direct object. However, syntactic relations are not always unambiguously determined by case in Polish, which occurs, for instance, due to case syncretism.[5] Feminine nouns do not have a separate accusative form in plural, but show a syncretism with the nominative. In such a case, it is word order that determines which NP is the subject and which is the direct object, as in (6c). The NP *pielęgniarki* 'nurses' is the subject due to its sentence-initial position whereas the post-verbal NP *nauczycielki* 'teachers' is the direct object.

(6) a. *Mari-a   bi-ł-a   Joann-ę.*
       Maria-NOM beat-PST-F Joanna-ACC
       'Maria beat Joanna.'
    b. *Mari-ę   bi-ł-a   Joann-a.*
       Maria-ACC beat-PST-F Joanna-NOM
       'Joanna beat Maria.'
    c. *Pielęgniark-i   widzia-ły   nauczycielk-i.*
       nurse.F-PL.NOM/ACC see-PST.F.PL teacher.F-PL.NOM/ACC
       'The nurses saw (the) teachers.'

With neuter nouns such as *okno* 'window', we observe a syncretism of the nominative, accusative, and vocative case in singular and plural. The same is true for the neuter noun *dziecko* 'child' in the singular. In the plural, there is one form *dzieci*, which is used for the nominative, accusative, vocative, and genitive case.

Neuter	singular	Plural	singular	plural
NOM	*okno*	*okna*	*dziecko*	*dzieci*
ACC				
VOC				
GEN	*okna*	*okien*	*dziecka*	
DAT	*oknu*	*oknom*	*dziecku*	*dzieciom*
LOC	*oknie*	*oknach*		*dzieciach*
INS	*oknem*	*oknami*	*dzieckiem*	*dziećmi*

Table 15: Case endings of neuter nouns like *okno* 'window' and *dziecko* 'child' in Polish.

---

[5] Babby (1991) shows mainly with Russian examples that there is no direct correlation between grammatical relations and case, which is also true for Polish.

5.2 Split case alternation

Table 16 demonstrates that masculine nouns behave differently depending on whether their referent is animate or not, which is not the case with neuter and feminine nouns. For singular masculine nouns, it can be observed that if the referent is inanimate, as in the case of *dom* 'house', we have a syncretism of the accusative with the nominative case, which is also found with neuter nouns. However, if the referent is animate, the accusative coincides with the genitive case like with *ptak* 'bird'. In plural, only with nouns which have human referents we find a syncretism of the accusative and genitive case. For all other referents (inanimate or animate but not human), the accusative coincides with the nominative.

	SG			PL		
	Inanimate 'house'	Animate 'bird'	Human 'student'	Inanimate 'house'	Animate 'bird'	Human 'student'
N	*dom*	*ptak*	*student*	*domy*	*ptaki*	*studenci*
A		*ptaka*	*studenta*			*studentów*
G	*domu*			*domów*	*ptaków*	
D	*domowi*	*ptakowi*	*studentowi*	*domom*	*ptakom*	*studentom*
L	*domu*	*ptaku*	*studencie*	*domach*	*ptakach*	*studentach*
V	*domie*			*domy*	*ptaki*	*studenci*
I	*domem*	*ptakiem*	*studentem*	*domami*	*ptakami*	*studentami*

Table 16: Case endings of masculine nouns like *dom/ptak/student* in Polish.

The different treatment of the nouns in table 16 is similar to the situation presented for Malayalam, where animacy also triggers differential object marking. However, in Polish we find this alternation only in the domain of masculine nouns in order to explicitly mark what the subject and what the direct object is and thus to avoid syntactic ambiguities.[6] With-

---

[6] There are some classes of masculine nouns in Polish which do not have animate referents, but still require the genitive case as direct objects in singular. Most of them are names and thus ICs such as names for dances like *krakowiak* 'Cracovienne', *polonez* 'polonaise', currencies like *dolar* 'dollar', *funt* 'pound', brands of cars like *trabant* 'Trabant', *fiat* 'Fiat' and cigarettes like *sport*, *giewont*, *wawel*, names for fungi *grzyb* 'mushroom', *maślak* 'boletus', names for viruses and bacteria *wirus* 'virus', *bakcyl* 'bacterium'. Further examples are names for corpse

out the case marking on *ptak* 'bird' in (7a) it would be unclear whether Jan saw the bird or the other way around. This kind of ambiguity does not arise with 'house'. With masculine nouns in plural, the split is only observable with human referents. For nouns with inanimate and non-human animate referents, there is a syncretism of the nominative and accusative case (7b).

(7)   a.   *Jan widział dom / ptak-a.*
           Jan see.PST.SG house.SG.ACC|NOM bird-SG.ACC|GEN
           'Jan saw a/the house/a/the bird.'
   b.   *Oni widzieli dom-y / ptak-I /*
           they see.PST.PL house-PL.ACC|NOM bird-PL.ACC|NOM
           student-ów.
           student-PL.ACC|GEN
           'They saw (the) houses/(the) birds/(the) students.'

With feminine nouns in the singular all direct objects are marked by a separate accusative form. However, this is not the case with feminine nouns in plural. With neuter nouns, there is no direct object marking split observable either. Almost all referents of neuter nouns are inanimate in Polish and no syntactic ambiguities could arise. There are only a few exceptions such as the neuter noun *dziecko* 'child' whose referent is animate (see table 15).

As was shown in Polish, the different marking of the object is triggered by the animacy of the referent of singular masculine nouns and by humanness of plural masculine nouns. This is a property of the noun's referent and the differential object marking does not interfere with definiteness, which is a property of NPs. As example (7) shows, there is no difference in definiteness between *house* and *bird*. Both NPs can receive a definite or indefinite reading. In (7), only masculine sortal concepts are presented. In the examples in (8), INs (8a) and FNs (8b) are used to show that masculine animate and masculine inanimate nouns in singular do

---

      trup 'corpse', *topielec* 'drowned person', *wisielec* 'hanged person' (see Tokarski 2001: 85 [1973], Nagórko 2006: 143) and some fruits/vegetables *banan* 'banana', *pomidor* 'tomato', *ziemniak* 'potato'. For a more detailed description of these exceptions see Grappin (1951) and Wierzbicka (1988: 447f.).

not differ with regard to definiteness, but only have a definite interpretation. With RNs (8c), in general a definite and indefinite interpretation is possible. This shows that differential case marking does not interfere with [±U] concept types.

(8) a. IN
    Jan widział księżyc / papież-a.
    Jan saw moon.M.ACC|NOM Pope-M.ACC|GEN
    'Jan saw the moon/the Pope.'
  b. FN
    Jan widział nos Ann-y / ojca Ann-y.
    Jan saw nose.M.ACC|NOM Anna-GEN father.M.ACC|GEN
    Anna-GEN
    'Jan saw Anna's nose/Anna's father.'
  c. RN
    Jan widział palec Ann-y / brat-a Ann-y.
    Jan saw finger.M.ACC|NOM Anna-GEN
    brother-M.ACC|GEN Anna-GEN
    'Jan saw a/the finger of Anna/ a/the brother of Anna.'

In Polish, there is also a group of verbs which requires all direct objects to be in genitive case.[7] Such verbs are, for example, verbs expressing desire or need (*życzyć* 'wish', *chcieć* 'want', *potrzebować* 'need', *szukać* 'look for'), some reflexive verbs (*bać się* 'be afraid of', *uczyć się* 'learn'), verbs expressing emotions (*nienawidzieć* 'hate'), and verbs expressing negative meaning (*zakazywać* 'forbid') (Fisiak et al. 1978: 65).[8] In (9), the three genitive objects show that the genitive case does not only allow for an indefinite reading of the NPs.

---

[7] Verbs which require a genitive object are also found in other Slavic languages. However, the Slavic languages differ in the number of such verbs and the question of obligatoriness. For a Slavic comparison see Kagan (2013: 15ff.).
[8] For a detailed description of the verb groups that require all direct object in genitive case see Engel et al. (1999: 235f.), Błaszczak (2001: 61, note 38), and Skibicki (2007: 32).

(9)   *Jan szuka   mieszkani-a / ulic-y   Warszawskiej/*
        Jan look_for.PRS flat-GEN   street-GEN Warsaw
        swoj-ego klucz-a.
        his-GEN key-GEN
        'Jan is looking for a/the flat/Warsaw street/his key.'

For some of these verbs, Fisiak et al. (1978: 85, n. 8) mention that "in colloquial Polish genitive alternates with accusative" exist such as with *potrzebować* 'need' and *szukać* 'look for', which is also observed by Buttler et al. (1971: 305). The results of my questionnaire support this observation showing that for *potrzebować* the combination with accusative and genitive objects are equally accepted by most speakers. Direct objects in genitive case with *szukać* are accepted by all speakers, whereas only half of my informants accept the direct object in accusative case.

5.2.2 Negation

Negation is another factor which triggers differential object marking. Polish is well known for the fact that the genitive case is obligatory with direct objects of negated sentences such as in (10b) instead of the accusative in affirmative sentences[9] (10a). It is interesting to observe that the direct objects in (10a) as well as (10b) can have a definite or indefinite interpretation and that the factor for the alternation is determined by negation and not by definiteness.

(10)   a.   *Widzę dziewczyn-ę.*
               see.1SG girl-SG.ACC
               'I see a/the girl.'
        b.   *Nie widzę dziewczyn-y / (*dziewczyn-ę).*
               NEG see.1SG girl-SG.GEN   girl-SG.ACC
               'I do not see a/the girl.'

---

[9] As mentioned at the end of the previous section, there are also verbs which always require the direct object in genitive case independent of the presence of negation. For a detailed analysis of negation in Polish see Błaszczak (2001). Furthermore, Harrer-Pisarkowa (1959) gives a diachronic analysis of the distribution of accusative and genitive objects in negated sentences in Polish.

5.2 Split case alternation

With the bare IN *Maria* in (11) and the FN *matka* 'mother' in (12), we get a definite reading in affirmative and negated sentences if not marked explicitly as indefinite. With the RN *siostra* 'sister' (13), the NP allows for a definite or indefinite reading. Only feminine nouns are used in the examples in order to provide a morphological distinction between the accusative and genitive cases:

(11) a. *Widzę Mari-ę.*
          see.1SG Maria-ACC
          'I see Maria.'
     b. *Nie widzę Mari-i / (*Mari-ę).*
          NEG see.1SG Maria-GEN   Maria-ACC
          'I do not see Maria.'

(12) a. *Widzę matk-ę Mari-i.*
          see.1SG mother-ACC Maria-GEN
          'I see Maria's mother.'
     b. *Nie widzę matk-i Mari-i.*
          NEG see.1SG mother-GEN Maria-GEN
          'I do not see Maria's mother.'

(13) a. *Widzę siostr-ę Mari-i.*
          see.1SG sister-ACC Maria-GEN
          'I see a/the sister of Maria.'
     b. *Nie widzę siostr-y Mari-i.*
          NEG see.1SG sister-GEN Maria-GEN
          'I do not see a/the sister of Maria.'

In Upper Silesian, just like in standard Polish, the genitive of negation is obligatory (14).

(14) Upper Silesian
    a. *Widza dziołch-a.*
       see.1SG girl-SG.ACC
       'I see a girl.'
    b. *Niy widza dziołch-y / (*dziołch-a).*
       NEG see.1SG girl-SG.GEN   girl-SG.ACC
       'I do not see a girl.'

In Russian, in contrast to Polish and Upper Silesian, the direct object in negated sentences can be marked by genitive or accusative case, resulting in a fluid case alternation (15):

(15) Russian (Timberlake 1986: 342)
    a. *Ja ne našel cvet-y.*
       I NEG found flower-PL.ACC
       'I did not find the flowers.'
    b. *Ja ne našel cvet-ow.*
       I NEG found flower-PL.GEN
       'I did not find any flowers.'

According to Timberlake (1986), "the accusative in the plural example above [15] would be used most naturally in a definite sense [...], while the genitive would be used in an indefinite sense" (Timberlake 1986: 342), which is also confirmed by my Russian informants. This topic has been focused on during previous decades and there are many authors who have investigated Russian examples such as in (15). Kagan (2013), among others, argues that there are several properties of the direct object which influence the choice of the case such as abstract vs. concrete noun, the number of the noun, definiteness, specificity, proper vs. common noun (Kagan 2013: 10ff.). With respect to definiteness, she says that the "genitive is more likely to be assigned to indefinite objects than to definite ones" (Kagan 2013: 12). For further literature on this topic, see Partee & Borschev (2007), Kagan (2013) and the literature cited therein.

Czech represents another extreme, since in negated sentences the direct object is usually in accusative case and the genitive case is regarded as archaic (Franks & Dziwirek 1993: 294f., Short 1993: 511, Janda &

Townsend 2000: 69, Mendoza 2004: 230), although the genitive case was the normal case for the direct objects of negated sentences in Old Czech (Short 1993: 511). In Serbo-Croatian, the genitive of negation is also no longer productive (16), according to Franks (1995: 205):[10]

(16) Serbo-Croatian (Franks 1995: 207)
    a. *nisam   čitao   nijedan   časopis*
       NEG.AUX.1SG read.M.SG not_even_one.ACC magazine.ACC
       'I didn't read even one magazine'
    b. **nisam   čitao   nijednog   časopisa*
       NEG.AUX.1SG read.M.SG not_even_one.GEN magazine.GEN

This brief comparison shows that there are significant differences between the Slavic languages concerning the choice of case for direct objects of negated sentences and that, for instance, in Russian this also interacts with definiteness.

5.2.3 Summary

In section 5.2, I have shown that the case alternation is triggered by animacy/humanness and negation in Polish. Here, definiteness does not play a role since the direct objects can receive a definite or indefinite interpretation. Table 17 which summarizes the results reveal that accusative and genitive objects can get a definite or indefinite reading. The table also shows that inherently unique concept types are interpreted as definite if used as bare NPs.

---

[10] In Slovenian, the genitive of negation is obligatory in contrast to Serbo-Croatian (Franks 1995: 207).

	[−U] concepts		[+U] concepts	
	ACC/NOM	GEN	ACC/NOM	GEN
Masc. SG nouns with animate referents/ Masc. PL nouns with human referents	–	definite/ indefinite	–	definite
Masc. SG nouns with inanimate referents/ Masc. PL nouns with non-human referents	definite/ indefinite	–	definite	–
Sentence negation	–	definite/ indefinite	–	definite

Table 17: Split case alternations in Polish and their interaction with the definiteness of direct objects.

5.3 Fluid case alternation

In the following subsections, there are three main points of investigation. The first deals with the question as to where we really find a fluid case alternation in Polish. The case alternation between accusative and genitive is very restricted. I will present two classes of verbs which are said to allow for a case alternation: (i) verbs of giving and taking and (ii) the two strictly incremental theme verbs *eat* and *drink*. These two groups of verbs are often classed together. As I showed in the previous chapter on aspect, incremental theme verbs behave differently from verbs of giving and taking with respect to definiteness. For this reason, I will discuss them separately here. The second question has to do with whether the case alternation can be attributed to definiteness or to other factors. I will show that there is a difference in definiteness between accusative and genitive direct objects. This is an effect of the partitive function of the genitive case. What partitivity is will be discussed in the next section. The third point deals with the question as to whether the four concept types distinguished by Löbner play a role.

One remark has to be made concerning the Polish examples cited in this section. The translations of the examples are taken from the cited authors and are not my own. Sometimes the translations are in German and in such cases I translated the German sentences into English not changing the definiteness of the direct object. The translations of the authors are a crucial point, which will be discussed later.

5.3.1 Verbs of giving and taking

In this section, I discuss verbs such as *kupić* 'buy', *sprzedać* 'sell', *brać* 'take', *przynieść* 'bring', *dać* 'give', *podać* 'pass', *dostać* 'get', and *pożyczyć* 'lend/borrow', most of which are found in Levin's (1993:138) class of 'Verbs of Change of Possession'.[11] For these verbs, it is often argued that they allow for a fluid case alternation (Bystroń 1893: 24, Kempf 1970, Buttler et al. 1971: 310, Laskowski 1972: 55, Lesz 1973, Brooks 1975: 379, Fisiak et al. 1978: 69, Topolińska 1981: 83, 1984: 316f., Franks & Dziwirek 1993: 289, Tokarski 2001: 72 [1973], and Rozwadowska & Willim 2004: 132f.), which is illustrated by the examples in (17)[12,13]

(17) a. *Kupi-ł-am*^{PF} *chleb*
 buy-PST-1SG bread.ACC
 'I bought the bread'
 b. *Kupi-ł-am*^{PF} *chleb-a*
 buy-PST-1SG bread-GEN
 'I bought some bread'
 (Franks & Dziwirek 1993: 289)

---

[11] Lesz (1973: 64f.) calls such verbs 'verba dandi and accipiendi'.
[12] It is not clear from the translations in (17) whether the direct object is used as a mass or count noun. Furthermore, the given translation of the direct object in (17) is not the only possible one. In (17a), *chleb* can also be translated as 'bread' or 'a bread'. In (17b), *chleba* can also be translated as 'bread' or 'some of the bread'. The possible interpretations of the direct objects in (17) will be discussed in more detail later in this section.
[13] The total number of my informants for the questionnaire on case alternation was 54. Only 12 informants judged the sentence with the genitive object in (17b) as felicitous. The acceptability of such sentences will be discussed later in more detail.

5 Differential object marking and case alternation

The case alternation as in (17) is only observable with mass and plural nouns (Laskowski 1972: 55; Sadziński 1991: 155, 1995/96: 49, 88; Rozwadowska & Willim 2004: 133). Singular count nouns in genitive case are ungrammatical (18a) and the alternation is also restricted to perfective verbs (18b)

(18) a. *Kupi-ł-am^{PF} jabłk-a.
         buy-PST-1SG apple-SG.GEN
     b. *Kupowa-ł-am^{IMPF} chleb-a
         buy.IMPF-PST-1SG bread-GEN

Some authors like Bystroń (1893: 25), Kempf (1970: 190f.), Buttler et al. (1971: 318), Laskowski (1972: 55), Lesz (1973: 62, 64, 69), Fisiak et al. 1978: 86, n. 11, Wierzbicka (1988: 448f.), and Tokarski (2001: 73 [1973]) argue that singular count nouns allow for a case alternation. The direct object in genitive case is said to signal that the speaker only wants to have the knife in (19) for a short period of time in contrast to the accusative case.[14] However, sentence (19b) is not accepted by almost all of my informants due to the genitive direct object, which is contrary to Reiter (1977: 360), who takes it to be grammatical. Furthermore, the NP nóż 'knife' in (19a) can also have an indefinite reading, contrary to Reiter.

(19) a. Daj^{PF} mi nóż.
         give.IMP me knife.ACC
         'Give me the/a knife.'
     b. *Daj^{PF} mi noż-a.
         give.IMP me knife-GEN

After having presented what is claimed in the literature with respect to the possible fluid case alternation, the question arises with which of these verbs do we really find a case alternation? The work with my in-

---

[14] The same is argued for similar constructions mentioned by Lesz (1973: 64) such as pożyczyć ołówka 'to borrow/lend pencil' or dobyć miecza 'to draw a sword'. In my investigation, it turned out that the verb dobyć is equally accepted with a genitive and accusative object. With pożyczyć, there is a strong tendency for the accusative case especially with count nouns as direct objects. With mass nouns, half of my informants allow a genitive object.

formants clearly shows that the case alternation as in (17) is falling out of use. For instance, the genitive direct object in (17b) is regarded as highly odd by about 80 % of my informants.

My observation that the genitive case is being replaced by the accusative is supported by earlier analyses carried out by Kempf (1970: 193f.), Buttler et al. (1971: 304ff.), and Lesz (1973: 71). Lesz (1973: 64f.) notes that in her questionnaire the informants prefer the accusative case especially in the colloquial speech of the young generation, too. In 79 % of cases, her informants chose the accusative and only 15 % the genitive case, which shows a strong dominance of the accusative case. Also Rozwadowska & Willim (2004: 132, note 12) emphasize that there is interspeaker variation concerning the acceptability of genitive objects.

We can turn now to the question as to how definiteness is connected to case alternation. Examples such as (17) suggest that NPs marked by the accusative case in Polish correspond to definiteness while the genitive case is connected to indefiniteness. This is explicitly claimed or repeated by authors such as Sadziński (1977: 41, 1991: 155, 1995/96: 48f., 86), Piskorz (2011: 159), and Witwicka-Iwanowska (2012: 35). In (20a), the accusative is said to lead to a definite reading of the direct object whereas the genitive case in (20b) leads to an indefinite reading.

(20) a. *Kupiec kupi-ł^{PF} mąk-ę.*
merchant buy-PST flour-ACC
'The merchant bought the flour'
b. *Kupiec kupi-ł^{PF} mąk-i.*
merchant buy-PST flour-GEN
'The merchant bought flour'
(Sadziński 1995/6: 49)

However, this assumption is only partially correct, a fact which has to do with a wrong and misleading translation of the examples given above. The accusative object in (20a) can have a definite or indefinite reading whereas in (20b) the genitive object is indefinite, as a result of the partitive genitive. Piñón (2003) points out that "the partitive genitive in Polish refers to *proper parts* of some object(s), essentially equivalent to *some of the x* in English" (Piñón 2003: 389). This means that the NP marked by the genitive case expresses partitivity. Koptjevskaja-Tamm (2001b) defines partitivity as the "selection of a subset from a [definite] superset" (Koptjevskaja-Tamm 2001b: 527), which is illustrated in (21). The NP *that good tea* refers to the superset and some part of it is selected by *some of*. Due to the fact that the selected subset is indefinite, the whole partitive NP is indefinite (Löbner 2011: 291).

(21)   *some of that good tea* (Koptjevskaja-Tamm 2001b: 527)

An example of a partitive NP in Polish is given in (22) reflected in the first reading of the Polish sentence given in (i). However, it has to be emphasized that (22) can also have a second reading, namely a pseudo-partitive one given in the second translation (ii).

(22)   *Dał-em^{PF} mu   zup-y.*
        gave-1SG PRON.DAT.3SG soup-GEN
        (i) 'I gave him some of the soup.'
        (ii) 'I gave him (some) soup.'

In contrast to partitive constructions, pseudo-partitive constructions do not express a selected subset from a given superset but only "an AMOUNT of some substance" (Koptjevskaja-Tamm 2001b: 523).[15] Thus, with pseudo-partitive constructions we have an unspecified quantity and no given superset. This is exactly what is expressed in the second reading in (22), which is also observed by Rozwadowska & Willim (2004: 125, 136, 139) for Polish.[16]

In contrast to the partitive genitive, accusative objects can have a definite or indefinite reading, as in (23).

(23)   *Dał-em^{PF} mu   zup-ę.*
        gave-1SG PRON.DAT.3SG soup-ACC
        'I gave him (the) soup.'

---

[15] For a detailed analysis of partitive and pseudo-partitive constructions in the Circum-Baltic languages see Koptjevskaja-Tamm (2001b).
[16] For Rozwadowska & Willim (2004: 136f.), Polish examples like (22) cannot have a partitive reading as claimed by Piñón (2003), but only a pseudo-partitive one. I argue that both interpretations are possible depending on the context. The superset can, for instance, be provided by the context.

So far, I have shown that for Polish the accusative object can be definite or indefinite and the partitive genitive marking leads to an indefinite reading of the direct object. The partitive genitive is restricted to perfective verbs of giving and taking and mass or plural nouns as direct objects.

Now I want to show that the acceptability of genitive objects varies from example to example depending on the verb and the direct object. The combination of the verb *dać* 'give' with the genitive object *cukier* 'sugar' in (24a) is judged by 17 of 54 informants as highly odd in contrast to the genitive object *mąka* 'flour' with the same verb *dać* 'give', which was highly odd for 26 of 54 informants. With the verbs *sprzedać* 'sell' or *kupić* 'buy' the genitive object is accepted by even fewer informants. Example (20b), with the verb *kupić* 'buy' and the genitive object *mąka* 'flour', is considered by 44 of 54 informants as highly odd. The reasons for the different acceptability are unclear. In order to make sure that there were no other factors which might affect the acceptability of the considered sentences, the questionnaire also included the same sentences with accusative objects. These sentences with an accusative object were felicitous for all informants, with the exception of one informant who regarded the sentence (24a) as odd due to some unknown reason.

(24) a. *Daj mi cukru - nie pijam gorzk-iej*
give.IMP me sugar.GEN NEG drink.1SG.PRS bitter-GEN
herbat-y.
tea-GEN
'Give me some (of the) sugar - I do not drink bitter tea.'
b. *Jeśli chcesz mi pomóc, to daj mi*
if want.2SG.PRS me help.INF then give.IMP me
mąk-i.
flour-GEN
'If you want to help me, then give me some (of the) flour.'

Now the question could arise what about other Slavic languages. Do they behave like Polish or do we find a totally different picture? For Russian, Steube & Späth (1999: 157) make similar observations as I do for Polish. The Russian example (25a) shows that the direct object in the accusative case can have a definite or indefinite reading and the genitive case can have a partitive and pseudo-partitive reading (25b).[17]

(25) Russian (Steube & Späth 1999: 157)
    a.   *Daj*^{PF} *mne xleb.*
          give.IMP me bread.ACC
          'Give me a/the bread.'
    b.   *Daj*^{PF} *mne xleb-a.*
          give.IMP me bread-GEN
          'Give me some (of the) bread.'

Similarly to Polish, singular count nouns in Russian cannot be used with the partitive genitive (26a). Furthermore, due to other restrictions not all nouns can be marked with the partitive genitive (26b); some lead to ungrammatical constructions, according to Kagan (2013: 4f.).

(26) Russian (Kagan 2013: 4f.)
    a.   **Ja kupil*^{PF} *tebe   jabloka.*
          I bought you.DAT apple.SG.GEN
          'I bought an apple for you.'
    b.   **Ja kupil*^{PF} *tebe   knig.*
          I bought you.DAT book.PL.GEN
          'I bought some books for you.'

Franks (1995: 207) shows that the partitive genitive is also productive for Serbo-Croatian (27).[18]

---

[17] For Kagan (2013: 3), the partitive genitive does not seem to have a partitive reading, but only a pseudo-partitive one in Russian (i):

(i) a. *Ja kupil*^{PF} *tebe   jabloki.*
        I bought you.DAT apples.PL.ACC
        'I bought (the) apples for you.'
    b. *Ja kupil*^{PF} *tebe   jablok.*
        I bought you.DAT apples.PL.GEN
        'I bought you some apples.'
        (Kagan 2013: 3)

[18] For Slovenian, Franks (1995: 207) points out that the partitive genitive is restricted.

(27) Serbo-Croatian (Franks 1995: 207)
   daj   mi   sira,   mesa   i   vode
   give me.DAT cheese.GEN meat.GEN and water.GEN
   'give me some cheese, meat, and water'

Still, the partitive genitive is more restricted in Polish than in Russian. According to Filip (p.c.), the genitive case in Czech is odd and obsolete in Bohemia, but still in use in Eastern Moravia[19] (28).

(28) Czech (Filip, p.c.)
   Dej   mi   ?cukru   a   ?vody
   give.IMP me   sugar.GEN and water.GEN
   'Give me some sugar and water'

In the Upper Silesian dialect, many verbs of giving and taking are highly odd with genitive objects (29a). The verb *dać* can be combined with a direct object which is marked by the partitive genitive; however, this is not true for all direct objects (29b). (29c) shows that there are also other verbs for which a case alternation is available.

(29) Upper Silesian
   a. ??Łon kupioł / sprzedoł / wzion monk-i.
       he   bought   sold   took flour-GEN
       'He bought/sold/took some flour.'
   b. Dej   mi   cukru   / monk-i   / cukerk-ów/
      give.IMP me   sugar.GEN flour-GEN sweet-PL.GEN
      *jabek.
      apple.PL.GEN
      'Give me some sugar/flour/sweets.'
   c. Łon mi przinios wod-y.
      he me brought   water-GEN
      'He brought me some water.'

---

[19] The western and central territories of the Czech Republic are part of Bohemia while the eastern territory is part of Moravia. Standard Czech is based on the languages spoken in Bohemia (Janda & Townsend 2000: 2f.). The different varieties of Czech and the question of standard Czech is very complex and a comprehensive discussion is given by Bermel (2000).

5 Differential object marking and case alternation

The last question to be addressed here is whether the concept types play a role. It is difficult to answer this question since the referents of the direct objects in such constructions are often things to eat and drink or represent other sortal concepts. Furthermore, in the previous chapter I already discussed the difficulty of determining whether a mass noun is a [+U] concept. Löbner (p.c.) assumes that *blood* is an RN and *skin* an FN. There seem to be no examples of INs which could be used as direct objects such as in (30). What is demonstrated in (30a) is that the assumed RN *krew* 'blood' is interpreted as definite in the accusative case whereas in the genitive case the RN gets an indefinite reading. The genitive object is not accepted by all of my informants, which is indicated by the question mark. In (30b), the assumed FN *skóra* 'skin' only has a definite interpretation in accusative case and the genitive object is not accepted by my informants.

(30) a. *Dosta-ł-em*^{PF} *krew* / *(?krwi)* *moj-ej* *siostr-y.*
 get-PST-1SG blood.ACC blood.GEN my-GEN sister-GEN
 'I got my sister's blood/(some) of my sister's blood.'
 b. *Sprzeda-ł-em*^{PF} *skór-ę* / *(*skór-y)* *moj-ego* *tygrys-a.*
 sell-PST-1SG skin-ACC skin-GEN my-GEN tiger-GEN
 'I sold the skin of my tiger.'

5.3.2 The incremental theme verbs *eat* and *drink*

With the strictly incremental theme verbs *eat* and *drink* in Polish, we find a similar situation as with the verbs in the previous section. Authors such as Wierzbicka (1967: 2238), Engel et al. (1999: 233f.), and Witwicka-Iwanowska (2012: 176) claim that there is a fluid alternation available between the accusative and genitive cases. (31a) shows that a bare mass noun in accusative is interpreted as definite if combined with a perfective strictly incremental theme verb. This has already been shown in the chapter on aspect, but this is a difference to the verbs of the previous section where the accusative object of a perfective verb of giving and taking can receive a definite interpretation or not depending on the context. In (31b), the genitive object has only an indefinite reading due to the (pseudo-)partitive interpretation.[20] Hence, we have a contrast in definiteness between (31a) and (31b) caused by the case alternation.[21] However, the construction in (31b) is only accepted by about 25 % of my informants, which shows that the partitive genitive also seems to be falling out of use with strictly incremental theme verbs. With an imperfective strictly incremental theme verb, the accusative object allows for a definite and indefinite reading (31c) and a genitive object is regarded as ungrammatical (31d). Also the combination of a perfective strictly incremental theme verb with a singular count noun in genitive case is ungrammatical (31e).

(31)	Perfective verb	Imperfective verb
ACC	a. *Wy-pił-em*^{PF} *mlek-o.* WY-drank-1SG milk-ACC 'I drank the milk.'	c. *Pił-em*^{IMPF} *mlek-o.* drank-1SG milk-ACC 'I was drinking (the) milk.'
GEN	b. ?*Wy-pił-em*^{PF} *mlek-a.* WY-drank-1SG milk-GEN 'I drank some (of the) milk.'	d. *Pił-em^{IMPF} *mlek-a.* drank-1SG milk-GEN
	e. *Z-jadł-em^{PF} *jabłk-a.* Z-ate-1SG apple-SG.GEN	

Here again, I would like to check whether concept types are sensitive to these constructions in Polish. However, similar problems arise as in the previous section. The examples in (32) reveal that again only a definite interpretation is possible with the accusative object. Having the RN as the genitive object in (32a) is considered by 25 % of my informants as acceptable, whereas the genitive object with the FN in (32b) is regarded as ungrammatical. Again, I was not able to find any INs which could enter this construction.

---

[20] For Piñón (2003: 389), only a partitive reading is possible and for Rozwadowska & Willim (2004) only a pseudo-partitive one.
[21] The sentences in (31a) and (31b) also differ with respect to (a)telicity. The accusative object in (31a) leads to a telic predication since a time span adverbial, such as *w minutę* 'in a minute', can be added. The combination of the genitive object with a time span adverbial is incompatible showing its atelicity.

(32)   a. *Wampir wy-pi-ł*^{PF} *krew / (?krwi) swoj-ej*
           vampire WY-drink-PST blood.ACC blood.GEN his-GEN
           ofiar-y.
           victim-GEN
           'The vampire drank his victim's blood/(some) of his victim's blood.'

   b. *Z-jadł-em*^{PF} *skór-ę / (*skór-y) tej ryb-y.*
       Z-eat.PST-1SG skin-ACC skin-GEN DEM fish-GEN
       'I ate the skin of this fish.'

It is interesting to observe Slavic variation in the distribution of the partitive genitive. In contrast to Polish, in Russian the perfective verb with a genitive object is totally acceptable (33b). In Russian, we find the same picture as in Polish with only one difference. According to Kagan (2013: 3), (33b) only allows for a pseudo-partitive reading.

(33)	Perfective verb	Imperfective verb
ACC	a. *Ja vy-pil*^{PF} *vod-u.* I VY-drink.PST water-ACC 'I drank the water.'	c. *Ja pil*^{IMPF} *vod-u.* I drink.PST water-ACC 'I drank/was drinking (the) water.'
GEN	b. *Ja vy-pil*^{PF} *vod-y.* I VY-drink.PST water-GEN 'I drank some water.'	d. **Ja pil*^{IMPF} *vod-y.* I drink.PST water-GEN

(Kagan 2013: 3, 5)

Also in Russian, the partitive genitive cannot be used with singular count nouns as direct objects (34a)[22]. Even if the verb is perfective and the direct object is not a singular count noun, there are restrictions for the use of the partitive genitive (34b) (Kagan 2013: 4f.).

---

[22] Example (34a) is my own.

(34) a. *Ja s''el^{PF} jabloka.
       I   ate   apple.SG.GEN
   b. *Ja s'jel^{PF} jablok.
       I   ate   apple.PL.GEN
       'I ate some apples.' (Kagan 2013: 5)

In Croatian and Serbian, the case alternation is also possible with imperfective verbs (Reiter 1977: 358, Mendoza 2004: 229), which is exemplified by the Croatian example in (35). Furthermore, we can see that – according to Mendoza – the case alternation interacts with the definiteness of the direct object. It is claimed that the marking of the direct object with the accusative results in a definite reading of *water* in (35b) whereas the genitive case leads to an indefinite interpretation (35a). Such examples should be checked with Croatian native speakers once more in order to elucidate if really only a definite reading is possible in (35b) and if (35a) also allows a partitive reading.

(35) Croatian (Mendoza 2004: 229)
   a. On pije^{IMPF} vod-y.
      he drink   water-GEN
      'He drinks water'
   b. On pije^{IMPF} vod-u.
      he drink   water-ACC
      'He drinks the water'

In Czech, the genitive object is obsolete and odd with the perfective verb *vypít* 'drink' (36a). This is at least true for Bohemian Czech, according to my work with my Czech informants in Prague. The combination of the imperfective verb *pít* 'drink' is not accepted (36b):

(36) Czech
   a. ?Petr vy-pil^{PF} vod-y.
      Petr drink.PST water-SG.GEN
      'Petr drank some water.'
   b. *Petr pil^{IMPF} vod-y.
      Petr drink.PST water-SG.GEN
      'Petr drank some water.'

5 Differential object marking and case alternation

There is also a general tendency in (Bohemian) Czech to avoid the genitive in other contexts such as with direct objects of negated sentences or the cases described in 5.3.1 (Janda & Townsend 2000: 69, Franks & Dziwirek 1993: 294f.).

In Upper Silesian, the direct object in the genitive case is accepted neither with perfective nor with imperfective incremental theme verbs (37b, d). Furthermore, perfective incremental verbs cannot be combined with bare plural and mass nouns as they are not inherently quantized. The only interpretation of (37a) is a kind-denoting reading. The only combination possible is an imperfective verb and direct object in the accusative (37c):[23]

(37)	Perfective verb	Imperfective verb
ACC	a. #Łon wy-pioł^{PF} mlyk-o. he WY-drink.PST milk-ACC 'He drank [something of the kind] milk.'	c. Łon pioł^{IMPF} mlyk-o. he drink.PST milk-ACC 'He drank/was drinking milk.'
GEN	b. *Łon wy-pioł^{PF} mlyk-a. he WY-drink.PST milk-GEN	d. *Łon pioł^{IMPF} mlyk-a. he drink.PST milk-GEN

The Slavic variation described above can be summarized in table 18. From the top to the bottom, the languages allow for more contexts of fluid case alternations of bare direct objects with the incremental theme verbs *eat* and *drink*. Upper Silesian is most restrictive and does not allow a genitive object. Furthermore, perfective verbs cannot combine with all accusative direct objects, but only with those which are quantized either inherently as with singular count nouns or they must be quantized by a definite article with mass and plural nouns. In contrast, Czech always allows for a direct object of a perfective verb to be accusative. In Russian, a fluid case alternation can be observed with perfective verbs in contrast to Serbian and Croatian, which also show this pattern with imperfective verbs. For Bohemian Czech, the genitive object is regarded as odd by my informants. However, Filip (p.c.) emphasizes that this is only the case in Bohemian Czech whereas genitive objects are still acceptable in Moravia,

---

[23] For a more detailed analysis of Upper Silesian see Czardybon & Fleischhauer (2014).

especially Eastern Moravia so that we have a cline from West to East. In Polish, only accusative objects are acceptable for increasing numbers of speakers.

	IMPF + ACC	PF + ACC	PF + GEN	IMPF + GEN
Upper Silesian	+	(+)	–	–
Polish	+	+	(+)	–
(Bohemian) Czech	+	+	(+)	–
Russian	+	+	+	–
Serbian/Croatian	+	+	+	+

Table 18: The distribution of the partitive genitive with *eat* and *drink* in the investigated Slavic languages.

The explanation for this variation must be left an open question. The fact that genitive objects are obsolete in Bohemian Czech fits into the general picture since the accusative is strongly preferred over the genitive in many other contexts in Czech (as has been illustrated in this chapter). This is, however, not the case in Polish where the genitive is obligatory in many other contexts. Why is it then falling out of use in this context? This question has to be left for future work.

5.4 Conclusion

In the previous section, I showed that the genitive has a (pseudo-)partitive function in Polish. The partitive genitive is restricted to mass and plural nouns as direct objects of some perfective verbs in Polish. The Polish data also reveal that the partitive genitive is often not accepted by the majority of my Polish informants. The partitive genitive leads to an indefinite interpretation of the direct object. I tried to extend my investigation by including concept types other than SNs. For this task, I chose the assumed FN *skóra* 'skin', which cannot be marked by the partitive genitive and the assumed RN *krew* 'blood' that has an indefinite interpretation as a genitive object. I could not find any INs

5 Differential object marking and case alternation

which could enter the investigated construction with partitive genitive as well as the accusative case. The accusative direct object leads to a definite reading with the Polish verbs for *eat* and *drink* with SNs, RNs, and FNs. With the verbs of giving and taking, the accusative object can have a definite or indefinite interpretation depending on the context with sortal concepts. This shows that the accusative does not automatically lead to a definite interpretation as assumed by Sadziński (1977: 41, 1991: 155, 1995/96: 48f., 86). With the investigated relational and functional concepts only a definite interpretation is possible. This is summarized in table 19.

	ACC				GEN			
	SN	RN	FN	IN	SN	RN	FN	IN
Perfective verbs of giving and taking	def./ indef.		def.	?	(indef.)		*	?
Perfective *eat* and *drink*	def.							

Table 19: Summary of the fluid case alternations in Polish and their interaction with definiteness.

Although the partitive genitive seems to be falling out of use in Polish, the genitive of negation is still obligatory. Table 20 summarizes the distribution of the genitive of negation and partitive genitive for the investigated Slavic languages.[24] What can be observed is that the distribution of the genitive of negation on the one hand and the partitive genitive are independent of each other. One cannot predict that if a language marks direct object of negated sentences with the genitive then this language also has a partitive genitive, or vice versa. This is also supported by the Slovenian and Serbian/Croatian data.

---

[24] '++' stands for obligatory, '+' for optional, '(+)' for restricted, and '–' for no use.

	Genitive of negation	Partitive genitive with verbs of giving and taking	Partitive genitive with the verbs for *eat* and *drink*
Bohemian Czech	–	(+)	(+)
Slovenian	++	–	–
Upper Silesian	++	(+)	–
Standard Polish	++	(+)	(+)
Russian	+	+	+
Serbian/Croatian	–	+	+

Table 20: Summary of the distribution of the genitive of negation and partitive genitive.

6 Information structure

Information structure is one of the most often discussed strategies to achieve definiteness in articleless languages. This chapter is structured as follows: Section 6.1 provides the theoretical background for this chapter. How information structure, definiteness, and the concept types in Polish interact is the focus of section 6.2. In section 6.3, Polish is compared to other Slavic languages. I will restrict my discussion to NPs in declarative sentences.

6.1 Theoretical background

The first section explains what information structure is. Section 6.1.2 is concerned with the thetic/categorical distinction. Mathesius' and Lambrecht's definitions of the bipartite structure of categorical sentences will be discussed in sections 6.1.3 and 6.1.4, respectively.

6.1.1 What is information structure?

Information structure, a term introduced by Halliday (1967), also called 'functional sentence perspective' by the linguists of the Prague School such as Mathesius (1929), concerns the packaging of information in a sentence or utterance. Therefore, it is about the way we convey information and not what the content is about (Chafe 1976: 27). The aim is to achieve an optimal transfer of information. Example (1) displays an optimal information packaging since a referent of the NP *a new car* is introduced in the first sentence and afterwards the personal pronoun *it* is used that refers back to it. If the personal pronoun were used before introducing the car to which the pronoun refers, we would not have an optimal transfer because the hearer would not know to which referent the pronoun refers at the moment of perceiving the first sentence.

(1)   I bought a new car. It was very expensive.

Depending on the background and aim of the conversation, the information has to be structured differently. Although the sentences in (2) have the same content, they differ in the packaging of information, resulting from a different word order and the different placement of sentence stress. Only the sentence in (2b) is an appropriate answer to the question *Where did Mary fly yesterday?* Why only this sentence is an appropriate answer will be discussed in the following sections.

(2)   a.   *Mary flew to London YESTERDAY.*
      b.   *To LONDON Mary flew yesterday.*
      c.   *Yesterday, MARY flew to London.*

6.1.2 Thetic sentences

The distinction between thetic and categorical[1] is crucial when discussing information structure. Thetic sentences are undivided and the sentence only comprises new information (Sasse 1987, Lambrecht 1994: 144, Rosengren 1997). As Rosengren (1997: 439) points out, the sentence is "all-focused and all-comment", which means that the sentence consists only of new information. Detailed definitions of the terms 'comment' and 'focus' are discussed in the following two sections. In Polish, declarative intransitive sentences with a VS structure are thetic (3a). The subjects of thetic sentences can also be preverbal, but they have to bear the sentence stress (3b) (cf. Lenertová & Junghanns: 2007: 398f.).

(3)   a.   Umarł   STUDENT.
           die.PST.3SG student
           'A/the student died.'
      b.   STUDENT umarł.
           student   die.PST.3SG
           'A/the student died.'

---

[1] The terminological distinction goes back to Brentano and Marty at the end of the 19th century (Sasse 1987: 511).

As (3) shows, thetic sentences can comprise definite NPs since *student* 'student' can have a definite or indefinite reading depending on whether its referent was mentioned earlier in the discourse or is definite due to the speech situation. Furthermore, the NP *student* 'student' can be replaced by the IN *papież* 'pope' and only a definite interpretation would be available, which would not change the thetic status of the sentence.

6.1.3 Mathesius' (1929) definition of theme and rheme

In contrast to thetic sentences, categorical sentences are bipartite (Rosengren 1997: 439). There are different terms for the two parts of the sentence such as topic-comment, theme-rheme, background-focus, and many more. As one of the first authors, Mathesius (1929, 1975), analysing English and Czech, pointed out that a sentence or utterance can normally be divided into a theme and a rheme[2]. He goes on to define them as follows:

> One part expresses what is given by the context or what naturally presents itself, in short what is being commented upon. [...] this part is called the theme of the utterance. The second part contains the new element of the utterance, i. e. what is being stated about something; this part is called the rheme of the utterance. The usual position of the theme of an utterance is the beginning of the sentence, whereas the rheme occupies a later position, i.e. we proceed from what is already known to what is being made known. (Mathesius 1975: 156 [1961])

In his definition of theme and rheme, three factors play a role (i) aboutness, (ii) new/given information, and (iii) position within the sentence. If we apply Mathesius' definition of theme and rheme to example (4), *Robert* in the second sentence represents the theme because it is at the beginning of the sentence, given information due to its previous mention and it is commented upon, namely that he ate an apple. In contrast, *ate an apple* is the rheme being at the end of the sentence, it is new information and it says something about Robert.

---

[2] According to Bogusławski (1977: 7, note 1) the terms 'theme' and 'rheme' were introduced by Ammann (1911).

(4) *What did Robert do? Robert ate an apple.*

Since Mathesius, various approaches to information structure have been developed. For a detailed overview of the various approaches see von Heusinger (2002b), who also summarizes the different terms which are used for the bipartite structure defined by Mathesius. It has to be stressed that there is no generally accepted definition of the bipartite structure.

6.1.4 Lambrecht's (1994) definition of topic and focus

I follow Lambrecht's (1994) definition of topic and focus for the bipartite structure because it is widespread and also used in syntactic theories such as Role and Reference Grammar by Van Valin (1993: 23f.; 2005, chapter 3) and Van Valin & LaPolla (1997, chapter 5). Lambrecht defines topic as follows:

> The topic of a sentence is the thing which the proposition expressed by the sentence is ABOUT" (Lambrecht 1994: 118). [...] "If a topic is seen as a matter of standing interest or concern, a statement about a topic can count as informative only if it conveys information which is RELEVANT with respect to this topic (Lambrecht 1994: 119).

There is an inherent relationship between topic and pragmatic presupposition (5):

(5) "PRAGMATIC PRESUPPOSITION: The set of propositions lexicogrammatically evoked in a sentence which the speaker assumes the hearer already knows or is ready to take for granted at the time the sentence is uttered." (Lambrecht 1994: 52)

From the definition of the topic, which is connected to aboutness and relevance, it follows that the topic must be part of the pragmatic presupposition since it is already under discussion (Lambrecht 1994: 150). Example (6) is to illustrate Lambrecht's definition of topic.

(6) *(What did the children do next?) The children went to SCHOOL.* (Lambrecht 1994: 121)

In (6), the sentence is about the referent of the NP *the children* and it adds to the addressee's knowledge about the children, namely that they went to school. Furthermore, the sentence pragmatically presupposes that the children are a "matter of standing current interest and concern" (Strawson 1964: 97), because they are under discussion and taken for granted due to their previous mention. This is why the NP *the children* is the topic of the sentence.

The topic of a sentence can only be determined if the discourse context is taken into consideration since one has to know what is already presupposed and under discussion (Lambrecht 1994: 120). For this reason, Lambrecht makes use of the question-answer test as in (6). The NP *the children* is the topical NP in the answer because its referent is mentioned in the question and thus is already established and taken for granted in the answer. There are also other tests which help to determine the topic and focus of a sentence (Bogusławski 1977: 183f.; van Dijk 1977: 116f.; Reinhart 1981: 56f., 64f.; Nilsson 1982: 3). In (6), we saw that we can ask for the focus. The focus in (6) is *went to school*. Furthermore, topical NPs can be pronominalized. This is shown in (7) with Lambrecht's modified example:

(7)   *(What did the children do next?) They went to SCHOOL.*

For Lambrecht (1994: 200f.), it is the aboutness and relevance aspects that are crucial for defining a topic, and not the syntactic position as is assumed, for example, by Halliday (1967: 212) or Mathesius as shown above.[3] Lambrecht (1994: 118, 146ff.) also points out that the grammatical subject does not necessarily have to be the topic. This will also be supported by the Polish data in section 6.2. The focus is defined by Lambrecht as follows.

---

[3] Lambrecht (1994: 200f.) provides arguments against the claim that the first constituent of a sentence is the topic, such as the change of sentence stress to the first constituent. Furthermore, there are languages with an unmarked focus-topic structure such as in Toba Batak, an Austronesian language with a strict VOS word order. For a detailed discussion of Toba Batak see Van Valin (1999: 518-520).

> The focus is that portion of a proposition which cannot be taken for granted at the time of speech. It is the UNPREDICTED or pragmatically NON-RECOVERABLE element in an utterance. The focus is what makes an utterance into an assertion. (Lambrecht 1994: 207)

> PRAGMATIC ASSERTION: The proposition expressed by a sentence which the hearer is expected to know or take for granted as a result of hearing the sentence uttered. (Lambrecht 1994: 52)

The focus is the part of the proposition which is asserted or added. The added proposition in (6) is that the referent of the topical NP *the children* went to school.

Lambrecht (1994: 221ff.) proposes a classification of different focus structures into argument, predicate, and sentence focus.[4] As the term reveals, with predicate focus the predicate is the focus while the subject is the topic, which is shown by Lambrecht's example in (8). The NP *my car* serves as the topic because it is given information. The referent of the topical NP is already mentioned in the question. The predicate *broke down* is the focus. So we have a topic-focus structure.

(8)   What happened to your car?
      My car/it broke DOWN.
      (Lambrecht 1994: 223)

In sentence focus constructions, the whole sentence represents the focus and no topic is present (9). Such sentences were called 'thetic' at the beginning of this chapter.

(9)   What happened?
      My CAR broke down.
      (Lambrecht 1994: 223)

With argument focus, only one constituent is the focus such as in (10) the NP *my car*. The constituent can be a subject or an object NP. The

---

[4] Lambrecht (1994: 223) illustrates the three types of focus structure with English, Italian, French, and Japanese examples. Here, only the English examples will be discussed.

topic is *broke down* since it is already mentioned in the question and thus taken for granted.

(10) *I heard your motorcycle broke down?*
My CAR broke down.
(Lambrecht 1994: 223)

In (10), the NP *my car* is the focus due to bearing the sentence stress[5] and not being granted for the hearer. In (10), we have a focus-topic structure due to the sentence stress on *car*.

After the definition of topic and focus, I will discuss how definiteness is related to it. If the topic is a presupposed or given proposition and taken for granted, this would mean that topical NPs must be definite or generic. This is substantiated by Gundel's (1988) cross-linguistic investigation of 30 languages. She comes to the conclusion that "the topic of a sentence is typically definite or generic" (Gundel 1988: 213). However, focal NPs cannot automatically be associated with indefiniteness. They can be definite or indefinite as pointed out by Lyons (1999: 232f.). This is illustrated by a Japanese example in (11), in which the topical NP *neko* 'cat' marked by the topic marker *wa* can only be definite in contrast to the focal NP *kingyo* 'goldfish' which allows a definite and indefinite reading.

(11) Japanese (Gundel 1988: 213)[6]
Neko wa kingyo o ijitte iru.
cat TOP goldfish OBJ play_with AUX
'The/*a cat is playing with the/a goldfish.'

---

[5] According to Chafe (1976: 31), the focus is more stressed than the topic, which means that the added proposition is highlighted.
[6] The example has been adapted by adding the auxiliary verb *iru*. Otherwise, the sentence is incomplete, according to Yuka Höfler (p.c.).

6.2 Information structure in Polish

In the following, I will show that the information structure, or topic-focus structure, of a Polish sentence is associated with word order and the placement of sentence stress.[7] In section 6.2.1, I will present the unmarked topic-focus structure in Polish and how this interacts with definiteness. Section 6.2.2 deals with the results of a quantitative study by Czardybon et al. (2014), which supports my claim that not every preverbal NP has to be interpreted as definite or generic, but there is a complex interaction between word order, information structure, and definiteness. How the concept types interact with information structure in Polish is focused on in section 6.2.3, followed by a discussion of the interaction and ranking of information structure, concept types, and explicit markers of (in)definiteness.

6.2.1 The unmarked topic-focus structure and its influence on definiteness

In Polish, the topic is normally found preverbally whereas the focus is post-verbal, i.e. in an unmarked sentence, the topic precedes the focus in Polish (Engel et al. 1999: 494f., Grzegorek 1984: 22, 92, Ożóg 1990: 142, Szwedek 1976b: 62). For illustration, an example taken from the Polish National Corpus is given in (12):

(12) Kobiet-a   znalazła dom.^{C}
      woman-NOM find.PST house
      'The woman found a house.'

---

[7] In Polish, there are no morphological markers for topics such as in Japanese or focus markers such as in the Indo-Iranian language Marathi or Duala, a Bantu language (For a discussion see Gundel 1988: 220-221). However, there are lexical means such as in English *as for, as concerns* or their Polish equivalents such as *jeżeli/jeśli chodzi/idzie o, co się tyczy, co do, odnośnie*, which introduce the topic, but will not be discussed here. For a discussion see Grochowski (1984) and Ożóg (1990: 142f.).

In (12), the preverbal NP *kobieta* 'woman' is the topic of the sentence. She is taken for granted and under discussion since she is given by the context due to a previous mention. As a topical NP, *kobieta* 'woman' could also be pronominalized by *ona* 'she' or the NP could be completely omitted. The NP *dom* 'house' is focal because it is a new piece of information which is not mentioned in the previous context or part of the speech situation. As mentioned above, only within a given context of utterance is it possible to determine the topic and the focus of a sentence.

For Polish, Błaszczak, among others, points out that "in a post-verbal position (i.e., in the so-called rhematic part of a sentence) a nominal phrase not accompanied by any determiner (i.e., any indefinite or demonstrative pronoun) is in principle ambiguous (definite or indefinite)" (Błaszczak 2001:11). Furthermore, she writes that "[i]n a preverbal position a nominal is normally interpreted as definite" (Błaszczak 2001:15).[8] It is crucial to say that Błaszczak's observation only holds if we have an unmarked sentence stress, which is towards the end of the sentence (Szwedek 1975: 101f.; Szwedek 1976a: 80f.; Gebert 2009: 308). Example (12) is taken from written Polish, where sentence stress is not indicated. The focal NP only has an indefinite reading in this example. However, Błaszczak is correct in claiming that in general focal NPs can also be definite. This is shown in (13) which is a modification of example (12):

(13) *Kobiet-a   znalazła DOM.*
    woman-NOM find.PST house.ACC
    'The/(*a) woman found a/the house.'

---

[8] In Polish, topics can also be generic as in (i). The topical NP *tramwaj* 'tram' refers to the whole class of trams and not to an individual one. In the following discussion, generic NPs as topics will not be taken into consideration.

(i) *Tramwaj jest   środkiem komunikacji miejskiej.*
    tram   COP   means_of_transport   municipal
    'The tram is a means of public transport.'

6 Information structure

In Polish, as in most Slavic languages, the word order can be changed due to its rich case morphology (Sussex & Cubberley 2006: 404f.). This has already been demonstrated in the previous chapter on differential object marking and case alternation. The unmarked word order is SVO in Polish as in (13), but all six word order combinations are possible (14). Siewierska & Uhlířová (1998: 107f., 121) analyse the word order of transitive sentences in Polish based on a corpus of written Polish with 1450 clauses and they state that in about 69 % SVO is found.

(14) a. OVS
Dom znalazła KOBIET-A.
house.ACC find.PST woman-NOM
'The/a woman found the/(*a) house.'
b. SOV
Kobiet-a dom ZNALAZŁA.
woman-NOM house.ACC find.PST
'The/(*a) woman found the/(*a) house.'
c. OSV
Dom kobiet-a ZNALAZŁA.
house.ACC woman-NOM find.PST
'The/(*a) woman found the/(*a) house.'
d. VSO
Znalazła kobiet-a DOM.
find.PST woman-NOM house.ACC
'A/the woman found a/the house.'
e. VOS
Znalazła dom KOBIET-A.
find.PST house.ACC woman-NOM
'A/the woman found a/the house.'

The five sentences in (14) differ in what is the topic and what the focus in the sentences. This also means that they differ in the context they can occur. All preverbal unstressed NPs are topical NPs. In (14a), it is the NP *dom* 'house', in (14b) and (14c) the NPs *dom* 'house' and *kobieta* 'woman', and in (14d) and (14e) we have thetic sentences with no topical NPs. All topical NPs are interpreted as definite, whereas the focal NPs, which are post-verbal, allow for a definite or indefinite reading. In all sentences, we assume to have an unmarked sentence stress at the end of the sentence. These examples show that in Polish it is possible to topicalize NPs by placing them preverbally. It is also vital to emphasize that the definiteness restriction which is observed in (14) is only found with bare NPs, i.e. without any determiners such as demonstratives (*ten, tamten, ów, taki*), indefinite (*jakiś* 'some', *jakikolwiek* 'any', *niektóry* 'some', *niejaki* 'some', *jeden* 'one' (cf. Mendoza 2004)), or possessive pronouns, as well as quantifiers (*wszystek* 'all', *wiele/dużo* 'many/much', *kilka* 'a few/several', *parę* 'a few'). This is also part of Błaszczak's (2001) observation given above. In (15), the numeral *jeden* 'one' explicitly marks the preverbal noun *plakat* 'poster' as indefinite. The whole sentence is focal and thus we have a thetic sentence.

(15) *Jeden plakat wisiał na fasadzie dom-u   dokładnie*
      one   poster hung on façade   house-GEN directly
      naprzeciwko.
      opposite
      'One poster hung on the façade of the house directly opposite.'
      (Orwell, translated by Mirkowicz 2008: 8)

6.2.2 Czardybon et al.'s (2014) study on word order and definiteness

Czardybon et al. (2014) carried out a quantitative study to investigate the interaction between word order and definiteness in Polish and to see whether the previous qualitative studies can be substantiated. The question was: Is the definiteness of an NP associated with the position of the NP relative to the main verb? They made use of an annotated text sample of the first 479 sentences of the Polish translation of George Orwell's novel *Nineteen Eighty-Four*.[9] Two native speakers of Polish did the annotation work and had to decide whether the NPs are definite or indefi-

---

[9] The sentences were split into syntactic chunks and only sentences/clauses with exactly one main verb were used for the further investigation. Sentences with auxiliary verbs were excluded. This is why only about 47 % of the data could be used, which was also due to unclear chunkings of the sentences (Czardybon et al. 2014: 147).

nite.[10] Furthermore, in unclear cases they could choose the option "I don't know". Only bare NPs were used for this study, whereby 101 nouns were excluded due to the presence of demonstratives, indefinite, and possessive pronouns, numerals, quantifiers, superlatives, and ordinals (Czardybon et al. 2014: 146f.). The syntactic position and definiteness of the remaining 623 nouns is given in table 21:

	preverbal position	post-verbal position
definite	197	222
indefinite	49	155

Table 21: Correlation between syntactic position and definiteness of NPs (Czardybon et al. 2014: 147).

The results are statistically significant and show that the preverbal position is strongly connected to definiteness with 197 definite vs. 49 indefinite NPs. Indefinite NPs are predominantly found in post-verbal position with 155 NPs vs. 49 indefinite preverbal NPs. However, in post-verbal position we also find 222 definite NPs. This shows that there is no syntactic preference for definite NPs.[11] Thus, this investigation supports the claims of earlier qualitative studies that in the post-verbal position definite and indefinite NPs can be found. The high number of preverbal indefinite NPs is unexpected. About 20 % of all preverbal NPs are indefinite (Czardybon et al. 2014: 148f.).

One possible explanation for the high number of indefinite preverbal NPs could be that partitive constructions are used in the preverbal position. They can serve as topics because, although the whole construction is indefinite, there is a definite superset involved. In contrast to the bare partitive NPs discussed in chapter 5, the subset can be expressed explicitly such as by the numeral *jedna* 'one' as in (16). The superset *dziewczyny*

---

[10] Generic NPs were not included in the category for definite NPs, but there was a separate category for them.
[11] In the next section, I will show that inherently unique nouns in congruent and bare use are interpreted as definite independent of their syntactic position. This is why the concept types of the nouns given in table 21 have been annotated to provide a better picture of the connection between the syntactic position, concept types, and definiteness. The results are given in the next section.

'girls' is definite, in this case marked by a demonstrative, which is optional in such examples.

(16)　*Jedna z   tych dziewczyn powiedział-a   że   ma   na*
　　　　one   of DEM   girl.PL.GEN say.PST-F   that has PREP
　　　imię   Aniela.^C
　　　name   Aniela
　　　'One of these girls said that her name is Aniela.'

However, I checked the text sample of Czardybon et al. (2014) and none of the 49 indefinite preverbal NPs is a partitive construction. The explanation for the preverbal indefinite NPs is that they are focal since indefinite NPs implicate focal NPs. As I have argued above, focal NPs can be definite or indefinite. In (17), the preverbal indefinite NP *helikopter* 'helicopter' is part of a thetic sentence. The referents of the sentence are not taken for granted or under discussion up to this point and thus the whole sentence is focal.

(17)　*helikopter zniżył   się   pomiędzy dachy* [...]
　　　helicopter skim_down REFL between roofs
　　　'a helicopter skimmed down between the roofs [...]'
　　　(Orwell, translated by Mirkowicz 2008: 8)

A similar situation is found in (18), which also represents a thetic sentence. The focal NP *sygnał trąbki* 'trumpet call' has an indefinite reading and would bear the sentence stress in spoken Polish. This again shows that the claim that all preverbal NPs have to be interpreted as definite does not apply to thetic sentences, but only to categorical ones with an unmarked information structure. Consequently, thetic sentences should be excluded from the investigation. In my text sample, 18 of the 49 indefinite preverbal NPs (and thus about 40 %) are part of thetic sentences.

(18)　*Sygnał trąbk-i,   czysty i   piękny,   przeciął*
　　　signal trumpet-GEN clear   and beautiful cut_through.PST
　　　zatęchłe powietrze.
　　　stagnant air
　　　'A trumpet call, clear and beautiful, floated into the stagnant air.'
　　　(Orwell, translated by Mirkowicz 2008: 33)

In spoken Polish, stressing the preverbal NP leads to argument focus (19b)[12] and thus changes the unmarked topic-focus structure (19a). This has also an influence on the definiteness of the NPs. In (19a), the topical NP *kobieta* 'woman' is preverbal and unstressed and thus can only be interpreted as definite. In (19b), the preverbal NP bears the sentence stress, which leads to argument focus and the fact that the NP can have a definite or indefinite reading. This shows that the topic-focus structure can be overwritten by sentence stress.[13]

(19) a. *Kobiet-a   kupi-ł-a   KSIĄŻK-Ę.*
       woman-NOM buy-PST-F book-ACC
       'The/(*a) woman bought a/the book.'
    b. *KOBIET-A   kupi-ł-a   książk-ę.*
       woman-NOM buy-PST-F book-ACC
       'The/a woman bought the book.'

What has been shown so far is that topical NPs in Polish can be found preverbally, which is the unmarked position for topics, and postverbally, but they never bear the sentence stress. Focal NPs can also occur pre- and post-verbally, but their unmarked position is post-verbal. This shows that the relevant feature for the explanation of the distribution of definite and indefinite NPs is not the syntactic position, although there is a tendency due to the unmarked position of topical NPs, but it is the distinction between topical and focal NPs. Topical NPs are definite[14] whereas focal NPs can be definite or indefinite. This is summarized in table 22.

---

[12] The sentence in (19b) can also have a thetic reading, which is neglected here.
[13] For more information on the interaction between sentence stress and word order in Polish, see Szwedek (1974, 1976a).
[14] As mentioned previously, topical NPs can also be generic NPs or partitive NPs, which are not of interest here and are thus neglected.

	Preverbal NP	**Post-verbal NP**
Stressed NP	Focus: definite/ indefinite	Focus: definite/ indefinite
Unstressed NP	Topic: definite	Focus: definite/indefinite Topic: definite

Table 22: Interaction between word order, sentence stress, and definiteness of the Polish bare NP.

In the literature, there are often incorrect observations with regard to preverbal NPs and their (in)definite interpretation. Weiss (1983: 235) and Topolinjska (2009: 184f.) argue that it is a rule for preverbal NPs to be definite. In detail, Topolinjska claims that a preverbal NP in Polish such as *nauczyciel* 'teacher' in her quotation below has to be translated by a definite article in Macedonian, which has postponed definite articles:

> A Polish sentence of the type *Nauczyciel wszedł do klasy* [teacher came into classroom] has to be translated into Macedonian as *Učitelot vleze vo oddelenieto* [teacher.DEF came into class.DEF] 'The teacher came into the classroom' and this is the unique valid translation. Preverbal, i.e. unmarked position of the nominative NP signalizes that we are speaking about an identified teacher. (Topolinjska (2009: 184f.)

I have demonstrated that it is only a strong tendency, but not a general rule for preverbal NPs to be definite. This is only the case if the NP is topical. With respect to the (in)definite interpretation of post-verbal NPs there is no consensus in the Polish literature. For Szwedek (1974: 209, 1976b: 62), sentence-final NPs can only have an indefinite reading, which is also claimed by Topolinjska (2009: 184) writing

> Finally, in a sentence of the type *Do klasy wszedł jakiś nauczyciel* lit. 'In the classroom came a (some) teacher' the post-verbal, marked position of the nominative NP, even without the lexical determiner [*jakiś*], signalizes the /– definite/ use.
> (Topolinjska 2009: 184)

Topolinjska's claim is not correct concerning the Polish example she gives. If the indefinite pronoun *jakiś* 'some' is omitted, the post-verbal

NP *nauczyciel* 'teacher' does not necessarily have to be interpreted as indefinite, but also allows for a definite reading in an appropriate context. This is why I follow Weiss (1983: 235), Mendoza (2004: 217) and Błaszczak (2001: 11), who argue that the post-verbal position allows for a definite and indefinite reading. Their claim for the unmarkedness of the post-verbal position is also supported by the investigation by Czardybon et al. (2014) presented above as well as examples like the one in (20). The definite interpretation of *kierowca* 'driver' is due to the fact that it is inherently unique. This clearly shows that the sentence-final position can also be associated with definiteness.

(20)   *Gdy samochód obok   nas przejeżdżał, mogliśmy*
       when   car   next_to us pass.PST   can.PST.3PL
      zobaczyć kierowc-ę.
      see   driver-ACC
      'As the car passed by us we were able to see the/(*a) driver.'

The discussion so far has clearly shown that a straightforward association between preverbal position and definiteness on the one hand and post-verbal position and indefiniteness on the other cannot be maintained.

Authors who associate the preverbal position with definiteness and post-verbal position with indefiniteness in Polish assume that demonstratives and indefinite pronouns are obligatory to overwrite definiteness by word order. Contrary to Sadziński (1982: 88), it is not the case that indefinite pronouns such as *jakiś* 'some' are obligatory to mark a preverbal NP as indefinite. This was already shown by the examples (17) and (18), in which the NPs are indefinite despite their preverbal position. Further evidence for the non-obligatoriness of indefinite pronouns in preverbal NPs is mentioned by Sadziński (1977: 82) himself in his analysis of translations of German texts into Polish. He points out that there are exceptions where an indefinite subject NP in German is not translated by using an indefinite pronoun with a preverbal NP in Polish. His explanation of these exceptions is that the translator has simply neglected to use them. My explanation is that they are simply not obligatory and can also be left out. On the other hand, demonstratives can explicitly mark a sentence-final NP as definite. However, this marking of definiteness is not obligatory in most cases, as with the [–U] concept *książka* 'book' in (19b). This is why Szwedek's (1974: 208) claim cannot be maintained:

> nouns with indefinite interpretation appear in sentence final position only (unless explicitly marked indefinite in some other way). This is why the pronoun *ten* is obligatory with a noun in this position if the noun is to be interpreted as definite. Nouns with definite interpretation appear in non-final positions (again, unless explicitly marked otherwise). (Szwedek 1974: 208)

Szwedek's quotation also shows that the distinction of concept types is crucial. In (20), the sentence-final NP *kierowca* 'driver' is a [+U] concept and only allows for a definite interpretation. The use of a demonstrative in this DAA example is not possible. The interaction between information structure and concept types is the topic of the next section.

6.2.3 The concept type distinction and information structure

So far, mostly sortal nouns have been analysed, whose definiteness is influenced by information structure. In (21), examples of individual nouns are given, such as the proper name *Jan* as well as the lexical IN *papież* 'Pope'. We have an unmarked sentence stress at the end of the sentence. The topical NP is *Jan* in (21a) while the rest of the sentence represents the focus, thus we have predicate focus. In (21b), the word order is changed to OVS, which makes *papież* 'pope' the topical NP, while *Jan* is focal. Thus, the sentences differ with respect to what is topic and what focus and thus the contexts in which the sentences can be uttered differ. In (21a), the referent of the NP *Jan* is taken for granted and given information whereas in (21b) it is the referent of the NP *papież* 'pope'. However, information structure does not interact with the definiteness of INs. Independently of whether they are topical or not, they can only have a definite interpretation as singular bare NPs. This also holds for other INs. The NP *papież* 'pope' can be replaced by the INs *księżyc* 'moon', *słońce* 'sun', or toponyms such as *Londyn* 'London' and *Polska* 'Poland' and all of them can only have a definite reading.

(21) a. *Jan widział PAPIEŻ-A.*
 Jan see.PST pope-ACC
 'Jan saw the/(*a) Pope.'
 b. *Papież-a widział JAN.*
 pope-ACC see.PST Jan
 'Jan saw the/(*a) Pope (It was Jan, who saw the Pope).'

Functional nouns behave similarly to individual nouns. They are interpreted as definite independent of whether they are the focus, as in (22a) with the FN *matka* 'mother', or the topic as in (22b).[15] Here again, this observation is also true of other FNs such as *ojciec* 'father', *kolor* 'color', *wysokość* 'height', *właściciel* 'owner' and many more. In (22), the FN is the possessee while the possessor *dziewczyna* 'girl' is realized as a genitive attribute. Since the possessor is a sortal noun, its definiteness is influenced by information structure. As part of the focus, it can be definite or indefinite (22a), whereas it can only have a definite reading as part of the topical NP (22b).[16]

(22) a. *Jan widział matk-ę DZIEWCZYN-Y.*
 Jan see.PST mother-ACC girl-GEN
 'Jan saw the/(*a) mother of a/the girl.'
 b. *Matk-ę dziewczyn-y widział JAN.*
 mother-ACC girl-GEN see.PST Jan
 'Jan saw the/(*a) mother of the/(*a) girl.'

Relational nouns such as *członek* 'member' in (23) behave like sortal nouns with respect to the interaction of definiteness and information

---

[15] FNs which are used without an explicit possessor also allow for an indefinite reading. The sentence in (i) can be uttered, for example, by a teacher to another teacher after a parents' evening and the FN *matka* 'mother' allows for an indefinite reading:

(i) *Przyszła do mnie matka i mówi* [...]
 came to me mother and say.3SG
 'A/the mother came to me and said [...]'

[16] The whole complex NP (possessee + possessor) as in (22) with *matka dziewczyny* 'the mother of a/the girl' is only definite if both nouns have a definite interpretation. According to Löbner (2011: 302f.), such a complex NP has unique reference iff all nouns within the NP have unique reference.

structure. As part of the focus, they can have a definite or indefinite interpretation (23a), while as part of the topical NP they have a definite interpretation (23b). The possessor *organizacja* 'organization' in (23) is a sortal noun and shows the same behaviour as the [−U] concept *członek* 'member'.

(23) a. *Jan widział członka ORGANIZACJ-I.*
Jan see.PST member.ACC organization-GEN
'Jan saw the/a member of the/an organization.'
b. *Członka organizacj-i widział JAN.*
member.ACC organization-GEN see.PST Jan
'Jan saw the member of the organization.'

The interaction of the four concept types with information structure provides evidence for the concept type distinction. Bare NPs with [+U] concept types have a definite reading only, independently of whether they are the topic or focus, whereas bare NPs with [−U] concepts are definite as topical NPs but definite or indefinite as focal NPs. Table 23 summarizes this result:

	[+U]		[−U]	
	IN	FN	RN	SN
Topical NP	definite		definite	
Focal NP			definite/indefinite	

Table 23: Interaction of concept types, information structure, and definiteness.

The result of table 24 might help to provide a clearer picture of the quantitative study presented in the previous section. This is why the nouns were annotated by two Polish native speakers with respect to inherent uniqueness and relationality: in order to make it possible to determine the underlying concept type of the nouns. The number of nouns in table 24 is smaller than in table 21 because nouns were not included, for example, if there was no agreement among the annotators. For more details concerning the annotation procedure and further reasons for excluding nouns see Czardybon & Horn (2015).

	preverbal position				post-verbal position			
definite	IN	73	[+U]	106	IN	65	[+U]	128
	FN	33			FN	63		
	RN	14	[−U]	73	RN	14	[−U]	81
	SN	59			SN	67		
indefinite	IN	3	[+U]	8	IN	8	[+U]	38
	FN	5			FN	30		
	RN	3	[−U]	19	RN	12	[−U]	100
	SN	16			SN	88		

Table 24: Correlation between syntactic position, definiteness of NPs, and underlying concept type.

If we only focus on [−U] concept types which are sensitive to information structure, we can see that there is a small tendency for definite NPs to be placed post-verbally (73 preverbal vs. 81 post-verbal definite NPs). Definite NPs with underlying [−U] concept types in post-verbal position are due to anaphoric use (24a), NPs as heads of DAAs (24b), or NPs modified by complements establishing uniqueness (24c).

(24) a. *Zanurzył stalówk-ę w atramencie i   zawahał się.*
        dip-PST   pen-ACC in ink.LOC and falter-PST REFL
        'He dipped the pen into the ink and then faltered.'
        (Orwell, translated by Mirkowicz 2008: 13)
    b. *Przemierzył pokój i   wszedł   do maleńkiej*
        cross-PST   room and enter.PST to tiny.GEN
        kuchni.
        kitchen.GEN
        'He crossed the room into the tiny kitchen.'
        (Orwell, translated by Mirkowicz 2008: 11)
    c. *Wrócił   do pokoj-u i   usiadł   przy*
        come_back to room-GEN and sit_down.PST at
        stolik-u   na lewo od teleekran-u.
        table.DIM-GEN on left   from telescreen-GEN
        'He went back to the living room and sat down at the small table that stood to the left of the telescreen.'
        (Orwell, translated by Mirkowicz 2008: 11)

In (24a), the referents of the definite NPs *stalówka* 'pen' and *atrament* 'ink' have been introduced in the previous discourse and are mentioned again. The anaphoric NPs are placed post-verbally. In (24b), the NPs *pokój* '(living) room' and *kuchnia* 'kitchen' are heads of a DAA. The anchor *mieszkanie* 'flat' has been mentioned before, which is the flat of the protagonist called Winston. The NPs are also post-verbal, but interpreted as definite. In (24c), the uniqueness establishing PP *na lewo od teleekranu* 'to the left of the telescreen' leads to a definite interpretation of the post-verbal NP *stolik* 'small table'.

The number of indefinite NPs with [−U] concept types in post-verbal position is higher than the ones with definite NPs (81 definite post-verbal vs. 100 indefinite post-verbal NPs). This also shows that the post-verbal position in general allows for a definite or indefinite reading. In contrast, the preverbal position is strongly associated with definiteness (73 definites vs. 19 indefinites). Indefinite NPs with [−U] concept types are found predominantly in post-verbal position (100 indefinite post-verbal vs. 19 indefinite preverbal NPs).

There is also a small syntactic preference of definite NPs with [+U] concept types for the post-verbal position (128 post-verbal vs. 106 pre-verbal nouns). What table 24 also reveals is that bare NPs with [+U] concepts can be indefinite in preverbal (8 nouns) as well as in post-verbal position (38 nouns). This can be explained due to incongruent uses, for example, using an FN without a possessor as in (25) or using them in plural. The NPs *twarz* 'face' in (25a) is post-verbal while the FN *głos* 'voice' in (25b) is preverbal and both have an indefinite reading. The NPs are modified by an adjective, but even without the adjectives the NPs would be interpreted as indefinite.

(25) a. *Przedstawiał tylko ogromn-ą twarz,* [...]
      depict.PST simply enormous-ACC face.ACC
      'It depicted simply an enormous face, [...]'
      (Orwell, translated by Mirkowicz 2008: 7)

    b. *W mieszkani-u przejęty głos czytał kolumny cyfr* [...]
      in flat-LOC fruity voice read.PST column figure.PL
      'Inside the flat a fruity voice was reading out a list of figures'
      (Orwell, translated by Mirkowicz 2008: 8)

6.2.4 The ranking of concept types, information structure, and determiners

So far, it has been shown that there are different strategies to express definiteness in Polish. These strategies interact in a complex way, which will be the topic in this section as well as in chapter 7. The question which will be investigated is what happens if two or more definiteness strategies come into conflict. Which strategy has the strongest impact and rules out the others and thus can be ranked highest? The previous section revealed that information structure has no influence on the definiteness of inherently unique nouns (FNs and INs) if they are used as bare singular NPs. This is why the [+U] concept types should be ranked higher than information structure (26).

(26) [+U] concept types > information structure

On the other hand, we have seen that the definiteness of [−U] concepts is influenced by information structure. As part of topical NPs, they only allow for a definite interpretation. This is why information structure should be ranked higher than [−U] concept types (27):

(27) [+U] concept types > information structure > [−U] concept types

It has to be emphasized that [+U] concept types can be used as indefinite NPs. But explicit marking is often required, such as indefinite pronouns. In (28), the IN *papież* 'Pope' has an indefinite reading due to the presence of the indefinite pronoun *jakiś* 'some'.

(28) [...], że   jakiś   papież zrobił z   Rzymu naj-większy
      that INDEF pope   made   from Rome SPL-bigger
      burdel świat-a?^{C}
      brothel world-GEN
      'that some/(*the) Pope made Rome into the biggest brothel in the world.'

The explicit marking of indefiniteness overwrites the unique reference of [+U] concepts. But it also overwrites the definite reading given by information structure with [−U] concept types. The SN *kobieta* 'woman' is preverbal and unstressed and would be interpreted most naturally as a definite and topical NP if it were not preceded by the indefinite determiner *jakiś* 'some'.

(29) *Jakąś kobiet-ę widział JAN.*
INDEF.ACC woman-ACC see.PST Jan
'Jan saw some woman.'

These examples illustrate that the explicit marking of definiteness by means of determiners should be ranked higher than concept type and information structure (30).

(30) definite and indefinite determiners
> [+U] concept types
> information structure
> [–U] concept types

This was the first step towards a ranking of definiteness strategies. In chapter 7, a ranking of all investigated strategies will be given which will serve as the basis for the construction of a decision tree.

6.3 Slavic comparison

Information structure in Slavic languages has been a topic of interest for some decades. However, it is not always the case that the interaction of definiteness with information structure is focused on. Authors such as Junghanns & Zybatow (2009) and Yokoyama (2009) are only interested in the expression of information structure in Slavic without even mentioning that it interacts with definiteness, in contrast to Späth (2006), Sussex & Cubberley (2006: 418), and Topolinjska (2009: 184f.). In this section, I will compare the Polish data to other Slavic languages. For this comparative part, I have chosen three Slavic languages representing each Slavic branch: Slovene (South Slavic), Czech (West Slavic), and Russian (East Slavic).

In Slovene, Russian, and Czech, it can also be observed that information structure influences the (in)definite interpretation of bare NPs. In Polish, post-verbal and stressed NPs are focal and can be either definite or indefinite. The same holds for Czech (31a). For the Russian postverbal NP *poezd* 'train' in (31b), Gladrow only gives an indefinite interpretation. For him, nouns which bear the sentence stress are interpreted as indefinite in Russian (Gladrow 1972: 648f.). According to Späth (2006: 59), the post-verbal stressed NP in (31b) can also have a definite reading. Slovene seems to differ from the other Slavic languages since, according to Sussex & Cubberley, only an indefinite reading is possible. It should be checked whether the post-verbal NP in Slovene really allows only for an indefinite reading.

(31) a. Czech (Cummins 1999: 179)[17]
         Přišel   TElegram.
         arrived telegram
         'A/the telegram has arrived.'
      b. Russian (Pospelov 1970, quoted after Gladrow 1972: 649; Späth 2006: 59)[18]
         prišel   POEZD
         arrived train
         'The/a train arrived'
      c. Slovene (Sussex & Cubberley 2006: 420)
         stric je   darovál knjigo[19]
         uncle AUX gave   book
         'uncle gave a book'

As in Polish, unstressed preverbal NPs are topical and get a definite interpretation in Czech (32a), Russian (32b), and Slovene (32c).

(32) a. Czech (Cummins 1999: 177)
         Postava stoí   v zahradě.[20]
         figure stands in garden
         'The/*a figure is standing in the garden.'

---

[17] Cummins (1999: 177, note 6) indicates sentence stress by bold face. To be consistent, I use capital letters and changed his Czech examples in this section accordingly.
[18] Pospelov indicates sentence stress by italics. I use capital letters instead.
[19] Sussex & Cubberley (2006: 419f.) do not indicate the sentence stress in (31c), but they give the information that we have a neutral stress.
[20] Cummins does not indicate the sentence stress in this sentence.

b. Russian (Pospelov 1970, quoted after Gladrow 1972: 649)
       poezd PRIŠEL
       train arrived
       'The train arrived'
   c. Slovene (Sussex & Cubberley 2006: 420)
       knjigo je   daroval STRIC[21]
       book   AUX give.PST uncle
       'the book was given by uncle'[22]

Three remarks concerning the examples in (32) have to be made. First, in the Czech example (32a), only a definite interpretation is given by Cummins for the post-verbal NP *zahradě* 'garden'. This is in contrast to the post-verbal NP *telegram* 'telegram' in (31a), which can have a definite or indefinite reading. The different behaviour with respect to definiteness seems to be due to the fact that the NP *zahradě* 'garden' is part of a PP. Also in Polish, bare nouns in PPs behave differently from nouns which are not part of a PP (33):

(33) a. *Książka   leży   na STOLE.*
          book.NOM lie.3SG.PRS on table
          'The book is lying on the table.'
      b. *Na stole leży   KSIĄŻKA.*
          on table lie.3SG.PRS book.NOM
          'A/the book is lying on the table.'

In both examples, the noun *stół* 'table' has a definite interpretation independently of its placement in the sentence. This does not mean that nouns in PPs always have a definite reading. Since nouns embedded in PPs seem to behave differently they will not be discussed in the following.

---

[21] Sussex & Cubberley (2006: 420) use bold face to indicate sentence stress in the Slovene examples. I use capital letters instead.

[22] Sussex & Cubberley (2006: 419) point out that the OVS word order in Slovene can be used to topicalize the direct object. In English, this is achieved by a passive construction (32c). The Slovene sentence is not a passive construction.

The second remark concerns the post-verbal NP *stric* 'uncle' in the Slovene sentence (32c). This NP seems to be interpreted here as a name and is therefore not influenced by information structure as an IN and not used with a definite article in the English translation.

Third, Cummins (1999: 177f.) points out that in colloquial Czech preverbal bare NPs such as in (32a) require the demonstrative *ten* in many contexts. This is also a tendency in literary Czech (Uhlířová 1987: 110, quoted after Cummins 1999: 178). Furthermore, *ten* is obligatory with fronted NPs such as with *knížku* 'book' in (34) (Cummins 1999: 178, 198).

(34) Czech
      Tu knížku jsem   v pracovně NE-viděl.[23]
      DET book   AUX.1SG in office   NEG-saw
      'I did not see the book in the office.' (Cummins 1999: 198)

This is in contrast to Polish, where the preverbal position is sufficient for achieving a definite reading of an NP. The occurrence of a demonstrative to explicitly mark the NP as definite is not necessary.

For Polish, I showed that shifting the sentence stress to the preverbal NP changes the topic-focus structure of the sentence. This is why the preverbal NP is no longer interpreted as a topical NP, but becomes a focal one. A stressed preverbal NP allows for an indefinite but also a definite reading in Polish. The sentences in (35) have the same structure as the ones in (32), but the sentence stress is shifted to the preverbal NPs. Russian and Slovene differ from Polish since the preverbal stressed NPs can only have an indefinite reading, see (35b) and (35c). Czech also differs from Polish because a preverbal bare NP can only have an indefinite reading, if it is modified (35a) (Cummins 1999: 178f.). However, there is interspeaker variation in the acceptability of the sentence since Cummins (1999: 178) writes "[f]or some [speakers], contrastive intonation can overcome position rules and introduce a specific indefinite." Without bearing the sentence stress, the preverbal NP *neznámá postava* would be definite (Cummins 1999: 178). To get an indefinite NP in preverbal position which is accepted by all speakers, an indefinite pronoun *nějaká*

---

[23] The translation of *tu* as a definite article by Cummins (1999: 198) could be understood as if Czech had a definite article, which is not the case.

'some' has to be used in (35a), according to Cummins (1999: 178). In Polish, the effect of word order can be overridden by sentence stress without any problem. No modifier or indefinite pronoun has to be added to the stressed preverbal NP in order to achieve an indefinite reading of the NP. The contrast between Polish and Czech reveals that the preverbal position in Czech is more associated with definiteness than in Polish.

(35) a. Czech (Cummins 1999: 179)
?NEznámá POstava stoí   v zahradě.
unknown figure   stands in garden
'A strange figure is standing in the garden.'
b. Russian (Pospelov 1970, quoted after Gladrow 1972: 649)
POEZD prišel
train   arrived
'A train arrived'
c. Slovene (Sussex & Cubberley 2006: 420)
KNJIGO je   daroval stric
book   AUX gave   uncle
'it was a book that uncle gave'

Table 25 summarizes the results of the interaction between information structure and definiteness in the four languages investigated:

	Topical NP	Focal NP	
	preverbal and unstressed	post-verbal and stressed	preverbal and stressed
Polish	definite	definite/indefinite	definite/indefinite
Russian			indefinite
Czech			(indefinite)[24]
Slovene		indefinite	indefinite

Table 25: Summary of the interaction between information structure and definiteness in Polish, Czech, Slovene, and Russian with [–U] nouns.

---

[24] The brackets indicate that an indefinite interpretation is not accepted by all Czech informants even if the NP is modified.

6 Information structure

For Polish, I demonstrated that bare NPs with INs only allow for a definite reading independently of their placement within the sentence. The same holds for other Slavic languages. This is exemplified by the post-verbal IN *solnce* 'sun' from Russian (36a) and the post-verbal FN *konec* 'end' from Czech (36b):

(36) a. Russian (Fedorov 1958: 191, quoted after Birkenmaier 1979: 58n)
vzošlo solnce
rose sun
'the sun rose'
b. Czech
To je konec (toho) filmu.
DEM COP end DEM film.GEN
'This is the end of the film.'

It has been shown that the (in)definite reading of inherently non-unique concepts depends on information structure in articleless Slavic languages. What about languages with articles? Does information structure influence the definiteness of NPs in such languages? For Polish, I demonstrated that explicit marking such as definite and indefinite determiners can overwrite the influence of information structure. It is not surprising that in languages with articles, which explicitly mark an NP as definite or indefinite, information structure does not interact with definiteness.

The following German examples illustrate this point. Independently of their syntactic position, NPs can be definite or indefinite marked by the definite or indefinite article.[25] (37a) shows that preverbal unstressed and post-verbal stressed NPs can be definite or indefinite, whereas (37b) exemplifies that the same holds for preverbal stressed and post-verbal unstressed NPs.

---

[25] Only indefinite singular count nouns are marked by the indefinite article in German. Indefinite plurals and mass nouns are not marked as indefinite explicitly.

(37) German
    a. *Die/eine Frau liest das/ein BUCH.*
       DEF/INDEF woman read.3SG DEF/INDEF book
       'The/a woman is reading the/a book.'
    b. *Die/eine FRAU liest das/ein Buch.*
       DEF/INDEF woman read.3SG DEF/INDEF book
       'The/a woman is reading the/a book.'

The same can be observed in Bulgarian, which is illustrated by (38).[26] In both examples, either the preverbal or the post-verbal NP can be stressed or not, which does not change the definiteness of the NPs:[27]

(38) Bulgarian[28]
    a. *Žena-ta čete edna kniga.*
       woman-DEF read.PRS.3SG one book
       'The woman is reading a/one book.'
    b. *Edna kniga čete žena-ta.*
       one book read.PRS.3SG woman-DEF
       'The woman is reading a/one book.'

6.4 Conclusion

Information structure primarily concerns an optimal structuring of the information one wants to convey. We started with the distinction between thetic and categorical sentences, whereby the latter consist of a topic and a focus. The results of table 23 are integrated into figure 3.

---

[26] There is much debate about whether *edin* in Bulgarian has the status of an indefinite article or is still a numeral for 'one'. For a discussion see Geist (2013).
[27] Although Bulgarian has lost almost all morphological case marking it has a "free" word order (Junghanns & Zybatow 2009: 685).
[28] I owe these examples to Syuzan Sachliyan.

6 Information structure

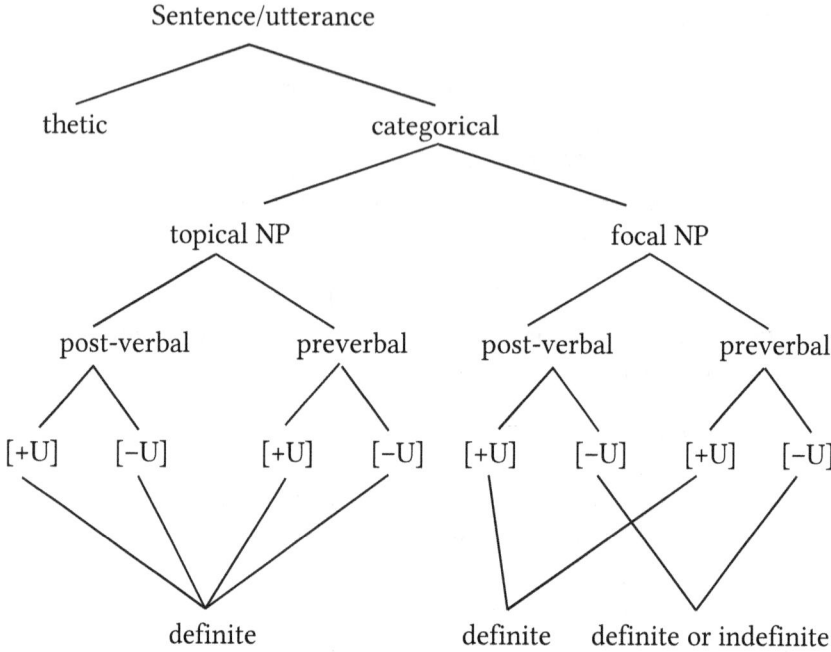

Figure 3: The interaction between information structure, word order, concept types, and definiteness in Polish.

The topic contains the presupposed proposition, thus information which is taken for granted and given for the speaker and the hearer, whereas the focus is the added or new proposition. It has been shown that information structure is associated with word order and sentence stress in Polish and other Slavic languages. In Polish unmarked sentences, topical NPs are found preverbally while focal NPs are post-verbal. However, topical NPs can also be post-verbal and focal NPs preverbal, which shows that we can find topical and focal NPs in all syntactic positions. Topical NPs can only be interpreted as definite (or generic, or partitive) regardless of the concept types. In contrast, focal NPs can be definite or indefinite if the noun is not a [+U] concept type. Inherently unique nouns keep their unique reference even as focal NPs as long as they are not explicitly marked as indefinite or used incongruently such as in plural or without a possessor in the case of FNs.

6.4 Conclusion

The quantitative study carried out by Czardybon et al. (2014) provides evidence against the claim that every preverbal NP is definite. This is only a tendency due to the unmarked preverbal position of topical NPs which are definite. The correlation between the syntactic position of an NP and its definiteness is thus more complex since this depends on the topic-focus structure, which can be changed to focus-topic by, for example, shifting the sentence stress to the preverbal NP or by using explicit marking. Regarding figure 3 from the bottom, an indefinite preverbal NP implicates a focal use of this NP, whereas a definite preverbal NP can be focal or topical.

The comparative study revealed that there is micro-variation with respect to the definiteness of focal NPs in the Slavic languages. This chapter also provides the first step towards a ranking of the investigated definiteness strategies, which interact in a complex way and will be a crucial point of investigation in the next chapter.

7 Conclusion

7.1 Summary

This thesis aimed at providing a detailed and comprehensive investigation of the expression of definiteness in the rather underrepresented language Polish. I analysed four definiteness strategies with which unique reference can be established. My analysis was based on Löbner's (1985, 2011) distinction of the four concept types, which turned out to be a relevant factor for the explanation of some definiteness phenomena. One goal of this thesis was to investigate the interaction between the four concept types and the four definiteness strategies, which has not been done before to the best of my knowledge.

I started with the analysis of demonstratives, which are one of the few explicit strategies for the determination on NP level. The first and central result of my study is that the distribution and frequency of the determiner *ten* differs in spoken and written Polish. For spoken Polish, I argued that although it is unstressed and frequently occurs in anaphoric contexts it has not achieved the article status due to its non-obligatoriness. However, it is developing towards the grammaticalization of an (anaphoric) definite article. Grammaticalization happens gradually and *ten* seems to be rather at the end of such a development. Written Polish differs from spoken Polish in that the determiner *ten* is used less frequently and is restricted to pragmatic uniqueness. I did not analyse Polish in isolation, but the aim was to investigate variation between the Slavic languages. The comparative part showed that the East Slavic languages represented by Russian and the South Slavic language Croatian are similar to written Polish. The investigated determiners in the West Slavic languages (Czech, Upper Sorbian variety, Upper Silesian) have a broader use than the East and South Slavic demonstratives. For Upper Silesian and the Upper Sorbian variety, a definite article is attested since

7 Conclusion

their determiners are not only obligatory with anaphoric NPs, but also extended to [+U] concept types. The Czech demonstrative *ten* is similar to *ten* in spoken Polish.

For the next two strategies, aspect and case alternation, the VP was at the focus of investigation. In chapter 4 on aspect, I contributed to the research by providing evidence against the claim that every perfective verb enforces a definite interpretation of the direct object. I have shown that there are a number of factors which have to be met in order to impose definiteness on the direct object. Here, I want to highlight only the most important ones and not repeat them all. I pointed out that the definiteness enforcement is dependent on the semantics of the prefixes that are combined with the verb (cf. Filip 1992, 2005b) as well as the properties of the direct object (cf. Wierzbicka 1967, Krifka 1989, Filip 1993/1999). Even if we have a strictly incremental theme verb, this does not automatically lead to a definite interpretation of the direct object. The direct object has to be a bare plural or mass noun and the verb must not be prefixed by accumulative *na-* or delimitative *po-*. Another finding was that there are also other than strictly incremental theme verbs such as incremental and non-incremental theme verbs with which also only a definite reading of the direct object is available. It is not totally clear why there are some non-incremental theme verbs that enforce definiteness; this issue will have to be left for future research.

In chapter 5 on differential object marking and case alternation, it turned out that the case alternation between accusative and genitive with some verbs can be explained in terms of definiteness. In some contexts, the genitive has a partitive function and leads to an indefinite reading of the NP while the accusative object can have a definite or indefinite interpretation. In other contexts, negation or the animacy of the referents are responsible for the case alternation, independent of definiteness. Consequently, a straightforward connection between genitive and indefiniteness, likewise also between accusative and definiteness, cannot be assumed.

After the investigation of definiteness strategies at NP and VP level, the last step was the sentence level. Chapter 6 dealt with the topic-focus structure and how it interacts with definiteness. In a sentence with an unmarked topic-focus structure, topical NPs are preverbal in Polish. Since topics are given, they are definite, generic or partitive. I have shown that the interaction between word order and information structure is complex and not as straightforward as is often assumed in the literature. The claim that preverbal NPs are always definite cannot be maintained, which became apparent, for example, from the quantitative study carried out by Czardybon et al. (2014). The study shows that topical and focal NPs can be pre- and post-verbal. The unmarked topic-focus structure can be changed, for example, by shifting the sentence stress to the beginning of the sentence. This is why we also find indefinite focal NPs in preverbal position.

There are two further definiteness strategies in the Slavic languages that I did not discuss for Polish: (i) possessive adjectives and (ii) the opposition between long vs. short adjectival endings. In Bosnian, for example, there is an opposition between a long and a short form of the adjectival endings in attributive use. The long form is associated with definiteness while the short one indicates indefiniteness (1a).[1] With respect to the distribution of the adjectival endings, one can observe that only the long form is grammatical in the combination with demonstratives (1b).

(1) Bosnian
    a. *Mlad-i/ mlad poštar je htjeo predate*
       young-DEF young.INDEF postman AUX wanted deliver
       pismo.
       letter
       'The/a young postman wanted to deliver a letter.'
    b. *ovaj skup-i/ (*skup) televizor*
       DEM.PROX expensive-DEF expensive.INDEF television
       'this expensive television'

Two different paradigms of the adjectival declension are also found in the two Baltic languages Lithuanian and Latvian (Lyons 1999: 83f.). Lithuanian, for example, differs with respect to the distribution of the long

---

[1] For more information on this topic see Townsend & Janda (1996: 177f.) and Mendoza (2004: 209f.) and the literature cited therein.

7 Conclusion

form from Bosnian in that the short form of the adjective is found if combined with a demonstrative (2):[2]

(2) Lithuanian (Elsbrock 2010: 30)
šita graži/ ??gražioji mergina
DEM handsome.INDEF handsome.DEF girl
'this handsome girl'

The opposition of short vs. long forms of adjectives and their association with definiteness in the Slavic languages can be attributed to a development in Protoslavic. Here the long forms were formed by the suffixation of the anaphoric pronoun for third person $jь$ to the short adjectives. The long forms indicated definiteness in contrast to the short forms which signalled indefiniteness (Panzer 1991: 163f., Mendoza 2004: 209). This situation is still to be found in the South Slavic languages (Slovene, Serbian, Croatian, Bosnian)[3] (Panzer 1991: 118, 131). In all other Slavic languages, the opposition was given up or is extremely restricted to predicative uses and is no longer associated with definiteness. In Polish, only the long forms are found (with some exceptions). The short forms have only been preserved for some adjectives (*gotów* 'ready', *pełen* 'full', *pewien* 'certain') and only for the nominative singular masculine form in predicative use. The long form can replace the short form (3):

(3) On jest gotów/ gotow-y.
PRON.M.SG COP.PRS.3SG ready ready-NOM.SG.M
'He is ready.'

The second definiteness strategy is represented by possessive adjectives, which are possessors derived from nouns by special suffixes. They are found in many Indo-European languages and are also attested, for example, in Ancient Greek and Latin (Löfstedt 1956; Wackernagel 1908; Watkins 1967). Most Slavic languages make extensive use of possessive adjectives (Corbett 1995). However, the frequency of them among the

---

[2] See Elsbrock (2010) for a detailed analysis.
[3] Slovene has the smallest repertoire for expressing the opposition, since we only find a long and a short adjectival ending in the nominative singular masculine (Rehder 2009: 236, Panzer 1991: 118, Priestly 1993: 412)

Slavic languages varies. They are often used in Slovene, Serbian/Croatian, Upper Sorbian, and Czech (Ivanova 1975: 9f., 1976: 151, quoted after Corbett 1995: 271). What can be observed is that an NP with a possessive adjective is definite, as the Russian example in (4) demonstrates:

(4) Russian (Babyonyshev 1997: 197)
    koškina/ myškina miska
    cat.POSS.SG.F.NOM mouse.POSS.SG.F.NOM bowl.SG.F.NOM
    'the cat's/the mouse's bowl'

There are language-specific restrictions as to when the possessor is expressed by a possessive adjective or a genitive attribute. In Upper Sorbian, the possessive adjective can only be used if the possessor is human, singular, and definite (Corbett 1995: 268; Koptjevskaja-Tamm 2001a: 967). In Polish, possessive adjectives have not been discussed as a definiteness strategy because they are very restricted (Birnbaum & Molas 2009: 153, Corbett 1987: 327, Pisarkowa 1977: 84). Ivanova (1975, 1976, quoted after Corbett 1995: 271) shows that only 3 % of the adnominal constructions are expressed by possessive adjectives in modern Polish. Szliferstejnowa (1960) compares different stages of Polish and concludes that possessive adjectives used to be productive in Old Polish. She points out that the use of the possessive adjectives in Polish became gradually less productive by comparing texts from the 14th and the 17th century. The frequency of possessive adjectives fell from 54.3 % to 40 % and this process has continued (Szliferstejnowa 1960: 41).

The concept types and determination approach by Löbner turned out to be a useful theoretical framework for explaining central aspects of the definiteness phenomena discussed in Polish. The fundamental distinction between the four concept types is reflected in Polish and other Slavic languages by exhibiting a different morphosyntactic behaviour. In written Polish, we find a split between [+U] and [−U] concept types since the demonstrative *ten* is restricted to [−U] concepts. A similar split is found in Russian and Croatian. It was also shown in section 3.4.4 that the demonstrative *ten* can be used with [+U] concepts such as *Pope*.

However, in such cases we have a shift from [+U] to [−U] and a contrastive use of the demonstrative.

In spoken Polish and the other investigated Slavic languages, the determiners are also extended to [+U] concept types, which is the domain of definite articles. Furthermore, bare [+U] concept types in congruent use, i.e. INs in singular and FNs in singular with a definite possessor, only allow for a definite reading as focal NPs; this is in direct contrast to [−U] concept types, which can also have an indefinite interpretation. The same picture is found in other Slavic languages. The study of Polish and other Slavic languages provides evidence for the distinction between [+U] and [−U] concept types and contributes to a broader typological study by, for example, Gerland & Horn (2015) and Ortmann (2014), in particular.

7.2 Questions for future research

The results of this thesis suggest several directions for future research. One question which directly follows is whether we also find Polish (Slavic) evidence for the distinction between [+R] and [−R] concept types (for typological evidence see Löbner 2011, Ortmann 2015). The distinction between relational and non-relational nouns is usually associated with the (in)alienability approach, which is proposed by a huge number of typologists (Chappell & McGregor 1996, Heine 1997, Nichols 1988, Seiler 1983, Stolz et al. 2008, Velazquez-Castillo 1996). To illustrate what (in)alienability means, an example of adnominal possession in Ewe, a Kwa language spoken in Togo and Ghana, is given in (5), which has two morphosyntactic constructions expressing adnominal possession depending on the noun for the possessee:

(5)   Ewe (Kwa, Niger-Kordofanian; Ameka 1996: 790, 796)
        a.   *ŋútsu má ɸé tú xóxó lá*
            man DEM POSS gun old DEF
            'that man's old gun'
        b.   *ɖeví-á-wó tɔ́gbé dze dɔ*
            child-DEF-PL grandfather fall sickness
            'The grandfather of the children has fallen sick'

(5a) is an example of alienable possession, whereas (5b) represents an inalienable construction. These two constructions differ in that in (5a) the possessive relation is marked explicitly by the possessive marker ɸé, while in (5b) the possessive marker is absent and we find juxtaposition of the possessor 'children' and the possessee 'grandfather'.[4] This shows that there is a split in Ewe, where the relational noun *grandfather* is juxtaposed to its possessor whereas with the non-relational noun *man* a possessive marker has to occur,[5] which marks the shift from [−R] to [+R] explicitly. This is not the case in (5b) with the NP grandfather which is already relational and need not be shifted.

It would be interesting to check whether Polish and other Slavic languages also have an asymmetrical treatment of [+R] and [−R] concept types. For Polish, Rothstein (2001: 747f. [1993]) observes, for example, that only alienably possessed subjects can be used in sentences like in (6) (Rothstein 2001: 747f. [1993]): In (6a), the subject is an inherently non-relational noun *książka* 'book', in contrast to the relational nouns *matka* 'mother' and *ręka* 'hand' in (6b), which cannot be used as subjects. According to my informants (6b) is only highly odd and thus less accepted than (6a), but not ungrammatical as claimed by Rothstein.

(6) a. *Ta książka jest moja/ Janka*
 DEM book COP.3SG.PRS POSS.PRON Janek.GEN
 'That book is mine/Janek's.'
 b. **Matka/ Ręka jest moja/ Janka*
 mother hand COP.3SG.PRS POSS.PRON Janek.GEN
 'The mother/The hand is mine/Janek's.'
 (Rothstein 2001: 748 [1993])

Another research question is to look for statistical evidence for the concept type distinction. The claim of the CTD approach is that the four concept types show a predisposition for certain modes of determination.

---

[4] Juxtaposition as a means of inalienable possession is also found in many other languages such as Djaru, Yidiny, Mandarin Chinese (Chappell & McGregor 1996: 5), Acholi (Bavin 1996: 844), and Tinrin (Osumi 1996: 439).

[5] This is the case for all kinship terms in Ewe. However, not all [+R] concept types are treated inalienably, such as terms for body parts which require the presence of the possessive marker as in (5a) (Ameka 1996: 783).

Löbner assumes that the underlying concept type of a noun is preserved by congruent determination whereas incongruent determination leads to shifts. He hypothesizes that congruent determination is more frequent than incongruent determination and thus that there are characteristic determination profiles for the concept types (Löbner 2011). For ICs, for instance, it is expected that they occur in a high percentage of uses with singular definite and non-possessive determination. To test this claim in a corpus, the underlying concept type of the nouns has to be annotated as well as the mode of determination with which the nouns are used. For German, this investigation has been carried out and showed statistically significant results (cf. Brenner et al. 2014, Horn & Kimm 2014, Horn 2015, in prep.). For Polish, I have carried out a pilot study where I used a text sample consisting of the first 479 sentences (almost 2500 noun tokens) of the Polish translation of George Orwell's novel *Nineteen Eighty-Four*. Two Polish native speakers annotated the modes of determination and decided, for instance, whether the nouns occur in a possessive construction or not and whether they are marked or interpreted as definite or indefinite.[6] In a second and independent step, the underlying concept type was annotated (for a detailed description of the annotation procedure in Polish see Czardybon & Horn 2015). The annotation of the determination has been completed, but the annotation of the concept types is still ongoing so that no result can be presented at this point.

7.3 The decision tree

One of the central aims of this thesis is to investigate the complex interaction of the four definiteness strategies with each other. In chapter 6 *Information structure*, I took the first steps towards a ranking of the four definiteness strategies. One can ask the question which strategy is the most important one, i.e. which overrides or cancels the definiteness of the others and thus has the strongest impact on the definiteness of an

---

[6] For possession, the annotation was based on surface determination such as possessive pronouns. Since in most cases definiteness is not indicated explicitly in Polish, the annotation for definiteness was based on the native annotators' judgements of definiteness, and thus on their intuitions.

NP? So far, I have come to the ranking in (7), where determiners such as indefinite pronouns are ranked higher than [+U] concept types, since they override their unique reference and they also rule out the definite reading given by information structure such as with topical NPs. [+U] concept types are not influenced by information structure in contrast to [−U] concept types and thus information structure is ranked in between.[7]

(7)   definite and indefinite determiners
          > [+U] concept types
              > information structure
                  > [−U] concept types

However, we are still left with the question as to where aspect and case alternation fit into the hierarchy. (8) shows that the partitive genitive has to be ranked higher than determiners. Despite the presence of a demonstrative, the partitive construction is indefinite. We have a definite superset, namely *this soup*, but the whole construction is indefinite because the partitive genitive indicates that some unspecified and indefinite part or subset of the definite superset is selected:

(8)   Daj   mi tej zup-y.
      give.IMP me DEM soup-GEN
      'Give me some of this soup.'

The ranking of aspect is difficult, since it is not only perfective aspect, but there are a number of factors which are responsible for enforcing a definite reading of the direct object. For simplicity, I will speak of 'perfective aspect' to cover all factors which are needed for the enforcement of definiteness. Indefinite pronouns can override the definiteness imposed by the perfective aspect as in (9). This is why determiners should be ranked higher than perfective aspect. The indefinite reading of *mleko* 'milk' in (9) is only due to the indefinite pronoun *jakiś* 'some'. Without the pronoun only a definite reading would be available.

---

[7] Superlatives and ordinals which lead to a definite interpretation of an NP will not be considered in the ranking, but they will be included in the decision tree at the end of this chapter.

7 Conclusion

(9) Jan wy-pił^{PF} jakieś MLEKO.
    Jan WY-drink.PST INDEF milk
    'Jan drank some/(*the) milk.'

The perfective aspect excludes the indefinite interpretation of focal NPs as in (10). Although the NP *mleko* 'milk' is the focus in (10), being post-verbal and stressed, it only allows for a definite reading. This illustrates that perfective aspect should be ranked higher than focal NPs, but lower than determiners.

(10) Jan wy-pił^{PF} MLEKO.
     Jan WY-drink.PST milk
     'Jan drank the/(*some) milk.'

The definite interpretation of bare [+U] concept types in congruent use is not changed by aspect (11), but with [−U] concepts this is the case (10). In (11), the NP with the IN *słońce* 'sun' is definite despite being the focal direct object of an imperfective verb.

(11) Jan widział^{IMPF} SŁOŃCE.
     Jan see.PST   sun
     'Jan saw the/(*a) sun.'

Example (12) shows that topical NPs that make up part of the information structure have to be ranked higher than what I will call '(im)perfective aspect'. '(Im)perfective aspect' is used here as a cover term for all imperfective verbs but also those perfective verbs which do not enforce a definite reading of the direct object. Despite the fact that the direct object *mleko* 'milk' is combined with an imperfective verb, it is definite due to being topical. This is why topical NPs should be ranked higher than (im)perfective aspect. The final ranking is given in (13).

(12) Mleko pił^{IMPF} JAN.
     milk drink.PST Jan
     'Jan drank/was drinking the/(*some) milk.'

(13)   partitive genitive
           > determiners
               > [+U] concept types
                   > topical NP, perfective aspect
                       > (im)perfective aspect, focal NPs
                           > [–U] concept types

Perfective aspect and topical NPs are ranked at the same level because they do not represent conflicting strategies. They both lead to a definite interpretation, which is demonstrated in (14). The NP *mleko* 'milk' is the topic and the direct object of a strictly incremental theme verb. It can only have a definite reading.

(14)   Mleko wy-pił^{PF} JAN.
       milk   WY-drink.PST Jan
       'Jan drank the/(*some) milk.'

The ranking in (13) can be compared to the one proposed by Mendoza (2004: 247). She distinguishes between primary and secondary means of expression. Primary means determine the NP directly – such as articles, demonstratives, indefinite pronouns, and quantifiers – whereas secondary means are others – such as word order, intonation, aspect, and case. She ranks primary means higher than the secondary means (Mendoza 2004: 247ff.), for which she does not give a further hierarchy. Moreover, her claim is not correct that case is ranked lower than the primary means, as I have shown.

The problem with a ranking like the one in (13) is that, for example, although the partitive genitive is ranked as the highest strategy it is very restricted in its use. Only a few verbs allow partitive genitive objects and more and more Polish speakers regard them as ungrammatical. Furthermore, it does not depict all of the factors that are crucial for achieving a definite reading such as with perfective aspect. Here, many factors are needed to enforce a definite reading. This is why I come up with a decision tree including all factors which have an influence on the definiteness of an NP. Such a tree provides a more appropriate and detailed picture of the interaction between the definiteness strategies. Figure 4 presents the first part of the tree.

7 Conclusion

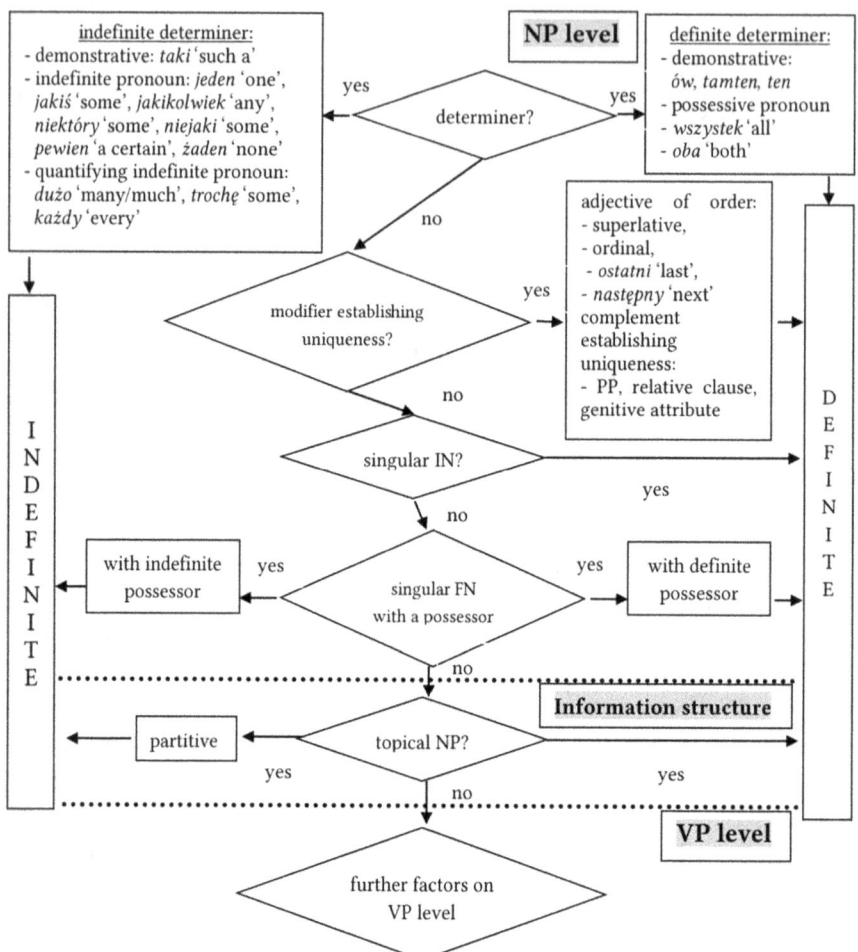

Figure 4: Decision tree for the (in)definiteness of NPs in Polish, part one.

7.3 The decision tree

Explicit marking at NP level is located at the top of the decision tree. There are definite and indefinite determiners which affect the definiteness of an NP. There are also quantifiers which have an influence on the definiteness of NPs. The two quantifiers (*wszystek* 'all' and *oba* 'both') lead to a definite reading of an NP whereas NPs with other quantifiers only allow for an indefinite reading.[8]

Furthermore, there are some classes of modifiers which have a definiteness effect on the NP such as superlatives or complements establishing uniqueness. Most modifiers, such as adjectives like *czerwony* 'red', do not influence the definiteness of the NP, but other factors are crucial, such as the underlying concept type. If INs are used congruently, i.e. in singular, the NP can only have a definite reading. And if INs are used incongruently, they are in need of explicit [−U] determination such as indefinite determiners or plural marking. This also holds for FNs. However, with bare FNs the non-possessive use alone can lead to an indefinite interpretation without explicit indefinite determination. The combination of a singular bare FN with an indefinite possessor NP leads to an indefinite reading of the whole NP, whereas the presence of a definite possessor argument results in a definite reading of the whole complex NP.

For [−U] concepts and [+U] concepts in incongruent use, information structure plays a role. As a topical NP, the NP can be interpreted as definite or partitive. If an NP is focal, there are other factors at VP level that are responsible for an (in)definite reading of an NP. This is illustrated in figure 5.

---

[8] Other quantifying pronouns such as *kilka* 'several' and *parę* 'a few' as well as numerals allow the combination with a definite determiner such as *ten* and can be part of a definite NP. Thus, they do not automatically lead to an indefinite interpretation of an NP.

7 Conclusion

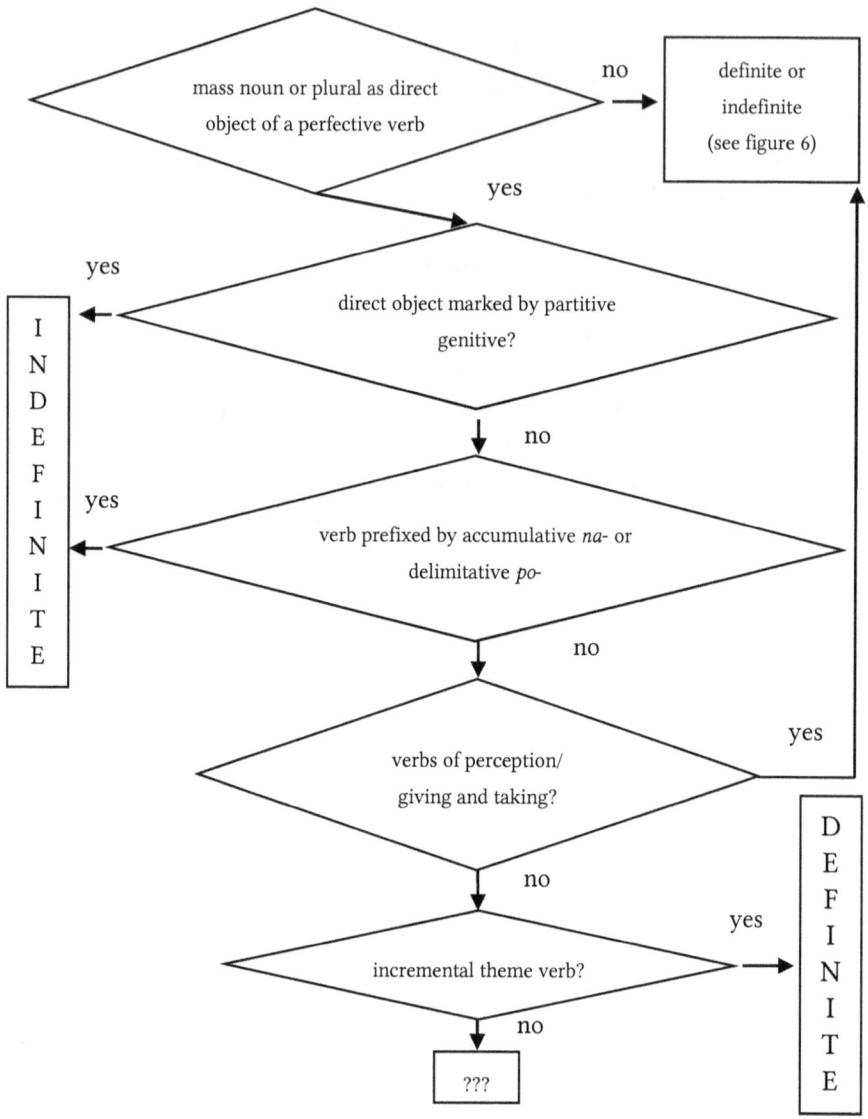

Figure 5: Decision tree for the (in)definiteness of NPs in Polish, part two.

Grammatical aspect can influence definiteness. A definite reading is only enforced if the NP is a cumulatively referring noun as the direct object of some perfective verbs.[9] The NP must not be marked by the partitive genitive, which automatically leads to an indefinite reading, and the perfective verb must not be prefixed by the accumulative *na-* or the delimitative *po-*. This effect is observable with incremental theme verbs, but not with verbs of perception and verbs of giving and taking. The box with the question marks indicates that further verb classes need to be investigated and it must be checked whether they behave like incremental theme verbs or like verbs of perception/giving and taking with regard to dcfinitcness. In all other cases, namely (i) the direct object is a singular count noun, (ii) the NP is not the direct object, but the subject, indirect object or an adjunct, or (iii) the verb is imperfective, the NP allows for a definite or indefinite reading. Whether the NP is definite or indefinite is determined by the linguistic and extralinguistic context, which is shown in figure 6:

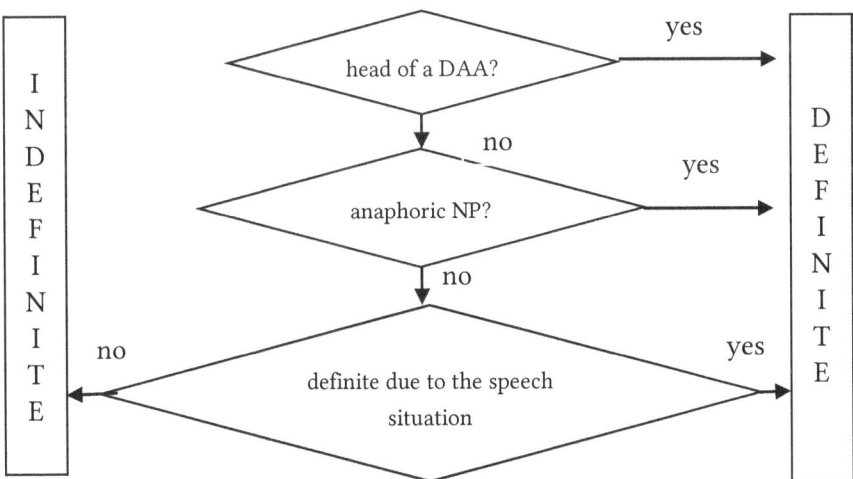

Figure 6: Decision tree for the (in)definiteness of NPs in Polish, part three.

---

[9] A test to distinguish between mass and count nouns in Polish is discussed in chapter 2.4, whereas tests to determine the grammatical aspect of a verb are given in chapter 4.2.

A definite interpretation can be found if the NP is the head of a definite associative anaphor, an anaphoric NP, or is part of the speech situation. Otherwise the NP is indefinite.

I have applied this decision tree to a text sample including 500 nouns and in 91 % of cases the tree leads to a correct result. There are some problematic cases which are not captured by the tree, such as nouns that make up parts of idioms and proverbs as well as generic uses of nouns. Such cases should be excluded from the beginning. In Polish, there are FNs which are pluralia tantum such as *plecy* 'back' or *usta* 'mouth', which cannot be used in singular. Consequently, they are not recognized as FNs in congruent use and might end up as being indefinite instead of definite. For some cumulatives being used as direct objects of a perfective verb, the decision tree does not provide a result since only some verb classes are included in the tree, which should be extended in this respect. The application and extension of the decision tree to other articleless Slavic, but also non-Slavic languages (e.g. Hindi, Finnish, Lithuanian, Chinese) could be another research question focusing on language diversity. What kinds of language-specific modifications are required? How can we integrate new strategies, such as possessive adjectives, that we find in other languages?

Despite the few cases that are not captured by the tree, it does provide a useful tool for the interpretation of NPs as definite or indefinite considering all investigated factors and their interaction, which, in turn, contributes to a better explanation and understanding of the linguistic category of definiteness in Polish and thus to a better description of the Polish grammar.

Appendix: The distribution of the Slavic determiners under investigation

This appendix presents the Slavic data (Croatian, Czech, and Russian) on the distribution of the determiners which are investigated in chapter 3. The data is structured concerning the hierarchical order of the different levels on the scale of uniqueness. The data have been provided by native speakers of the corresponding languages. A list of my informants for each language is given in the introduction.

Croatian

Anaphoric SNs:

(1) *Kupio je auto$_j$. Ali (taj) auto$_j$ je bio vrlo skup.*
buy.PST AUX car but DEM car AUX was very expensive
'He bought a car. But the car was very expensive.'

(2) *Novoga smo psa$_j$ kupili prošle godine. (Taj) pas$_j$ je*
new AUX dog buy.PST last year DEM dog COP
veoma umiljat.
very sweet
'We bought a new dog last year. The dog is very sweet.'

(3) *Moj prijatelj je kupio zanimljivu knjigu$_j$ o*
my friend AUX buy.PST interesting book about
životinjama. Rekao je da (ta) knjiga$_j$ nije bila
animals say.PST AUX that DEM book NEG was
skupa.
expensive
'My friend bought an interesting book about animals. He said that the book was not expensive.'

Appendix: The distribution of the Slavic determiners under investigation

In (4), there is interspeaker variation concerning the use of the demonstrative *tu*. Some prefer it while others regard it as optional.

(4) *Prošle sam godine na konferenciji u Španjolskoj upoznao*
last AUX year on conference in Spain meet.PST
jednu ženu$_j$. Dvije godine kasnije, dok sam bio na
one woman two years later while AUX was on
praznicima u Njemačkoj, sreo sam tu/(tu) ženu$_j$ opet.
holiday in Germany meet.PST AUX DEM woman again
'Last year I met a woman at a conference in Spain. Two years later while I was on holiday in Germany, I met the woman again.'

(5) *U jedan je sat neki čovjek$_j$ ušao u sobu. Kad*
at one AUX o'clock some man enter.PST in room when
sam ja ušao u 1:15 (taj) čovjek$_j$ je stajao kraj
AUX I enter.PST at 1:15 DEM man AUX stand.PST next_to
prozora.
window
'At one o'clock a man entered the room. When I entered at 1:15, the man was standing next to the window.'

(6) *U jedan je sat neki čovjek$_j$ ušao u sobu. Kad*
at one AUX o'clock some man enter.PST in room when
sam ja ušao u 1:15 kraj prozora je stajao taj
AUX I enter.PST at 1:15 next_to window AUX stand.PST DEM
čovjek$_j$.
man
'At one o'clock a man entered the room. When I entered at 1:15, the man was standing next to the window.'

SNs with complements establishing uniqueness:

(7) *Kako se zove (ona) ptica koja krade?*
how REFL call.3SG DEM.DIST bird REL steal.3SG
'What is the name of the bird that steals?'

Appendix: The distribution of the Slavic determiners under investigation

(8) *(Ona) žena koju sam jučer vidio bila je lijepa.*
 DEM.DIST woman REL AUX yesterday saw was AUX beautiful
 'The woman I saw yesterday was beautiful.'

(9) *(Onaj) čovjek koji je izumio telefon dobio je*
 DEM.DIST man REL AUX invent.PST telephone got AUX
 Nobelovu nagradu.
 Nobel Prize
 'The man who invented the telephone was awarded the Nobel Prize.'

Definite associative anaphors:

According to my Croatian informants, no determiners occur with definite associative anaphors or the other contexts of the scale that follow.

(10) *Jučer sam bio na bazenu. Ali voda je bila*
 yesterday AUX was on swimming_pool but water AUX was
 prehladna.
 cold
 'I was in the swimming pool yesterday. But he water was too cold.'

(11) *Kupili smo star auto i motor je stalno*
 have-1PL.PRS we old car and engine COP constantly
 pokvaren.
 broken
 'We bought an old car and the engine is constantly broken.'

(12) *Imam lijepu šalicu Ali ručka joj je otpala.*
 have.1SG.PRS nice cup but handle POSS.PRON COP broken
 'I have a nice cup, but the handle is broken.'

(13) *Jučer sam bio u kinu, i film je bio dosadan.*
 yesterday AUX was at cinema and film AUX was boring
 'I went to the cinema yesterday and the film was boring.'

Appendix: The distribution of the Slavic determiners under investigation

(14) *Nakon kina razgovarali smo o filmu.*
after cinema.GEN talk.PST AUX about film.
Dopali su nam se glumci.
like.PST AUX us REFL actor.PL
'After the cinema we talked about the film. We liked the actors.'

(15) *Kad sam ušao u autobus pitao sam vozača*
when AUX enter.PST in bus ask.PST AUX driver
koliko stoji karta.
how_much cost.3SG ticket
'When I got into the bus, I asked the driver how much a ticket costs.'

(16) *Prošli smo tjedan bili na vjenčanju našega susjeda.*
last AUX week were on wedding our.GEN neighbour.GEN
Mlada je bila prelijepa.
bride AUX COP beautiful
'Last week we were at our neighbour's wedding. The bride was beautiful.'

(17) *Kad je Jan ušao u crkvu obred je već bio*
when AUX Jan enter.PST in church service AUX already was
počeo. Svećenik je molio Očenaš.
start.PST priest AUX pray.PST Lord's Prayer
'When Jan entered the church, the service had already started. The priest was saying the Lord's Prayer.'

(18) *U subotu sam bio u francuskom restoranu. Hrana mi se*
in Saturday AUX was in French restaurant food me REFL
jako svidjela.
very like.PST
'I was in a French restaurant on Saturday. I liked the food a lot.'

(19) Nako što su vidjeli stan htjeli su razgovarati s
  after that AUX seen flat want.PST AUX talk with
  vlasnikom o cijeni.
  owner about price.
  'After seeing the flat, they wanted to talk with the owner about the price.'

(20) Dok smo stajali pred Empire State Building
  while AUX stand.PST in_front_of E.S.B.
  visina joj je bila dojmljiva.
  height POSS.PRON AUX was impressive
  'When we stood in front of the Empire State Building, the height was impressive.'

Complex ICs:

(21) Živim u najljepšem gradu u zemlji.
  live.1SG in most_beautiful city in country
  'I'm living in the most beautiful city in the country.'

(22) Knjiga se nalazi u drugoj ladici.
  book REFL lie.3SG in second drawer
  'The book lies in the second drawer.'

(23) Moram sići na sljedećoj stanici.
  must.1SG get_off on next stop
  'I have to get off at the next stop.'

(24) Posljednji je student otišao kući.
  last AUX student went home
  'The last student went home.'

Lexical INs/FNs:

(25) Sunce sja.
  sun shine.3SG.PRS
  'The sun is shining.'

(26) Ovo je   kraj filma
      DEM COP end film
      'This is the end of the film.'

(27) Udaljenost između Španjolske i   Njemačke iznosi
      distance   between Spain   and Germany amount.3SG
      oko   2000 km.
      about 2000 km
      'The distance between Spain and Germany is about 2000 km.'

(28) Papa je poglavar katoličke crkve.
      Pope COP head   Catholic church.GEN
      'The Pope is the head of the Catholic Church.'

Czech

Deictic SNs:

(29) To(hle) auto je hezké.
      DEM   car COP nice
      'This car is nice.'

Anaphoric SNs:

My Czech informants prefer the demonstrative *ten* with anaphoric SNs. However, *ten* is not considered as obligatory.

(30) Jan si   včera   koupil   knih-u$_j$. Když začal   číst,
      Jan REFL yesterday buy.PST book-ACC   when begin.PST   read
      vsiml   si,   že   už   tu   knih-u$_j$ četl.
      notice.PST   REFL that already DEM book-ACC   read.PST
      'Jan bought a book yesterday. When he began to read it he noticed that he had already read this book.'

(31) Koupil   si   auto$_j$. Ale to   auto$_j$ bylo moc drahé.
      buy.PST REFL car   but DEM car   was very expensive
      'He bought a car. But the car was very expensive.'

212

Appendix: The distribution of the Slavic determiners under investigation

(32) *Byl jednou jeden král$_j$ a ten král$_j$ měl tři*
was once one king and DEM king have.PST three
dcery.[1]
daughter.PL
'Once upon a time, there was a king and the king had three daughters.'

(33) *Pozoroval jsem, jak do pokoje vešel muž$_j$. Když jsem do*
observe.PST AUX how in room enter.PST man when AUX in
toho pokoje vstoupil, uviděl jsem, že ten muž$_j$ stojí u
DEM room enter.PST see.PST AUX that DEM man stand at
okna.
window
'I observed a man going into the room. When I entered, I saw that the man was standing at the window.'

SNs with complements establishing uniqueness:

In (35) and (36), there is interspeaker variation with respect to the optional and preferred use of *ten*. In all other examples of complements establishing uniqueness, the demonstrative is preferred (34), (37) or optional (38) and (39).

(34) *Znáte, doufám, toho učitele, co má chatu a auto?*[2]
know hope.1SG DEM teacher REL have.3SG house and car
'You know, I hope, the teacher who has a weekend house and a car?'

(35) *To je na tom/(tom) gauči, co na něm spí.*[3]
DEM COP on DEM couch REL on it sleep.3SG.PRS
'This is on the couch on which he is sleeping.'

---

[1] This example is taken from Berger (1993: 99).
[2] This example is taken from Berger (1993: 153).
[3] This example is taken from Berger (1993: 153) and has slightly been modified for testing the occurrence of *ten* with my informants.

Appendix: The distribution of the Slavic determiners under investigation

(36)   *To je ten/(ten) člověk, o kterém jsme mluvili.*[4]
       DEM COP DEM   man   about REL   AUX talk.PST
       'This is the man we talked about.'

(37)   *Ta žena, kterou jsem včera viděl, byla hezká.*
       DEM woman REL   AUX yesterday see.PST was beautiful
       'The woman I saw yesterday was beautiful.'

(38)   *Jak se jmenuje (ten) pták, který krade?*
       how REFL call.3SG DEM bird REL   steal.3SG
       'What is the name of the bird that steals?'

(39)   *Nobelovu cenu získal (ten) muž, který vynalezl telefon.*
       Nobel Prize   get.PST DEM man REL   invent.PST telephone
       'The man who invented the telephone was awarded the Nobel Prize.'

Definite associative anaphors:

(40)   *Včera jsem byla na plovárně, ale voda byla studená.*
       yesterday AUX was on baths   but water COP cold
       'I was in the swimming baths yesterday. But the water was cold.'

(41)   *Mám hezký hrnek, ale jeho ucho je ulomené.*
       have.1SG.PRS nice   cup   but POSS.PRON handle COP broken
       'I have a nice cup, but the handle is broken.'

---

[4] This example is taken from Berger (1993: 148).

(42) *Máme   staré auto. Proto   je   jeho   motor   pořád*
      have.3PL old   car   therefore COP POSS.PRON engine always
      pokažený.
      broken
      'We have an old car. Therefore, the engine is always broken.'

(43) *Včera   jsem byla v kině,   ale (ten) film byl nudný.*
      yesterday AUX was in cinema but DEM film was boring
      'I went to the cinema yesterday. But the film was boring.'

(44) *Když jsem nastoupil do autobusu, zeptal jsem se*
      when AUX get.PST   in bus   ask.PST AUX REFL
      řidiče, kolik   stojí jízdenka.
      driver how much cost ticket
      'When I got into the bus, I asked the driver how much a ticket costs.'

(45) *Po   kině   se   ještě bavili   o   (tom) filmu.*
      after cinema REFL still talk.PST about DEM film
      (Ti) herci   se   jim   líbili.
      DEM actor.PL REFL them please.PST
      'After the cinema we talked about the film. We liked the actors.'

(46) *Minulý týden jsme byli   na svatbě   mého   souseda.*
      last   week AUX were on wedding my.GEN neighbor.GEN
      (Ta)/Ø nevěsta byla překrásná.
      DEM   bride   was beautiful
      'Last week we were at our neighbour's wedding. The bride was beautiful.'

(47) *Když jsme stáli   před   Empire State Building,*
      when AUX stood in_front_of Empire State Building
      jeho velikost nás ohromila.
      POSS height   us stunned
      'When we stood in front of the Empire State Building, its height stunned us.'

(48) *Když přišel Jan do kostela, mše už začala.*
when came Jan to church service already start.PST
Kněz právě předříkával otčenáš.
priest just said Lord's Prayer
'When Jan came to the church the service had already started. The priest was saying the Lord's Prayer.'

(49) *Poté, co si prohlédla byt, chtěla*
after that what REFL inspect.PST flat want.PST
s majitelem mluvit o ceně.
with owner talk about price
'After seeing the flat, she wanted to talk with the owner about the price.'

(50) *V sobotu jsem byl ve francouzské restauraci. (To) jídlo*
in Saturday AUX was in French restaurant DEM food
mi moc chutnalo.
me very tasted
'I was in a French restaurant on Saturday. I liked the food a lot.'

Complex ICs:

With complex ICs, the demonstrative *ten* can appear, which leads to an indication of emotional involvement.

(51) *Bydlím v (tom) nejkrásnějším městě v zemi.*
live.1SG.PRS in DEM SPL.beautiful city in world
'I live in the most beautiful city.'

(52) *Kniha leží v (tom) druhém šuplíku.*
book lie.3SG in DEM second drawer
'The book lies in the second drawer.'

(53) *(Ty) poslední holky šly domů.*
DEM last girl.PL went home
'The last girls went home.'

Appendix: The distribution of the Slavic determiners under investigation

(54) Na (té) příští zastávce musím vystoupit.
      on DEM next stop must.1SG get_off
      'I have to get off at the next stop.'

(55) Máme na skladě (ty) nejnovější vzorky.[5]
      have.3PL.PRS on warehouse DEM SPL.late sample.PL
      'We have the latest samples in stock.'

(56) Přičemž otevřenost, nezakrývání nepříjemných věcí
      with openness non-concealment unpleasant things
      a hraní s otevřenými kartami je (tou) nejlepší
      and playing with open cards COP DEM best
      strategií.[6]
      strategy
      'With openness, the non-concealment of unpleasant things and playing with open cards are the best strategy.'

Lexical INs/FNs:

(57) Papež je hlavou církve.
      Pope COP head church.GEN
      'The Pope is the head of the church.'

(58) To je konec (toho) filmu.
      DEM COP end DEM film.GEN
      'This is the end of the film.'

(59) Vzdálenost ze Španělska do Německa je 2000 km.
      distance from Spain to Germany COP 2000 km
      'The distance from Spain to Germany is 2000 km.'

(60) Slunce svítí.
      sun shine.3SG.PRS
      'The sun is shining.'

---

[5] Taken from Zubatý (1916, quoted after Krámský 1972: 188). The example has slightly been modified in that the demonstrative is put in brackets in order to indicate its optionality.

[6] Taken from Berger (1993: 404).

Appendix: The distribution of the Slavic determiners under investigation

Russian

Anaphoric SNs:

(61) On kupil   mašin-u$_j$, no (èta) mašina$_j$ byla očen'
    he bought car-ACC but DEM car   was very
    dorogoj.
    expensive
    'He bought a car, but the car was very expensive.'

(62) Pered   domom   naxoditcja mašina$_j$. Ja uže
    in_front_of house.INS be.3SG.PRS car   I already
    včera   videl ètu mašin-u$_j$.
    yesterday saw DEM car-ACC
    'There is a car in front of the house. I already saw the car yesterday.'

(63) Ivan uvidel ženščin-u$_j$. (Èta) ženščina$_j$ byla prekrasna.
    Ivan see.PST woman-ACC DEM woman   was beautiful
    'Ivan saw a woman. The woman was beautiful.'

SNs with complements establishing uniqueness:

(64) Kak nazyvaetsja   (ta)   ptica, kotoraja voru-et?
    how be_called.3SG.PRS DEM.DIST bird REL   steal-3SG.PRS
    'What is the name of the bird that steals.'

(65) (Ta)   ženščina, kotoruju ja u-vide-l   včera,   byla
    DEM.DIST woman   REL   I U-see-PST yesterday was
    očen' krasivaja.
    very beautiful
    'The woman I saw yesterday was beautiful.'

Appendix: The distribution of the Slavic determiners under investigation

Definite associative anaphors:

According to my Russian informants, no determiners occur with definite associative anaphors or the other contexts of the scale that follow.

(66) *U menja est' krasivaja čaška, no (eë)   ručka*
at me is nice   cup   but POSS.PRON handle
slomana.
broken
'I have a nice cup, but the handle is broken.'

(67) *My kupi-li   star-uju mašin-u, poetomu (eë)   motor*
we buy-PST.PL old-ACC car-ACC therefore POSS.PRON engine
lomaetsja.
get_broken.3SG.PRS
'We bought an old car. Therefore, the engine is constantly broken.'

(68) *Včera   ja xodi-l v baccejn,   no voda byla očen'*
yesterday I go-PST to swimming_pool but water was very
xolodnoj.
cold
'I was in the swimming pool yesterday. But the water was too cold.'

(69) *My včera   xodi-li   v kino, no fil'm byl skučnym.*
we yesterday go-PST.PL to cinema but film was boring
'We went to the cinema yesterday. But the film was boring.'

(70) *Posle kino   my govorili o   fil'me.*
after cinema we talk.PST about film.
Nam ponravilis' aktery.
us please.PST actor.PL
'After the cinema we talked about the film. We liked the actors.'

219

Appendix: The distribution of the Slavic determiners under investigation

(71) *Kogda ja zašel   v avtobus, ja sprosil voditelja*
when I enter.PST in bus   I ask.PST driver
skol'ko   stoit   bilet.
how_much cost.3SG ticket
'When I got into the bus, I asked the driver how much a ticket costs.'

(72) *Na prošloj nedele my byli na cvad'be   našego*
on last   week we were on wedding our.GEN
soseda.   Nevesta byla krasivaja.
neighbour.GEN bride   COP beautiful
'Last week we were at our neighbour's wedding. The bride was beautiful.'

(73) *Kogda Džan zašel   v cerkov' služba uže   načalas'.*
when Jan enter.PST in church service already start.PST
Svjaščennik čital   molitvu.
priest   read.PST prayer
'When Jan entered the church, the service had already started. The priest was saying a prayer.'

(74) *Ja byl vo francuzskom restorane v subbotu. Eda mne*
I was in French   restaurant in Saturday food me
očen' ponravilas'.
very taste.PST
'I was in a French restaurant on Saturday. I liked the food a lot.'

(75) *Posle osmotra kvartiry oni xoteli   pogovorit' s*
after seeing flat   they want.PST talk   with
xozjainom o   cene.
owner   about price
'After seeing the flat, they wanted to talk with the owner about the price.'

Appendix: The distribution of the Slavic determiners under investigation

(76) *Kogda my stojali pered Empire State Building*
when we stand.PST in_front_of E.S.B
ego vysota vpečatljala.
POSS.PRON height impressive
'When we stood in front of the Empire State Building, the height was impressive.'

Complex ICs:

(77) *Mne nužno vyjti na sledujuščej ostanovke.*
me must get_off at next stop
'I have to get off at the next stop.'

(78) *Dve poslednie devočki pošli domoj.*
two last girl.PL went home
'The last two girls went home.'

(79) *Kniga lež-it vo vtorom jaščike.*
book lie-3SG.PRS in second drawer
'The book lies in the second drawer.'

Lexical INs/FNs:

(80) *Èto byl konec (ètogo) fil'ma.*
DEM COP end DEM film
'This is the end of the film.'

(81) *Rasstojanie meždu Germaniej i Rossiej...*
distance between Germany and Russia
'The distance between Germany and Russia...'

(82) *Solnce svet-it.*
sun shine-3SG.PRS
'The sun is shining.'

References

Abbott, Barbara (2010): *Reference*. Oxford University Press. Oxford.

Abraham, Werner (1997): The interdependence of case, aspect and referentiality in the history of German: the case of the verbal genitive. In: van Kemenade, Ans; Vincent, Nigel (eds.). *Parameters of Morphosyntactic Change*. Cambridge University Press. Cambridge. pp. 29–61.

Adach-Stankiewicz, Ewa; Bielska, M.; Cendrowska, A.; Chmielewski, M.; Filip, P.; Gudaszewski, G.; Kaczorowski, P.; Kostrzewa, Z.; Nowak, L.; Piszcz, A.; Seweryn, E.; Sobieszak, A.; Stańczak, J.; Szałtys, D.; Szefler, S.; Wysocka, A.; Zgierska, A. (2012): *Raport z wyników. Narodowy Spis Powszechny Ludności i Mieszkań 2011*. Zakład Wydawnictwa Statystycznych. Warszawa.
Downloadable at
http://www.stat.gov.pl/gus/5840_13164_PLK_HTML.htm (07/12/2012)

Aissen, Judith (2003): Differential object marking: Iconicity vs. economy. *Natural Language and Linguistic Theory* 21 (3). pp. 435–483.

Allan, Keith (1980): Nouns and Countability. *Language* 56 (3). pp. 541–567.

Ameka, Felix (1996): Body parts in Ewe grammar. In: Chappell, Hilary; McGregor, William (eds.). *The Grammar of Inalienability. A Typological Perspective on Body Part Terms and the Part-Whole Relation*. Mouton de Gruyter. Berlin. pp. 783–840.

Asher, Ronald; Kumari, T. (1997): *Malayalam*. Routledge. London/New York.

Asudeh, Ash (2005): Relational Nouns, Pronouns, and Resumption. *Linguistics and Philosophy* 28. pp. 375–446.

Babby, Leonard (1991): Noncanonical Configurational Case Assignment Strategies. In: Toribio, Almeida; Harbert, Wayne (eds.). *Cornell Working Papers in Linguistics.* pp. 1–55.

Babyonyshev, Maria (1997): The Possessive Construction in Russian: A Crosslinguistic Perspective. *Journal of Slavic Linguistics* 5 (2). pp. 193–233.

Bach, Emmon (1986): The Algebra of Events. *Linguistics and Philosophy* 9. pp. 5–16.

Bacz, Barbara (1991): On some article-like uses of the demonstrative *ten* (=this) in Polish. Could *ten* become an article? *Langues et Linguistique* 17. pp. 1–16.

Bale, Alan C.; Barner, David (2009): The Interpretation of Functional Heads: Using Comparatives to Explore the Mass/Count Distinction. *Journal of Semantics* 26. pp. 217–252.

Barker, Chris (1995): *Possessive Descriptions.* CSLI. Stanford.

Barker, Chris (2000): Definite Possessives and Discourse Novelty. *Theoretical Linguistics* 26. pp. 211–227.

Bartnicka, Barbara; Hansen, Björn; Klemm, Wojtek; Lehmann, Volkmar; Satkiewicz, Halina (2004): *Grammatik des Polnischen.* Verlag Otto Sagner. Munich.

Bauer, Winifred (1993): *Maori.* Routledge. London.

Bauernöppel, Josef; Fritsch, Hermann; Bielefeld, Bernhard (1970): *Kurze tschechische Sprachlehre.* Volk und Wissen. Berlin.

Bavin, Edith L. (1996): Body parts in Acholi: alienable and inalienable distinction and extended uses. In: Chappell, Hilary; McGregor, William (eds.). *The Grammar of Inalienability. A Typological Perspective on Body Part Terms and the Part-Whole Relation.* Mouton de Gruyter. Berlin. pp. 841–864.

Berger, Tilman (1993): *Das System der tschechischen Demonstrativpronomina. Textgrammatische und stilspezifische Gebrauchsbedingungen.* Unpublished habilitation thesis. Ludwigs-Maximilians-Universität Munich.

Bermel, Neil (2000): *Register variation and language standards in Czech.* LINCOM EUROPA. Munich.

Birkenmaier, Willy (1977): Aspekt, Aktionsart und nominale Determination im Russischen. *Zeitschrift für slavische Philologie* 39. pp. 398–417.

Birkenmaier, Willy (1979): *Artikelfunktionen in einer artikellosen Sprache. Studien zur nominalen Determination im Russischen.* Wilhelm Fink. Munich.

Birnbaum, Henrik; Molas, Jerzy (2009): Das Polnische. In: Rehder, Peter (ed.). *Einführung in die slavischen Sprachen.* WBG. Darmstadt. pp. 145–164.

Bisle-Müller, Hansjörg (1991): *Artikelwörter im Deutschen.* Niemeyer. Tübingen.

Bleam, Tonia (2005): The role of semantic type in differential object marking. *Belgian Journal of Linguistics* 19. pp. 3–27.

Błaszczak, Joanna (2001): *Investigation into the Interaction between the Indefinites and Negation.* Akademie Verlag. Berlin.

Bogusławski, Andrzej (1977): *Problems of the Thematic-rhematic Structure of Sentences.* PWN. Warszawa.

Borer, Hagit (2005): *The normal course of events.* Oxford University Press. Oxford.

Borik, Olga (2006): *Aspect and reference time.* Oxford University Press. Oxford.

Brenner, Dorothea; Indefrey, Peter; Horn, Christian; Kimm, Nicolas (2014): Evidence for four basic noun types from a corpus-linguistic and a psycholinguistic perspective. In: Gerland, Doris; Horn, Christian; Latrouite, Anja, Ortmann, Albert (eds.). *Meaning and grammar of nouns and verbs.* Düsseldorf University Press. Düsseldorf. pp. 21–48.

Breu, Walter (2004): Der definite Artikel in der obersorbischen Umgangssprache. In: Krause, Marion; Sappok, Christian (eds.): *Slavistische Linguistik 2002. Referate des XXVIII. Konstanzer Slavistischen Arbeitstreffens Bochum.* Otto Sagner. Munich. pp. 9–57.

Brooks, Maria (1975): *Polish Reference Grammar*. Mouton. The Hague/Paris.
Bunt, Harry C. (1981): *The Formal Semantics of Mass Terms*. PhD thesis. University of Amsterdam.
Buttler, Danuta; Kurkowska, Halina; Satkiewicz, Halina (1971): *Kultura Języka Polskiego. Zagadnienia poprawności gramatycznej*. PWN. Warszawa.
Bystroń, Jan (1893): *O użyciu genetivu w języku polskim*. Nakł. Akademii Umiejętności. Kraków.
Cabredo Hofherr, Patricia. (2014): Reduced Definite Articles with Restrictive Relative Clauses. In: Cabredo Hofherr, Patricia; Zribi-Hertz, Anne (eds.). *Crosslinguistic Studies on Noun Phrase Structure and Reference*. Brill. Leiden. pp. 172–211.
Chafe, Wallace (1976): Givenness, Contrastiveness, Definiteness, Subjects, Topics, and Point of View. In: Li, Charles (ed.). *Subject and Topic*. ACADEMIC PRESS, Inc. New York/San Francisco/London. pp. 25–56.
Chappell, Hilary; McGregor, William (1996): *The Grammar of Inalienability. A Typological Perspective on Body Part Terms and the Part-Whole Relation*. de Gruyter. Berlin.
Chen, Ping (2004): Identifiability and definiteness in Chinese. *Linguistics* 42 (6). pp. 1129–1184.
Cheng, Chung-Ying (1973): Comments on Moravscik's paper. In: Hintikka, Jaako; Moravscik, Julius; Suppes, Patrick (eds.). *Approaches to natural language*. Reidel. Dordrecht/Boston. pp. 286–288.
Chesterman, Andrew (1991): *On definiteness. a study with special reference to English and Finnish*. Cambridge University Press. Cambridge.
Chierchia, Gennaro (1998): Reference to kinds across languages. *Natural Language Semantics* 6. pp. 339–405.
Christian, R. F. (1961): Some Consequences of the Lack of a Definite and Indefinite Article in Russian. *The Slavic and East European Journal* 5 (19). pp. 1–11.

Christophersen, Paul (1939): *The articles. A study of their theory and use in English.* Munksgaard. Copenhagen.

Chvany, Catherine V. (1983): On 'Definiteness' in Bulgarian, English and Russian. *American contributions to the International Congress of Slavists/American Committee of Slavists.* pp. 71–92.

Cieschinger, Maria (2007): *Constraints on the Contraction of Preposition and Definite Article in German.* presented at the conferences *Concept Types and Frames in Language, Cognition, and Science* in Düsseldorf (20–22/08/2007) and The 8th Szlarska Poręba Workshop on *Lexical Concepts* in Amsterdam (23–27/02/2007).

Comrie, Bernard (1976): *Aspect.* Cambridge University Press. Cambridge.

Comrie, Bernard; Corbett, Greville (eds.) (1993): *The Slavonic Languages.* Routledge. London/New York.

Corbett, Greville (1987): The Morphology/Syntax Interface: Evidence from Possessive Adjectives in Slavonic. *Language* 63 (2). pp. 299–345.

Corbett, Greville (1995): Slavonic's Closest Approach to Suffixaufnahme: The Possessive Adjective. In: Plank, Frank (ed.). *Double Case. Agreement by Suffixaufnahme.* Oxford University Press. Oxford/New York. pp. 265–283.

Cummins, George (1999): Indefiniteness in Czech. *Journal of Slavic Linguistics* 6 (2). pp. 171–203.

Czardybon, Adrian (2010): *Die Verwendung des definiten Artikels im Oberschlesischen im Sprachvergleich.* Unpublished MA thesis. University Düsseldorf.

Czardybon, Adrian; Fleischhauer, Jens (2014): Definiteness & perfectivity in telic incremental theme predications. In: Doris Gerland; Christian Horn; Latrouite, Anja; Ortmann, Albert (eds.). *Meaning and Grammar of Nouns and Verbs.* Düsseldorf University Press. Düsseldorf. pp. 373–400.

Czardybon, Adrian; Hellwig, Oliver; Petersen, Wiebke (2014): Statistical Analysis of the Interaction between Word Order and Definiteness in Polish. In: Adam Przepiórkowski & Maciej Ogrodniczuk (eds.). *Proceedings of PolTAL 2014*. Springer. pp. 144–150.

Czardybon, Adrian; Horn, Christian (2015): Annotation of related properties in unrelated languages – adaptation and modification of a German noun type annotation procedure to Polish. *Prace Filologiczne* XLVII. Pp. 57-77.

Czochralski, Jan A. (1975): *Verbalaspekt und Tempussytem im Deutschen und Polnischen. Eine konfrontative Darstellung*. Państwowe Wydawnictwo Naukowe. Warszawa.

Dede, Müşerref (1986): Definiteness and Referentiality in Turkish Verbal Sentences. In: Slobin, Dan; Zimmer, Karl (eds.). *Studies in Turkish Linguistics*. John Benjamins. Amsterdam. pp. 147–163.

Dickey, Stephen M. (2000): *Parameters of Slavic Aspect. A Cognitive Approach*. CSLI Publications. Stanford.

Diessel, Holger (1999): *Demonstratives. Form, Function, and Grammaticalization*. Benjamins. Amsterdam.

Diessel, Holger (2012): Deixis and demonstratives. In: Maienborn, Claudia; von Heusinger, Klaus; Portner, Paul (eds.). *Semantics. An International Handbook of Natural Language Meaning* vol. 3. de Gruyter Mouton. Berlin/Boston. pp. 2407–2432.

Van Dijk, Teun (1977): *Text and Context. Explorations in the semantics and pragmatics of discourse*. Longman. London/New York.

Dixon, R. (1979): Ergativity. *Language* 55 (1). pp. 59–138.

Doetjes, Jenny (2012): Count/mass distinction across languages. In: Maienborn, Claudia; von Heusinger, Klaus; Portner, Paul (eds.). *Semantics. An International Handbook of Natural Language Meaning* Vol. 3. de Gruyter Mouton. Berlin/Boston. pp. 2559–2580.

Dončeva-Mareva, L. (1966): Der Artikel, ein Ausdrucksmittel der Opposition "Determiniertheit/Indeterminiertheit", und seine möglichen Äquivalente im Russischen (auf der Grundlage des Bulgarischen, Französischen, Deutschen und Englischen). *Zeitschrift für Slawistik* 11 (1). pp. 38–44.

Dowty, David (1979): *Word meaning and Montague grammar*. Reidel Publishing Company. Dordrecht/Boston/London.

Dowty, David (1991): Thematic Proto-Roles and Argument Selection. *Language* 67 (3). pp. 547–619.

Dryer, Matthew (2015a): Feature 37A: Definite Articles. In: *The World Atlas of Language Structures Online (WALS)*. Available at: http://wals.info/feature/37A#2/25.5/148.2 (01/04/2015)

Dryer, Matthew (2015b): Feature 38A: Indefinite Articles. In: *The World Atlas of Language Structures Online (WALS)*. Available at: http://wals.info/feature/38A#2/25.5/148.2 (01/04/2015)

Ebert, Karen H. (1971): *Referenz, Sprechsituation und die bestimmten Artikel in einem nordfriesischen Dialekt (Fering)*. Nordfriisk Instituut. Bredstedt.

Eckert, Eva (1993): *Varieties of Czech. Studies in Czech Sociolinguistics*. Rodopi. Amsterdam/Atlanta.

Elsbrock, Pilipp (2010): *Definiteness without definite articles – a study on Estonian, Finnish, Latvian and Lithuanian*. Magister thesis. University of Düsseldorf.

Engel, Ulrich; Rytel-Kuc, Danuta; Cirko, Lesław; Dębski, Antoni; Gaca, Alicja; Lurasz, Alina; Kątny, Andrzej; Mecner, Paweł, Prokop, Izabela; Sadziński, Roman; Schatte, Christoph; Schatte, Czesława; Tomiczek, Eugeniusz; Weiss, Daniel (1999): *Deutsch-polnische kontrastive Grammatik*. Julius Groos Verlag. Heidelberg.

Fedorov, A. V. (1958): *Vvedenie v teoriju perevoda*. Moscow.

Filip, Hana (1985): *Der Verbalaspekt und die Aktionsarten, dargelegt am Beispiel des Tschechischen*. Unpublished Magisterarbeit. University of Munich.

Filip, Hana (1992): Aspect and Interpretation of Nominal Arguments. In: Canakis, Costas; Chan, Grace; Marshall Denton, Jeanette (eds.). *Proceedings of the Chicago Linguistic Society (CLS)* 28. The University of Chicago. Chicago. pp. 139–158.

Filip, Hana (1993/1999): *Aspect, Eventuality Types and Noun Phrase Semantics.* Garland. New York/London.

Filip, Hana (2001): Nominal and verbal semantic structure – analogies and interactions. *Language Sciences* 23. pp. 453–501.

Filip, Hana (2004): The Telicity Parameter Revisited. In: Young, R. (ed.): *Semantics and Linguistic Theory XIV.* Cornell University. Ithaca/NY. pp. 92–109.

Filip, Hana (2005a): On Accumulating and Having it all. In: Verkuyl, Henk; de Swart, Henriette; van Hout, Angeliek (eds.): *Perspectives on Aspect.* Springer. Dordrecht. pp. 125–148.

Filip, Hana (2005b): Measures and Indefinites. In: Carlson, Gregory N.; Pelletier, Francis Jeffry (eds.): *Reference and Quantification.* CSLI Publications. Stanford. pp. 229–288.

Filip, Hana (2007): Events and Maximalization: The Case of Telicity and Perfectivity. In: Rothstein, Susan (ed.). *Theoretical and Crosslinguistic Approaches to the Semantics of Aspect.* John Benjamins. Amsterdam/Philadelphia. pp. 217–256.

Filip, Hana (2012): Lexical Aspect. In: Binnick, Robert (ed.). *The Oxford Handbook of Tense and Aspect.* Oxford University Press. Oxford. pp. 721–751.

Filip, Hana; Carlson, Gregory (1997): Sui Generis Genericity. In: *Penn Working Papers in Linguistics.* Vol. 4. The University of Pennsylvania. Philadelphia. pp. 91–110.

Fisiak, Jacek; Lipińska-Grzegorek, Maria; Zabrocki, Tadeusz (1978): *An introductory English-Polish contrastive grammar.* PWN. Warszawa.

Fleischhauer, Jens (2016): *Degree Gradation of Verbs.* Düsseldorf University Press. Düsseldorf.

Fleischhauer, Jens; Czardybon, Adrian (2016): The role of verbal prefixes and particles in aspectual composition. *Studies in Language* 40 (1). pp. 176-203.

Fontański, Henryk (1986): *Anaforyczne przymiotniki wskazujące w języku polskim i rosyjskim.* Uniwersytet Śląski. Katowice.

Forsyth, James (1970): *A Grammar of Aspect. Usage and Meaning in the Russian Verb.* Cambridge University Press. Cambridge.

Franks, Steven (1995): *Parameters of Slavic morphosyntax.* Oxford University Press. Oxford.

Franks, Steven; Dziwirek, Katarzyna (1993): Negated Adjunct Phrases are really Partitive. *Journal of Slavic Linguistics* 1 (2). pp. 280–305.

Friedrich, Svetlana (2009): *Definitheit im Russischen.* Peter Lang Verlag. Frankfurt am Main.

Gamerschlag, Thomas; Ortmann, Albert (2007): *The role of functional concepts in the classification of nouns and verbs.* Handout of a talk presented at the Conference "Concept Types and Frames 07". 21 August 2007. Heinrich-Heine-University. Düsseldorf.

Garey, Howard (1957): Verbal Aspect in French. *Language* 33. pp. 91–110.

Gebert, Lucyna (2009): Information structure in Slavic languages. In: Mereu, Lunella (ed.). *Information Structure and its Interfaces.* Mouton de Gruyter. The Hague. pp. 307–324.

Gehrke, Berit (2008a): Goals and sources are aspectually equal: Evidence from Czech and Russian prefixes. *Lingua* 118. pp. 1664–1689.

Gehrke, Berit (2008b): Ps in Motion: *On the semantics and syntax of P elements and motion events.* LOT. Utrecht.

Geist, Ljudmila (2013). Bulgarian *edin*: The Rise of an Indefinite Article. In: Junghanns, Uwe; Fehrmann, Dorothee; Lenertová, Denisa; Pitsch, Hagen (eds.). *Formal Description of Slavic Languages: The Ninth Conference. Proceedings of FDSL 9*, Göttingen 2011 (= Linguistik International; 28). Peter Lang. Frankfurt am Main. pp. 125–148.

Gerland, Doris; Horn, Christian (2015): Referential properties of nouns across languages. In: Gamerschlag, T., Gerland, D.; Osswald, R.; Petersen, W. (eds.). *Meaning, Frames, and Conceptual Representation.* DUP. Düseldorf. pp. 133–150.

Gillon, Brendan S. (1992): Towards a Common Semantics for English Count and Mass Nouns. *Linguistics and Philosophy* 15. pp. 597–639.

Gladrow, W. (1972): Das Zusammenwirken unterschiedlicher sprachlicher Mittel zum Ausdruck der Determiniertheit/Indeterminiertheit des Substantivs im Russischen. *Zeitschrift für Slawistik* 17 (5). pp. 647–656.

Golovačeva, A. V. (1979): Identifikacija i individualizacija v anaforičeskix strukturax. In: Nikolaeva, T.M. (ed.). Kategorija opredelennosti - neopredelennosti v slavjanskix i baltijskix jazykax. Nauka. pp. 175–203.

Grappin, Henri (1951): Comment en polonaise des génitifs sont devenus et deviennent des accusatifs. In: *Revue des études slaves.* Vol. 28. pp. 50–67.

Greenberg, Joseph (1978): How Does a Language Acquire Gender Markers? In: Greenberg, Joseph (ed.): *Universals of Human Language. Word Structure.* Vol. 3. Stanford University Press. Stanford. pp. 47–82.

Grochowski, Maceij (1984): On Lexical Units Introducing Sentence Themes. In: Lönngren, Lennart (ed.). *Polish Text Linguistics. The Third Polish-Swedish Conference held at the University of Uppsala, 30 May – 4 June 1983.* Slaviska institutionen vid Uppsala Universitet. Uppsala. pp. 10–19.

Grzegorek, Maria (1984): *Thematization in English and Polish. A study in Word Order.* Drukarnia Uniwersytetu IM. A. Mickiewicza. Poznań.

Gundel, Jeanette (1988): Universals of topic-comment structure. In: Hammond, Michael; Moravcsik, Edith; Wirth, Jessica (eds.). *Studies in Syntactic Typology.* John Benjamins. Amsterdam/Philadelphia. pp. 209–239.

Gvozdanović, Jadranka (2012): Perfective and Imperfective Aspect. In: Binnick, Robert (ed.). *The Oxford Handbook of Tense and Aspect.* Oxford University Press. Oxford. pp. 781–802.

Halliday, Michael (1967): Notes on transitivity and theme in English. Part 2. *Journal of Linguistics* 3. pp. 199–244.

Hammond, Lila (2005): *Serbian. An Essential Grammar.* Routledge. London/New York.

Harrer-Pisarkowa, Krystyna (1959): Przypadek dopełnienia w polskim zdaniu zaprzeczonym. *Język Polski* 39. pp. 9–32.

Hartmann, Dietrich (1982): Deixis and anaphora in German dialects: the semantics and pragmatics of two definite articles in dialectal varieties. In: Weissenborn, Jürgen; Klein, Wolfgang (eds.). *Here and there. Cross-linguistic studies on deixis and demonstration.* John Benjamins. Amsterdam. pp. 187–207.

Hauenschild, Christa (1985): *Zur Interpretation russischer Nominalgruppen. Anaphorische Bezüge und thematische Strukturen im Satz und im Text.* Verlag Otto Sagner. Munich.

Hauenschild, Christa (1993): Definitheit. In: Jacobs, Joachim; von Stechow, Armin; Sternefeld, Wolfgang; Vennemann, Theo. *Syntax. An International Handbook of Contemporary Research.* de Gruyter. Berlin/New York. pp. 988–998.

Hawkins, John A. (1978): *Definiteness and Indefiniteness. A Study in Reference and Grammaticality Prediction.* Croom Helm. London.

Hawkins, John (1991): On (in)definite articles: implications and (un)-grammaticality prediction. *Linguistics* 27. pp. 405–442.

Heim, Irene (1982): *The Semantics of Definite and Indefinite Noun Phrases.* Doctoral dissertation. University of Massachusetts.

Heine, Bernd (1997): *Possession. Cognitive sources, forces, and grammaticalization.* Cambridge University Press. Cambridge.

von Heusinger, Klaus (2002a): Specificity and Definiteness in Sentence and Discourse Structure. *Journal of Semantics* 19. pp. 245–274.

von Heusinger, Klaus (2002b): Information structure and the partition of sentence meaning. In: Hajičová, Eva; Sgall, Petr; Hana, Jiří; Hoskovec, Tomáš (eds.). *Travaux du Cercle Linguistique de Prague*. Vol. 4. John Benjamins. Amsterdam/Philadelphia. pp. 275–305.

von Heusinger, Klaus (2011): Specificity. In: Maienborn, Claudia; von Heusinger, Klaus; Portner, Paul (eds.). *Semantics. An International Handbook of Natural Language Meaning* vol. 2. de Gruyter Mouton. Berlin/Boston. pp. 1025–1057.

von Heusinger, Klaus & Kornfilt, Jaklin (2005): The case of the direct object in Turkish: Semantics, syntax and morphology. *Turkic Languages* 9. pp. 3–44.

Hiietam, Katrin (2003): *Definiteness and Grammatical Relations in Estonian*. PhD thesis. University of Manchester.

Hiietam, Katrin; Börjars, Kersti (2002): The Emergence of a Definite Article in Estonian. In: Nelson, Diane; Manninen, Satu (eds.). *Generative Approaches to Finnic and Saami Linguistics*. CSLI Publications. pp. 383–418.

Himmelmann, Nikolaus (1997): *Deiktikon, Artikel, Nominalphrase. Zur Emergenz syntaktischer Struktur*. Max Niemeyer Verlag. Tübingen.

Himmelmann, Nikolaus (2001): Articles. In: Haspelmath, Martin; König, Ekkehard; Oesterreicher, Wulf; Raible, Wolfgang (eds.). *Language Typology and Language Universals*. de Gruyter. Berlin/New York. pp. 831–841.

Hlebec, Boris (1986): Serbo-Croatian correspondents of the articles in English. *Folia Slavica* 8. pp. 29–50.

Hopper, Paul; Traugott, Elisabeth (1993): *Grammaticalization*. Cambridge University Press. Cambridge.

Horn, Christian (in prep.): *Nominal concept types and determination in German*. PhD thesis. University of Düsseldorf. Düsseldorf.

Horn, Christian (2015): Linguistic congruency of nominal concept types in German texts. In: Uhrig, P.; Herbst, T. (eds.). *Yearbook of the German Cognitive Linguistics Association.* Volume 3. Walter DeGruyter. Berlin/Boston. pp. 195–218.

Horn, Christian; Kimm, Nicolas (2014): Nominal concept types in German fictional texts. In: Gamerschlag, Thomas; Gerland, Doris; Osswald, Rainer; Petersen, Wiebke (eds.). *Frames and Concept Types. Applications in Language and Philosophy.* Studies in Linguistics and Philosophy. Springer. Dordrecht. pp. 343–362.

Isačenko, Aleksandr V. (1962): *Die russische Sprache der Gegenwart. Teil 1: Formenlehre.* Max Niemeyer Verlag. Halle.

Istratkova, Vyara (2004): *On multiple prefixation in Bulgarian.* Nordlyd 32.2. pp. 301–321.

Ivanova, T. A. (1975): Nekotorye aspekty sopostavitel'nogo analiza posessivnyx konstrukcji. (Namateriale sovremennyx slavjanskix literaturnyx jazykax.) *Slavjanskaja filologija* (Leningrad) 3. pp. 148–152.

Ivanova, T. A. (1976): K voprosu o sootnošenii upotrebljaemosti posessivnyx konstrukcii v sovremennyx slavjanskix jazykax. *Voprosy filologii* (Izdatel'stvo Leningradskogo universitet) 5. pp. 3–10.

Jackendoff, Ray (1996): The proper treatment of measuring out, telicity, and perhaps even quantification in English. *Natural Language and Linguistic Theory* 14, pp. 305–354.

Janda, Laura; Townsend, Charles (2000): *Czech.* LINCOM EUROPA. Munich.

Jarząbkowska, Patrycja Ewa (2012): *Pronomina in der polnischen Sprache polnischer Migranten in Deutschland.* Unpublished MA thesis. Christian-Albrechts-Universität zu Kiel.

Junghanns, Uwe; Zybatow, Gerhild (2009): Grammatik und Informationsstruktur. In: Kempgen, Sebastian; Kosta, Peter; Berger, Tilman; Gutschmidt, Karl (eds.). *The Slavic Languages.* de Gruyter. Berlin/New York. pp. 684–706.

Kagan, Olga (2013): *Semantics of Genitive Objects in Russian*. Springer. Dordrecht/Heidelberg/New York/London.

Kempf, Zdzisław (1970): Rozwój i zanik polskiego partitiwu. In: *Język Polski: organ Towarzystwa Miłośników Języka Polskiego*. pp. 181–194.

Koptjevskaja-Tamm, Maria (2001a): Adnominal possession. In: Haspelmath, Martin; König, Ekkehard; Oesterreicher, Wulf; Raible, Wolfgang (eds.). *Language typology and language universals*. Vol. 2. de Gruyter. Berlin. pp. 960–970.

Koptjevskaja-Tamm, Maria (2001b): "A piece of the cake" and "a cup of tea". Partitive and pseudo-partitive nominal constructions in the Circum-Baltic languages. In: Dahl, Östen; Koptjevskaja-Tamm, Maria (eds.). *The Circum-Baltic Languages*. Benjamins. Amsterdam/Philadelphia. pp. 523–568.

König, Ekkehard; van der Auwera, Johan (eds.) (1994): *The Germanic Languages*. Routledge. London.

Kornfilt, Jaklin (2003): Scrambling, subscrambling, and case in Turkish. In: Karimi, S. (ed.). *Word Order and Scrambling*. Blackwell. Oxford. pp. 125–155.

Krámský, Jiří (1972): *The article and the concept of definiteness in language*. Mouton. The Hague.

Krifka, Manfred (1986): *Nominalreferenz und Zeitkonstitution*. Fink. Munich.

Krifka, Manfred (1989): *Nominalreferenz und Zeitkonstitution. Zur Semantik von Massentermen, Individualtermen, Aspektklassen*. Fink. Munich.

Krifka, Manfred (1991): Massennomina. In: Wunderlich, Dieter; von Stechow, Arnim (eds.). *Semantik. Ein internationales Handbuch der zeitgenössischen Forschung*. de Gruyter. Berlin/New York. pp. 399–417.

Krifka, Manfred (1992): Thematic Relations as Links between Nominal Reference and Temporal Constitution. In: Sag, Ivan; Szabolcsi, Anna (eds.). *Lexical Matters*. Stanford University. pp. 29–53.

Krifka, Manfred (1998): The origins of telicity. In: Rothstein, S. (ed.): *Events and Grammar.* Kluwer Academic Publishers. Dordrecht/Boston/London. pp. 197-235.
Krifka, Manfred; Pelletier, Francis; Carlson, Gregory; ter Meulen, Alice; Chierchia, Gennaro; Link, Godehard (1995): Genericity: An Introduction. In: Carlson, Gregory; Pelletier, Francis (eds.). *The Generic Book.* The University of Chicago Press. Chicago/London. pp. 1-124.
Kryk, Barbara (1987): *On Deixis in English and Polish.* Lang Verlag. Frankfurt am Main.
Kuryłowicz, Jerzy (1975 [1965]): The evolution of grammatical categories. *Esquisses linguistiques* 2. pp. 38-54.
Lambrecht, Knud (1994): *Information structure and sentence form.* Cambridge University Press. Cambridge.
Laskowski, Roman (1972): *Polnische Grammatik.* VEB Verlag Enzyklopädie. Leipzig.
Laskowski, Roman (1998a): Kategorie morfologiczne języka polskiego – charakterystyka funkcjonalna. In: Grzegorczykowa, Renata; Laskowski, Roman; Wróbel, Henryk (eds.). *Gramatyka Współczesnego Język Poskiego. Morfologia.* Wydawnictwo Naukowe PWN. Warszawa. pp. 151-224.
Laskowski, Roman (1998b): Liczebnik. In: Grzegorczykowa, Renata; Laskowski, Roman; Wróbel, Henryk (eds.). *Gramatyka Współczesnego Języka Polskiego. Morfologia.* Wydawnictwo Naukowe PWN. Warsaw. pp. 341-360.
Laury, Ritva (1995): On the Grammaticization of the Definite Article *SE* in Spoken Finnish. In: Andersen, H. (ed.). *Historical Linguistics 1993. Selected Papers from the 11th International Conference on Historical Linguistics,* Los Angeles, 16-20 August 1993. Benjamins. Amsterdam/Philadelphia. pp. 239-250.
Laury, Ritva (1997): *Demonstratives in Interaction. The emergence of a definite article in Finnish.* Benjamins. Amsterdam/Philadelphia.

Lehmann, Christian (1991): Grammaticalization and related changes in contemporary German. In: Traugott, Elizabeth; Heine, Bernd (eds.). *Approaches to grammaticalization II.* John Benjamins. Amsterdam/Philadelphia. pp. 493–535.

Leiss, Elisabeth (2000): *Artikel und Aspekt. Die grammatischen Muster von Definitheit.* de Gruyter. Berlin.

Leko, Nedžad (1999): Functional categories and the structure of the DP in Bosnian. In: Dimitrova-Vulchanova, Mila; Hellan, Lars (eds.). *Topics in South Slavic Syntax and Semantics.* John Benjamins Publishing Company. Amsterdam. pp. 229–252.

Lenga, Gerd (1976): *Zur Kontextdeterminierung des Verbalaspekts im modernen Polnisch.* Verlag Otto Sagner. Munich.

Lesz, Maria (1973): Genetivus partitivus w języku polskim. In: *Rozprawy komisji językowej* 19. Łódzkie Towarzystwo Naukowe. pp. 61–75.

Levin, Beth (1993): *English verb classes and alternations.* University of Chicago Press. Chicago.

Li, Charles N.; Thompson Sandra A. (1975): The Semantic Function of Word Order: A Case Study in Mandarin. In: Li, Charles N. (ed.). *Word Order and Word Order Change.* University of Texas Press. Austin/London. pp. 163–195.

Li, Charles N.; Thompson Sandra A. (1981): *Mandarin Chinese. a functional reference grammar.* University of California Press. Berkeley.

Löbner, Sebastian (1985): Definites. *Journal of Semantics* 4. pp. 279–326.

Löbner, Sebastian (1998). Definite associative anaphora. In: Botley, Simon (ed.). *Approaches to discourse anaphora: proceedings of DAARC96 – Discourse Anaphora and Resolution Colloquium.* UCREL Technical Papers Series. Vol. 8. Lancaster University.

Löbner, Sebastian (2011): Concept types and Determination. *Journal of Semantics* 28. pp. 279–333.

Löbner, Sebastian (2013): *Understanding Semantics.* Routledge. London.

Löbner, Sebastian (2015): The semantics of nominals. In: Riemer, Nick (ed.). *The Routledge Handbook of Semantics*. Routledge. London/New York. pp. 293–302.

Löfsted, Einar (1956): *Syntactica. Studien und Beiträge zur historischen Syntax des Lateins. Part 1.* Gleerup. Lund.

Lubaś, Władysław (ed.) (1978): *Teksty języka mówionego mieszkańców miast Górnego Śląska i Zagłębia.* Uniwersytet Śląski. Katowice.

Lyons, Christopher (1999): *Definiteness.* Cambridge University Press. Cambridge.

Massam, Diane (ed.) (2012): *Count and Mass Across Languages.* Oxford University Press. Oxford.

Mathesius, Vilém (1926): Přívlastkové *ten, ta, to* v hovorové češtině [Attributive *ten, ta, to* in colloquial Czech]. *Naše řeč* 10. 39–41.

Mathesius, Vilém (1929): Zur Satzperspektive im modernen Englisch. *Archiv für das Studium der neueren Sprachen und Literaturen* 155. pp. 202–210.

Mathesius, Vilém (1975 [1961]): *A functional analysis of present day English on a general linguistic basis.* Mouton. The Hague.

Matthewson, Lisa (2004): On the Methodology of Semantic Fieldwork. *International Journal of American Linguistics* 70 (4). pp. 369–415.

McCawley, James D. (1975): Lexicography and the count-mass distinction. In: *Proceedings of the First Annual Meeting of the Berkeley Linguistics Society.* pp. 314–321.

Mehlig, Hans Robert (1988): Verbalaspekt und Determination. In: Slavistische Linguistik 1987: Referate des 13. Konstanzer Slavistischen Arbeitstreffens, Tübingen, 22–25/9/1987. Sagner. Munich. pp. 245–296.

Mendoza, Imke (2004): *Nominaldetermination im Polnischen. Die primären Ausdrucksmittel.* Unpublished habilitation thesis. Ludwig-Maximilians-Universität Munich.

Miodunka, Władysław (1974): *Funkcje zaimków w grupach nominalnych współczesnej polszczyzny mówionej.* Państwowe Wydawnictwo Naukowe. Kraków.

Mirkowicz, Tomasz (2008): *Rok 1984.* Warszawskie Wydawnictwo Literackie MUZA SA. Warszawa (translation of the novel *Nineteen Eighty-Four* by George Orwell).

Młynarczyk, Anna (2004): *Aspectual Pairing in Polish.* LOT. Utrecht.

Mourelatos, Alexander (1978): Events, Processes, and States. *Linguistics and Philosophy* 2. pp. 415–434.

Nagórko, Alicja (2006): *Zarys gramatyki polskiej.* Wydawnictwo Naukowe PWN. Warszawa.

Nichols, Johanna (1988): On alienable and inalienable possession. In: Shipley, William (ed.). *In Honor of Mary Haas. From the Haas Festival Conference on Native American Linguistics.* Mouton de Gruyter. Berlin. pp. 557–609.

Nilsson, Barbro (1982): *Personal Pronouns in Russian and Polish. A Study of Their Communicative Function and Placement in the Sentence.* Almqvist & Wiksell International. Stockholm.

Ortmann, Albert (2009): *Definite article asymmetries and concept types: semantic and pragmatic uniqueness.* Handout. CTF09. 25/08/2009.

Ortmann, Albert (2014): Definite article asymmetries and concept types: semantic and pragmatic uniqueness. In: Gamerschlag, Thomas; Gerland, Doris; Osswald, Rainer; Petersen, Wiebke (eds.). *Concept types and frames – Applications in Language, Cognition and Philosophy.* Springer. Dordrecht. pp. 293–322.

Ortmann, Albert (2015): Uniqueness and possession: Typological evidence for type shifts in nominal determination. In: *Logic, language, and computation. 10th International Tbilisi Symposium on Logic, Language, and Computation, TbiLLC 2013.* (Lecture Notes in Computer Science). Springer. Berlin/Heidelberg. pp. 234–256.

Osumi, Midori (1996): Body parts in Tinrin. In: Chappell, Hilary; McGregor, William (eds.). *The Grammar of Inalienability. A Typological Perspective on Body Part Terms and the Part-Whole Relation.* Mouton de Gruyter. Berlin. pp. 433–462.

Ożóg, Kazimierz (1990): *Leksykon metatekstowy współczesnej polszczyzny mówionej.* Drukarnia Uniwersytetu Jagiellońskiego. Kraków.

Panzer, Baldur (1991): *Die slavischen Sprachen in Gegenwart und Geschichte.* Lang. Frankfurt am Main.

Partee, Barbara (1983/1997): Genitives – A case study. Appendix to Theo M.V. Janssen, Compositionality. In: van Benthem, J.F.A.K.; ten Meulen, A. (eds.). *Handbook of Logic and Linguistics.* Elsevier. Amsterdam. pp. 464–470.

Partee, Barbara; Borschev, Vladimir (2007): Existential Sentences, BE, and the Genitive of Negation in Russian. In: Comorovski, I.; von Heusinger, K. (eds.). *Existence: Semantics and Syntax.* Springer. Dordrecht. pp. 147–190.

Pelletier, Francis Jeffry (1975): Non-singular References: some Preliminaries. *Philosophia* 5 (4). pp. 451–465.

Pelletier, Francis Jeffry (2010): Mass Terms: A Philosophical Introduction. In: Pelletier, Francis Jeffry (ed.). *Kinds, Things, and Stuff. Mass terms and Generics.* Oxford University Press. Oxford/New York. pp. 123–131.

Pelletier, Francis Jeffry (2012): Lexical nouns are both + MASS and + COUNT, but they are neither + MASS nor + COUNT. In: Massam, Diane (ed.). *Count and Mass Across Languages.* Oxford University Press. Oxford. pp. 9–26.

Pelletier, Francis Jeffry; Schubert, Lenhart K. (2002): Mass Expressions. In: Gabbay, D.; Guenthner, F. (eds.). *Handbook of Philosophical Logic.* Vol. 10. Kluwer Academic Publishers. Netherlands. pp. 1–87.

Peterson, John (2016): Multilingualism, multilectalism and register variation in linguistic theory. Extending the diasystematic approach. In: *Explorations of the Syntax-Semantics Interface. Studies in Language and Cignition.* Düsseldorf University Press. Düsseldorf. pp. 109–147.

Piernikarski, Cezar (1969): *Typy opozycji aspektowych czasownika polskiego na tle słowiańskim.* Zakład narodowy imienia ossolińskich. Wydawnictwo polskiej akademii nauk. Wrocław/Warsaw/Kraków.

Piñón, Christopher (1994): Accumulation and aspectuality in Polish. *Proceedings of the North East Linguistic Society* 24. pp. 49–506.
Piñón, Christopher (2001): A problem of aspectual composition in Polish. In: Zybatow, Gerhild; Junghanns, Uwe; Mehlhorn, Grit; Szucsich, Luka (eds.). *Current Issues in Formal Slavic Linguistics*. Peter Lang. Frankfurt am Main. pp. 397–414.
Piñón, Christopher (2003): Nominal reference and the imperfective in Polish and English. *Proceedings of the North East Linguistic Society* 23. pp. 383–397.
Pisarkowa, Krystyna (1968): Zaimek w polskim zdaniu. 2. Obserwacje przydawki zaimkowej. *Język polski.* pp. 12–33.
Pisarkowa, Krystyna (1969): *Funkcje składniowe polskich zaimków odmiennych*. Wydawnictwo Polskiej Akademii Nauk. Wrocław/Warszawa/Kraków.
Pisarkowa, Krystyna (1975): *Składnia Rozmowy Telefonicznej*. Wydawnictwo Polskiej Akademii Nauk. Wrocław/Warszawa/Kraków/Gdańsk.
Pisarkowa, Krystyna (1977): Über die Possessivität im Polnischen und Deutschen. In: Engel, Ulrich (ed.). *Deutsche Sprache im Kontrast*. Verlag Gunter Narr. Tübingen. pp. 83–99.
Piskorz, Kinga (2011): Entsteht ein bestimmter Artikel im Polnischen? In: Kotin, M.; Kotorova, E. (eds.). *History and Typology of Language Systems*. Winter Verlag. Heidelberg. pp. 159–168.
Pospelov, N. S. (1970): O sintaksičeskom vyraženii kategorii opredelennosti-neopredelennosti v sovremennom russkom jazyke. In: Issledovanija po sovremennomu russkomu jazyku. Moscow. pp. 182–189.
Priestly, T. M. S. (1993): Slovene. In: Comrie, Bernard; Corbett, Greville (eds.). *The Slavonic Languages*. Routledge. London/New York. p. 388–454.
Progovac, Ljiljana. (1998): Determiner phrase in a language without determiners. *Journal of Linguistics* 34. pp. 165–179.

Przepiórkowski, Adam; Bańko, Mirosław; Górski, Rafał L.; Lewandowska-Tomaszczyk, Barbara (eds.) (2012): *Narodowy Korpus Języka Polskiego*. Wydawnictwo Naukowe PWN. Warsaw.

Quine, Willard Van Orman (1960): *Word and object*. MIT Press. Cambridge.

Radeva, Vassilka; Walter, Hilmar; Penčev, Jordan; Comati, Sigrun (2003): *Bulgarische Grammatik. Marphologisch-syntaktische Grundzüge*. Buske Verlag. Hamburg.

Rehder, Peter (2009): Das Slovenische. In: Rehder, Peter (ed.). *Einführung in die slavischen Sprachen*. Wissenschaftliche Buchgesellschaft. Darmstadt. pp. 230–245.

Reinhart, Tanya (1981): Pragmatics and Linguistics: An Analysis of Sentence Topics. *Philosophica* 27 (1). pp. 53–94.

Reiter, Norbert (1977): Slavische Kasus- und deutsche Artikelopposition. *Zeitschrift für slavische Philologie* 39. pp. 357– 372.

Richardson, Kylie (2007): *Case and Aspect in Slavic*. Oxford University Press. Oxford.

Roberts, Craig (2003): Uniqueness in definite noun phrases. *Linguistics and Philosophy* 26. pp. 287–350.

Rosengren, Inger (1997): The thetic/categorical distinction revisited once more. *Linguistics* 35 (3). pp. 439–479.

Rothstein, Robert (2001) [1993]: Polish. In: Comrie, Bernard; Corbett, Greville (eds.). *The Slavonic Languages*. Routledge. London/New York. 686–758.

Rothstein, Susan (2010): Counting and the Mass/Count Distinction. *Journal of Semantics* 27. pp. 343–397.

Rozwadowska, Bożena, Willim, Ewa (2004): The role of the accusative/partitive alternation in aspectual composition in Polish. *Poznań Studies in Contemporary Linguistics* 39. pp. 125–142.

Russell, Bertrand (1905): On Denoting. *Mind* 14 (56). pp. 479–493.

Sachliyan, Syuzan (in prep.): *Definitheit im Bulgarischen und Mazedonischen*. PhD thesis. University of Düsseldorf.

Sadziński, Roman (1977): *Die deutsche Artikelkategorie und ihre Äquivalenzstruktur im Polnischen. Eine theoretische Grundlegung, exemplifiziert anhand des unbestimmten Artikels.* PhD thesis. Leipzig.

Sadziński, Roman (1982): Zur Wiedergabe der deutschen Artikel im Polnischen. In: Bahner, W.; Heidolph, K.-E.; Neumann, W.; Schildt, J. (eds.). *Linguistische Studien. Reihe A.* 102. pp. 84–92.

Sadziński, Roman (1985): Die Artikelkategorie im Deutschen – in Konfrontation mit dem Polnischen. In: Lipczuk, Ryszard (ed.). *Grammatische Studien. Beiträge zur germanistischen Linguistik in Polen.* Kümmerle Verlag. Göppingen. pp.163–173.

Sadziński, Roman (1991): Deutsche Artikelkategorie und deren Äquivalente im artikellosen Polnischen. In: Iwasaki, Eijirō (ed.). *Begegnung mit dem Fremden: Grenzen - Traditionen – Vergleiche. Akten des VIII. Internationalen Germanisten-Kongresses. Tokyo 1990.* Iudicium-Verlag. Munich. pp. 154–160.

Sadziński, Roman (1995/96): *Die Kategorie der Determiniertheit und Indeterminiertheit im Deutschen und im Polnischen.* WSP. Częstochowa.

Sasse, Hans-Jürgen (1987): The thetic/categorical distinction revisited. *Linguistics* 25 (3). pp. 511–580.

Scatton, Ernest (1984): *A Reference Grammar of Modern Bulgarian.* Slavica Publishers, Inc. Columbus.

Scatton, Ernest (1993): Bulgarian. In: Comrie, Bernard; Corbett, Greville (eds.). *The Slavonic Languages.* Routledge. London/New York. pp. 188–248.

Scholze, Lenka (2008): *Das grammatische System der obersorbischen Umgangssprache im Sprachkontakt.* Domowina-Verlag. Bautzen.

Schroeder, Christoph (2006): Articles and article systems in some areas of Europe. In: Bernini, Giuliano; Schwartz, Marcia (eds.). *Pragmatic Organization of Discourse in the Languages of Europe.* de Gruyter. Berlin. pp. 545–611.

Schwager, Magdalena (2007). *(Non-)Functional Concepts: Definite Articles in Bavarian.* Talk at the 8th Szklarska Poręba Workshop. Slides downloadable at: http://user.uni-frankfurt.de/~scheiner/papers/szklarska07.pdf.

Schwarz, Florian (2009): *Two Types of Definites in Natural Language.* PhD thesis. University of Massachusetts Amherst.

Seiler, Hansjakob (1983): *Possession as Operational Dimension of Language.* Gunter Narr Verlag. Tübingen.

Short, David (1993): Czech. In: Comrie, Bernard; Corbett, Greville (eds.). *The Slavonic Languages.* Routledge. London/New York. pp. 455–523.

Siewierska, Anna; Uhlířová, Ludmila (1998): An overview of word order in Slavic languages. In: Siewierska, Anna (ed.). *Constituent Order in the Languages of Europe.* de Gruyter. Berlin/New York. pp. 105–149.

Skibicki, Monika (2007): *Polnische Grammatik.* Buske. Hamburg.

Skudrzykowa. Aldona; Tambor, Jolanta; Urban, Krystyna; Wolińska, Olga (2001): *Gwara śląska – świadectwo kultury, narzędzie komunikacji. Sytuacja językowa w miastach Górnego Śląska.* „Śląsk" Wydawnictwo Naukowe. Katowice.

Smith, Carlotta (1991): *The parameter of aspect.* Kluwer. Dordrecht.

Solonicyn, Ju. V. (1962): Roditel'nyj neopredelennogo količestva pri perexodnyx glagolax. In: *Očerki po russkomu jazyku.* Kirov. pp. 93–98.

Späth, Andreas (2006): *Determinierung unter Defektivität des Determinierersystems.* de Gruyter. Berlin/New York.

Steube, Anita; Späth, Andreas (1999): Determination in German and Russian. In: Hajičová, Eva; Hoskovec, Tomáš; Leška, Oldřich; Sgall, Petr; Skoumalová, Zdena (eds.). *Prague Linguistic Circle Papers.* Vol. 3. Benjamins. Amsterdam/Philadelphia. pp. 145–164.

Stolz, Thomas; Kettler, Sonja; Stroh, Cornelia; Urdze, Aina (2008): *Split Possession.* John Benjamins. Amsterdam.

Strawson, P. (1964): Identifying reference and truth values. *Theoria* 30. pp. 96–118.

Studler, Rebekka (2004): Voller und reduzierter Artikel in der schweizerdeutschen DP. In: Bračič, Stojan (ed.). *Linguistische Studien im Europäischen Jahr der Sprachen.* Lang. Frankfurt am Main. pp.625–635.
Sussex, Roland; Cubberley, Paul (2006): *The Slavic Languages.* Cambridge University Press. Cambridge.
Swan, Oscar (2002): *A Grammar of Contemporary Polish.* Slavica. Bloomington/Indiana.
de Swart, Petrus Jacobus Franciscus (2007): *Cross-linguistic Variation in Object Marking.* LOT. Utrecht.
Szlifersztejnowa, Salomea (1960): *Przymiotniki dzierżawcze w języku polskim.* Wrocław.
Szwedek, Aleksander (1974): Some aspects of definiteness and indefiniteness of nouns in Polish. *Papers and Studies in Contrastive Linguistics* 2. pp. 203–211.
Szwedek, Aleksander (1975): *A Contrastive Analysis of Reference in English and Polish.* Wydawnictwo WSP.
Szwedek, Aleksander (1976a): The role of sentence stress in the interpretation of coreferentiality in English and Polish. *Papers and Studies in Contrastive Linguistics* 4. pp. 13–23.
Szwedek, Aleksander (1976b): *Word order, sentence stress and reference in English and Polish.* Linguistic Research. Edmonton/Alberta.
Szwedek, A. (1986): *A Linguistic Analysis of Sentence Stress.* Gunter Narr Verlag. Tübingen.
Tęcza, Zygmunt (2007): *Das Problem der Komparabilität beim Vergleich des deutschen bestimmten Artikels mit seinem Gegenspieler im Westslawischen.* Neisse-Verlag. Dresden. pp. 337–348.
Tenny, Carol L. (1994): *Aspectual roles and the syntax-semantics interface.* Kluwer Academic Publishers. Dordrecht/Boston/London.
Timberlake, Alan (1986): Hierarchies in the Genitive of Negation. In: *Case in Slavic.* Brecht, Richard; Levine, James (eds.). Slavica Publishers. Columbus. pp. 338–360.

Timberlake, Alan (2004): *A Reference Grammar of Russian.* Cambridge University Press. Cambridge.
Tokarski, Jan (2001 [1973]): *Fleksja polska.* Wydawnictwo Naukowe. Warsaw.
Topolińska, Zuzanna (1976): Wyznaczoność (tj. charakterystyka referencyjna) grupy imiennej w tekście polskim. *Polonica* II. pp. 33–72.
Topolińska, Zuzanna (1981): *Remarks on the Slavic Noun Phrase.* Wydawnictwo Polskiej Akademii Nauk. Wrocław.
Topolińska, Zuzanna (1984): Składnia grupy imiennej. In: Topolińska, Zuzanna (ed.). *Gramatyka współczesnego języka polskiego. Składnia.* Państwowe Wydawnictwo Naukowe. Warsaw. pp. 301–386.
Topolińska, Zuzanna (1986): Grammatical Functions of Noun Phrases in Balkan Slavic Languages and the So-called Category of Case. In: *Case in Slavic.* Brecht, Richard; Levine, James (eds.). Slavica Publishers. Columbus. pp. 280–295.
Topolinjska, Zuzanna (2009): Definiteness (Synchrony). In: Kempgen, Sebastian; Kosta, Peter; Berger, Tilman; Gutschmidt, Karl (eds.). *The Slavic Languages.* de Gruyter. Berlin/New York. pp. 176–187.
Townsend, Charles; Janda, Laura (1996): *Common and Comparative Slavic: Phonology and Inflection.* Slavica Publishers, Inc. Columbus.
Traugott, Elizabeth; Heine, Bernd (1991): Introduction. In: Traugott, Elizabeth; Heine, Bernd (eds.). *Approaches to grammaticalization II.* John Benjamins. Amsterdam/Philadelphia. pp. 1–14.
Trenkic, Danijela (2002): Establishing the definiteness status of referents in dialogue (in languages with and without articles). Working papers in *English and Applied Linguistics* 6. University of Cambridge. Cambridge. pp. 107–131.
Trenkic, Danijela (2004): Definiteness in Serbian/Croatian/Bosnian and some implications for the general structure of the nominal phrase. *Lingua* 114. pp. 1401–1427.
Uhlířová, Ludmila (1987): *Knížka o slovosledu.* Academia. Prague.

Van Valin, Robert D. Jr. (1993): *Advances in Role and Reference Grammar.* John Benjamins. Amsterdam/Philadelphia.

Van Valin, Robert Jr. (1999): A Typology of the Interaction of Focus Structure and Syntax. In: Raxilina, E.; Testelec, J. (eds.). *Typology and the Theory of Language: From Description to Explanation.* Moscow.

Van Valin, Robert D. Jr. (2005): *Exploring the syntax semantics interface.* Cambridge University Press. Cambridge.

Van Valin, Robert Jr. & LaPolla, Randy (1997): *Syntax.* Cambridge University Press. Cambridge.

Velazquez-Castillo, Maura (1996): *The Grammar of Possession. Inalienability, incorporation and possessor ascension in Guaraní.* John Benjamins. Amsterdam/Philadelphia.

Vendler, Zeno (1957): Verbs and times. *The Philosophical Review* 66 (2). pp. 143–160.

Verkuyl, Henk (1972): *On the compositional nature of the aspects.* Reidel Publishing Company. Dordrecht.

Verkuyl, Henk (1993): *A Theory of Aspectuality. The Interaction between Temporal and Atemporal Structure.* Cambridge University Press. Cambridge/New York/Melbourne.

Verkuyl, Henk (1999): *Aspectual Issues. Studies on Time and Quantity.* CSLI Publications. Stanford.

Verkuyl, Henk (2005): Aspectual composition: Surveying the ingredients. In: Verkuyl, Henk; de Swart, Henriette; Van Hout, Angeliek. *Perspectives on Aspect.* Springer. Dordrecht. pp. 19–39.

Wackernagel, Jacob (1908/1975): Genitiv und Adjektiv. In: *Mélanges de Linguistique offerts à M. Ferdinand de Saussure.* Slatkine Reprint. Genève (Collection Linguistique publiée par La Société de Linguistique de Paris – II). pp. 125–152.

Watkins, Calvert (1967): Remarks on the Genitive. In: *To Honor Roman Jakobson. Essays on the Occasion of his Seventieth Birthday 11 October 1966.* Vol. III. Mouton. The Hague/Paris. pp. 2191–2198.

Weiss, Daniel (1983): Indefinite, definite und generische Referenz in artikellosen slavischen Sprachen. In: Mehlig, Hans (ed.). *Referate des VIII. Konstanzer Slavistischen Arbeitstreffens.* Kiel 28/9–1/10/1982. Verlag Otto Sagner. Munich. pp. 229–261.

Wierzbicka, Anna (1967): On the Semantics of the Verbal Aspect in Polish. In: Jakobson, Roman. *To Honor Roman Jakobson. Essays on the Occasion of his Seventieth Birthday.* Mouton. The Hague. pp. 2231–2249.

Wierzbicka, Anna (1988): *The Semantics of Grammar.* John Benjamins. Amsterdam/Philadelphia.

Wiese, Heike (2012): Collectives in the intersection of mass and count nouns. In: Massam, Diane (ed.). *Count and Mass Across Languages.* Oxford University Press. Oxford. pp. 54–74.

Wisniewski, Edward J.; Lamb, Christopher A.; Middleton, Erica L. (2003): On the conceptual basis for the count and mass noun distinction. *Language and Cognitive Processes* 18 (5/6). pp. 583–624.

Wisniewski, Edward J. (2010): On Using Count Nouns, Mass Nouns, and Pluralia Tantum: What Counts?. In: Pelletier, Francis Jeffry (ed.). *Kinds, Things, and Stuff. Mass terms and Generics.* Oxford University Press. Oxford/New York. pp. 166–190.

Witwicka-Iwanowska, Magdalena (2012): *Artikelgebrauch im Deutschen. Eine Analyse aus der Perspektive des Polnischen.* Narr Verlag. Tübingen.

Wróbel, Henryk (1984): Functions of the Demonstrative Pronoun *Ten* in Spoken Polish. In: Lönngren, Lennart (ed.). *Polish Text Linguistics. The Third Polish-Swedish Conference held at the University of Uppsala, 30 May – 4 June 1983.* Slaviska institutionen vid Uppsala Universitet. Uppsala. pp. 41–52.

Wróbel, Henryk (1998): Kategorie morfologiczne języka polskiego – charakterystyka funkcjonalna. In: Grzegorczykowa, Renata; Laskowski, Roman; Wróbel, Henryk (eds.). *Gramatyka współczesnego język poskiego. Morfologia.* Wydawnictwo Naukowe PWN. Warsaw. pp. 151–224.

Yokoyama, Olga (2009): Discourse, Sentence Intonation, and Word Order. In: Kempgen, Sebastian; Kosta, Peter; Berger, Tilman; Gutschmidt, Karl (eds.). *The Slavic Languages.* de Gruyter. Berlin/New York. pp. 707–713.

Zubatý, Josef (1916): Ten. *Naše řeč* 10. pp. 289–294.

Sources from the internet:

National Corpus of Polish (NKJP): http://nkjp.pl/

www.ingramcontent.com/pod-product-compliance
Lightning Source LLC
Chambersburg PA
CBHW052130010526
44113CB00034B/1300